D0294816

MONARCHY

ALSO BY DAVID STARKEY

The English Court: From The Wars Of The Roses to The Civil War
Elizabeth
The Reign of Henry VIII: Personalities And Politics
Six Wives: The Queens of Henry VIII
The Monarchy of England: The Beginnings

MONARCHY

From the Middle Ages to Modernity

DAVID STARKEY

Harper*Press*

An Imprint of HarperCollins*Publishers*

Harper*Press*
HarperCollins*Publishers*
77–85 Fulham Palace Road,
Hammersmith, London W6 8JB

www.harpercollins.co.uk

Published by Harper*Press* 2006

1 3 5 7 9 8 6 4 2

Copyright © David Starkey 2006

David Starkey asserts the moral right to
be identified as the author of this work

A catalogue record for this book
is available from the British Library

ISBN-13 978-0-00-724750-9
ISBN-10 0-00-724750-8

Family trees: Artwork by Leslie Robinson

Endpapers: *Queen Elizabeth I in Coronation Robes* (detail)
*c.*1559 (panel), English School. *National Portrait
Gallery, London/The Bridgeman Art Library*

Set in PostScript Monotype Bell by
Rowland Phototypesetting Ltd,
Bury St Edmunds, Suffolk

Printed and bound in Great Britain by
Clays Ltd, St Ives plc

All rights reserved. No part of this publication may be
reproduced, stored in a retrieval system, or transmitted,
in any form or by any means, electronic, mechanical,
photocopying, recording or otherwise, without the prior
permission of the publishers.

To Hal and Susie Bagot,
under whose roof it was finished.
For friendship and hospitality.

CONTENTS

PICTURE CREDITS

Section I
Page 1
1. *King Edward IV*, by unknown artist, (oil on panel). *The National Portrait Gallery, London.*

2. *Elizabeth Woodville.* © *The President and Fellows of Queens' College.*

3. *King Richard III*, by unknown artist, late 16th century, (oil on panel). *The National Portrait Gallery, London.*

4. *Lady Margaret Beaufort*, by unknown artist, *c.*1600, (oil on panel). *The National Portrait Gallery, London.*

Pages 2–3
1. *King Henry VII*, by unknown artist, 1505, (oil on panel). *The National Portrait Gallery, London.*

2. *Elizabeth of York*, by unknown artist, *c.*1500, (oil on panel). *The National Portrait Gallery, London.*

3. *King Henry VIII*, (miniature), Horenbout Lucas, 1526–7. *The Royal Collection* © *2006, Her Majesty Queen Elizabeth II.*

4. *Catherine of Aragon*, (miniature), attributed to Horenbout Lucas, *c.*1525. *The National Portrait Gallery, London.*

5. *Meeting at the Field of the Cloth of Gold*, 7th June 1520. From an original by Hans Holbein, the Elder (oil on canvas), this copy by Friedrich Bouterwek. © *Chateau de Versailles, France/Lauros/Giraudon/The Bridgeman Art Library.*

Pages 4–5
1. *The Whitehall Mural*, or The Dynasty Portrait. From an original by Hans Holbein, this copy by Remigius van Leemput, late 17th century. *The Royal Collection* © *2006, Her Majesty Queen Elizabeth II.*

2. *The Great Bible*, title page, 1539. © *Lambeth Palace Library, London, UK/The Bridgeman Art Library.*

Pages 6–7

1. *The Family of Henry VIII*, by unknown artist, *c*.1545, (oil on canvas). *The Royal Collection © 2006, Her Majesty Queen Elizabeth II.*

2. *Thomas Cranmer*, by Flicke Gerlach, 1545, (oil on panel). *The National Portrait Gallery, London.*

3. *King Edward VI and the Pope*, by unknown artist, *c*.1570, (oil on panel). *The National Portrait Gallery, London.*

4. *Queen Mary I* by Hans Eworth or Ewoutsz, (fl.1520–74). © *Society of Antiquaries, London, UK/The Bridgeman Art Library.*

5. *Foxe's Book of Martyr's* (page detail), *c*.1500. © *Lambeth Palace Library.*

Page 8

1. *Queen Elizabeth I in Coronation Robes*, by unknown artist, *c*.1559, (panel). © *National Portrait Gallery, London, UK/The Bridgeman Art Library.*

2. *Mary, Queen of Scots* after a miniature, by unknown artist, *c*.1560–1565, (oil on panel). *The National Portrait Gallery, London.*

3. *James I* (in robes of state), van Somer Paul, *c*.1620. *The Royal Collection © 2006, Her Majesty Queen Elizabeth II.*

SECTION II
Page 1

1. *The Somerset House Conference*, by unknown artist, 1604, (oil on canvas). *The National Portrait Gallery, London.*

2. Right hand side of Diptych showing the Parliament of James I of England, VI of Scotland and the Gunpowder Plot, detail of the Gunpowder Plotters from the bottom right hand corner, by English School, 17th century, (oil on panel). © *St. Faith's Church, Gaywood, Norfolk, UK/The Bridgeman Art Library.*

3. Great Seal of James I (detail) by English School, 17th century, (engraving). © *Private Collection/ The Bridgeman Art Library.*

PICTURE CREDITS

Pages 2–3

1. *King Charles I and his Family,* by school of Sir Anthony van Dyck, (oil on canvas). © *Royal Hospital Chelsea, London, UK/The Bridgeman Art Library.*

2. *Archbishop William Laud,* after Sir Anthony van Dyck, *c.*1636, (oil on canvas). *The National Portrait Gallery, London.*

3. *Parliament Assembled at Westminster on 13th April 1640,* by unknown artist, 17th century, (engraving). © *Museum of London, UK/The Bridgeman Art Library.*

Pages 4–5

1. The Battle Plan of Naseby from *Anglia Rediviva,* 1647. © *The British Library, London.*

2. *Oliver Cromwell* by Walker Robert, *c.*1649, (oil on canvas). *The National Portrait Gallery, London.*

3. *Execution of Charles I (1600–49) at Whitehall, January 30th, 1649* (oil on canvas) by Coques, Gonzales, attr.to. © *Musee de Picardie, Amiens, France/Giraudon/The Bridgeman Art Library.*

4. *The Pourtraiture of his Royal Highness, Oliver, Late Protector etc, in his Life and Death, with a short view of his Government.* © *The British Library, London.*

Pages 6–7

1. *Coronation Procession of Charles II to Westminster from the Tower of London,* by Dirck Stoop, 1661. © *Museum of London, UK/The Bridgeman Art Library.*

2. *Charles II enthroned wearing the recreated Regalia,* by John Michael Wright, 1660–1670. *The Royal Collection* © *2006, Her Majesty Queen Elizabeth II.*

3. *The Royal Gift of Healing,* King Charles II healing the sick, by unknown artist, 1684. © *Heritage Image Partnership/The British Library.*

Page 8

1. *Dutch attack on the Medway: The* Royal Charles *carried into Dutch waters, 12th June 1667,* by Ludolf Bakhuizen, 1667, (oil on canvas). *National Maritime Museum, London.*

2. *Titus Oates*, by Robert White, 1679, (line engraving). *The National Portrait Gallery, London.*

SECTION III
Page 1
1. A perspective of Westminster Abbey from the High alter to the West end showing the manner of his Majesties crowning (James II). From *The History of the Coronation*, Francis Sandford, 1687. © *Lambeth Palace Library.*

Pages 2–3
1. *Louis XIV in Royal Costume*, by Hyacinthe Rigaud, 1701, (oil on canvas). © *Louvre, Paris, France/Giraudon/The Bridgeman Art Library.*

2. *King William III*, by unknown artist, *c.*1690, (oil on canvas). *The National Portrait Gallery, London.*

3. *Mary II as Princess of Orange*, attributed to Nicholas Dixon, *c.*1677. *The Royal Collection* © *2006, Her Majesty Queen Elizabeth II.*

Pages 4–5
1. *Apotheosis of William and Mary*, Ceiling of the Painted Hall, by Sir James Thornhill, 18th century. *Courtesy of the Greenwich Foundation for the Old Royal Naval College.*

2. *Queen Ann and William, Duke of Gloucester*, studio of Sir Godfrey Kneller BT, *c.*1694, (oil on canvas). *National Portrait Gallery, London.*

Pages 6–7
1. *John Churchill, 1st Duke of Marlborough, and Sarah, Duchess of Marlborough, with their children*, by Johann Closterman, (oil on canvas). © *Blenheim Palace, Oxfordshire, UK/The Bridgeman Art Library.*

2. *The Duke of Marlborough surveys his troops at the Battle of Oudenarde in the Spanish Netherlands, 30th June 1708*, tapestry woven by Judocus de Vos. © *Blenheim Palace, Oxfordshire, UK/The Bridgeman Art Library.*

3. View of Blenheim Palace from the column of Victory. © *Skyscan.*

Page 8

1. Rear wall painting of the Upper Hall at Greenwich glorifying George I and the House of Hanover, by Sir James Thornhill. *Courtesy of the Greenwich Foundation for the Old Royal Naval College.*

SECTION IV
Page 1

1. The pediment of the Temple of Concord and Victory, *c.*1735, at Stowe Landscape Garden. *Courtesy of John Bedington, 2006, Stowe Landscape Garden, The National Trust.*

2. *Robert Walpole, 1st Earl of Orford,* Studio of Jean Baptiste van Loo, 1740, (oil on canvas). *The National Portrait Gallery, London.*

3. *William Pitt the Elder, 1st Earl of Chatham,* studio of William Hoare, *c.*1754, (oil on canvas). *The National Portrait Gallery, London.*

Pages 2–3

1. *George Washington,* by Gilbert Stuart. © *Metropolitan Museum of Art, New York, USA/The Bridgeman Art Library.*

2. *Thomas Jefferson, 3rd President of the United States,* by James Sharples, *c.*1797, (oil on canvas). © *Bristol City Museum and Art Gallery, UK/The Bridgeman Art Library.*

3. Wren building of the College of William and Mary, Williamsburg, Virginia, USA. © *G.E. Kidder Smith/CORBIS.*

4. *George III in his Coronation Robes,* by Allan Ramsay, 1761. © *Scottish National Portrait Gallery, Edinburgh/Bridgeman Art Library.*

5. *Edmund Burke,* studio of Sir Joshua Reynolds, *c.*1767–69, (oil on canvas). *The National Portrait Gallery, London.*

6. The severed head of Louis XVI, King of France, in the hands of the executioner, (Stipple engraving). *Photo: akg-images, London.*

Pages 4–5

1. *The Plum Pudding in Danger,* by James Gillray, 1805, (colour engraving). © *Private Collection/The Bridgeman Art Library.*

2. *King George IV in Highland Dress,* 1830, (oil on canvas), Sir David Wilkie. *Apsley House, The Wellington Museum, London/The Bridgeman Art Library.*

3. *The Quadrant, Regent Street, from Piccadilly Circus,* published by

Ackermann, *c*.1835–50, (coloured aquatint). © *Private Collection/ The Stapleton Collection/The Bridgeman Art Library.*

Pages 6–7

1. *King William IV*, by Sir Martin Archer Shee, *c*.1800, (oil on canvas). *The National Portrait Gallery, London.*

2. *Sir Herbert Taylor, Private Secretary to King William IV*, by John Simpson, exhibited 1833, (oil on canvas). *The National Portrait Gallery, London.*

3. *The House of Commons, 1833*, by Sir George Hayter, 1833–1834, (oil on canvas). *The National Portrait Gallery, London.*

Page 8

1. *The Royal Family in 1846*, Franz Xavier Winterhalter, 1846. *The Royal Collection* © 2006, *Her Majesty Queen Elizabeth II.*

2. *Opening of the Great Exhibition by Queen Victoria on 1st May 1851*, Henry Courtney Selous, 1851–52. © *V&A Images, London.*

GENEALOGIES

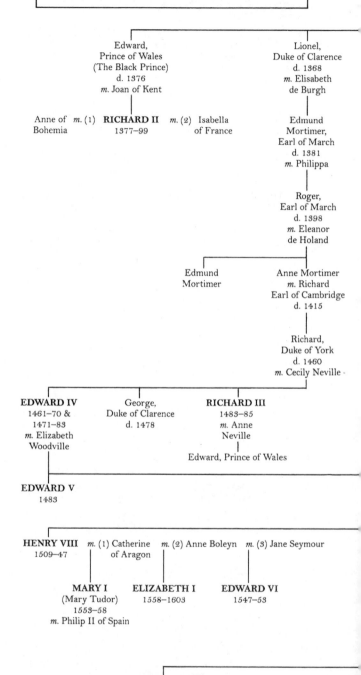

THE ENGLISH AND BRITISH MONARCHY
FROM THE MIDDLE AGES TO VICTORIA

Edward,
Prince of Wales
(The Black Prince)
d. 1376
m. Joan of Kent

Lionel,
Duke of Clarence
d. 1368
m. Elisabeth
de Burgh

Anne of   m. (1)   **RICHARD II**   m. (2)   Isabella
Bohemia   1377–99   of France

Edmund
Mortimer,
Earl of March
d. 1381
m. Philippa

Roger,
Earl of March
d. 1398
m. Eleanor
de Holand

Edmund
Mortimer

Anne Mortimer
m. Richard
Earl of Cambridge
d. 1415

Richard,
Duke of York
d. 1460
m. Cecily Neville

EDWARD IV
1461–70 &
1471–83
m. Elizabeth
Woodville

George,
Duke of Clarence
d. 1478

RICHARD III
1483–85
m. Anne
Neville

Edward, Prince of Wales

EDWARD V
1483

HENRY VIII   m. (1) Catherine   m. (2) Anne Boleyn   m. (3) Jane Seymour
1509–47   of Aragon

MARY I   **ELIZABETH I**   **EDWARD VI**
(Mary Tudor)   1558–1603   1547–53
1553–58
m. Philip II of Spain

JAMES I of England
JAMES VI of Scotland
1603–25
m. Anne of Denmark

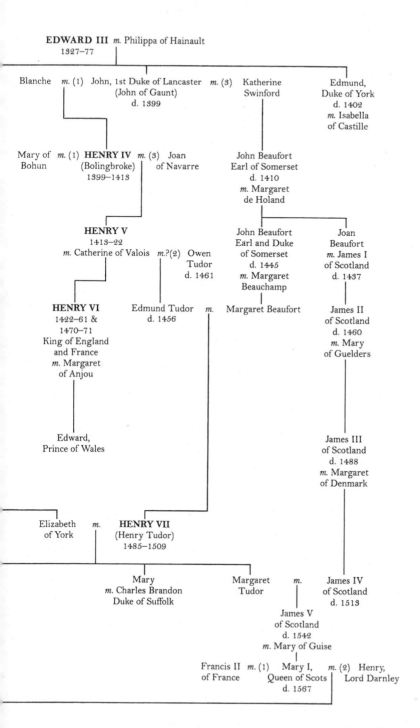

EDWARD III *m.* Philippa of Hainault
1327–77

Blanche   *m.* (1)   John, 1st Duke of Lancaster   *m.* (3)   Katherine   Edmund,
(John of Gaunt)   Swinford   Duke of York
d. 1399   d. 1402
m. Isabella
of Castille

Mary of   *m.* (1)   **HENRY IV**   *m.* (3)   Joan   John Beaufort
Bohun   (Bolingbroke)   of Navarre   Earl of Somerset
1399–1413   d. 1410
m. Margaret
de Holand

HENRY V   John Beaufort   Joan
1413–22   Earl and Duke   Beaufort
m. Catherine of Valois   *m.?*(2)   Owen   of Somerset   *m.* James I
Tudor   d. 1445   of Scotland
d. 1461   *m.* Margaret   d. 1437
Beauchamp

HENRY VI   Edmund Tudor   *m.*   Margaret Beaufort   James II
1422–61 &   d. 1456   of Scotland
1470–71   d. 1460
King of England   *m.* Mary
and France   of Guelders
m. Margaret
of Anjou

Edward,   James III
Prince of Wales   of Scotland
d. 1488
m. Margaret
of Denmark

Elizabeth   *m.*   **HENRY VII**
of York   (Henry Tudor)
1485–1509

Mary   Margaret   *m.*   James IV
m. Charles Brandon   Tudor   of Scotland
Duke of Suffolk   d. 1513

James V
of Scotland
d. 1542
m. Mary of Guise

Francis II   *m.* (1)   Mary I,   *m.* (2)   Henry,
of France   Queen of Scots   Lord Darnley
d. 1567

(continued overleaf)

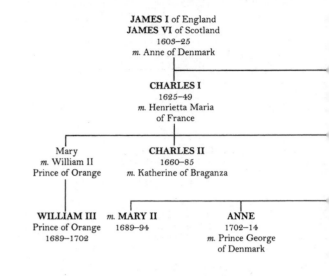

JAMES I of England
JAMES VI of Scotland
1603–25
m. Anne of Denmark

CHARLES I
1625–49
m. Henrietta Maria
of France

Mary
m. William II
Prince of Orange

CHARLES II
1660–85
m. Katherine of Braganza

WILLIAM III   *m.* **MARY II**
Prince of Orange   1689–94
1689–1702

ANNE
1702–14
m. Prince George
of Denmark

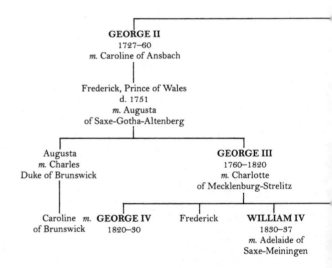

GEORGE II
1727–60
m. Caroline of Ansbach

Frederick, Prince of Wales
d. 1751
m. Augusta
of Saxe-Gotha-Altenberg

Augusta
m. Charles
Duke of Brunswick

GEORGE III
1760–1820
m. Charlotte
of Mecklenburg-Strelitz

Caroline   *m.* **GEORGE IV**
of Brunswick   1820–30

Frederick

WILLIAM IV
1830–37
m. Adelaide of
Saxe-Meiningen

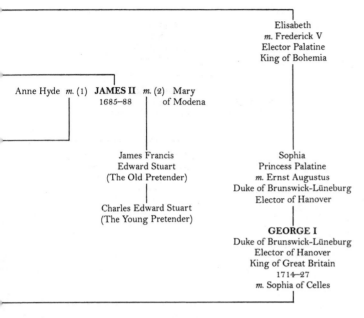

Elisabeth
m. Frederick V
Elector Palatine
King of Bohemia

Anne Hyde *m.* (1) **JAMES II** *m.* (2) Mary
1685–88 of Modena

James Francis
Edward Stuart
(The Old Pretender)

Charles Edward Stuart
(The Young Pretender)

Sophia
Princess Palatine
m. Ernst Augustus
Duke of Brunswick-Lüneburg
Elector of Hanover

GEORGE I
Duke of Brunswick-Lüneburg
Elector of Hanover
King of Great Britain
1714–27
m. Sophia of Celles

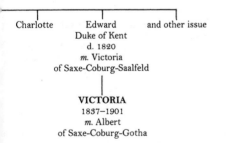

Charlotte   Edward   and other issue
Duke of Kent
d. 1820
m. Victoria
of Saxe-Coburg-Saalfeld

VICTORIA
1837–1901
m. Albert
of Saxe-Coburg-Gotha

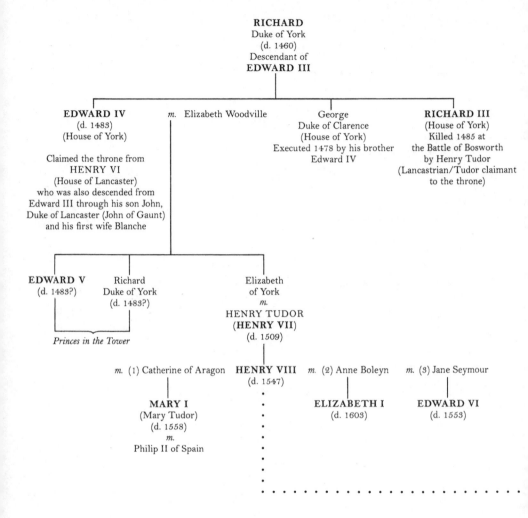

RICHARD
Duke of York
(d. 1460)
Descendant of
EDWARD III

EDWARD IV   *m.*   Elizabeth Woodville
(d. 1483)
(House of York)

Claimed the throne from
HENRY VI
(House of Lancaster)
who was also descended from
Edward III through his son John,
Duke of Lancaster (John of Gaunt)
and his first wife Blanche

George
Duke of Clarence
(House of York)
Executed 1478 by his brother
Edward IV

RICHARD III
(House of York)
Killed 1485 at
the Battle of Bosworth
by Henry Tudor
(Lancastrian/Tudor claimant
to the throne)

EDWARD V   Richard
(d. 1483?)   Duke of York
(d. 1483?)

Elizabeth
of York
m.
HENRY TUDOR
(**HENRY VII**)
(d. 1509)

Princes in the Tower

m. (1) Catherine of Aragon   **HENRY VIII**   *m.* (2) Anne Boleyn   *m.* (3) Jane Seymour
(d. 1547)

MARY I   **ELIZABETH I**   **EDWARD VI**
(Mary Tudor)   (d. 1603)   (d. 1553)
(d. 1558)
m.
Philip II of Spain

THE HOUSE OF YORK AND LANCASTER
THE HOUSE OF TUDOR

HENRY V
(House of Lancaster)
Died 1422
Descended from Edward III
through his son John,
Duke of Lancaster (John of Gaunt)
and his first wife Blanche

m.

Catherine of Valois *m.?* (2) Owen Tudor
d. 1461

HENRY VI
(House of Lancaster)
Killed 1471 at
the Battle of Tewkesbury
by Edward IV

Descended from Edward III
through his son John,
Duke of Lancaster (John of Gaunt)
and his first wife Blanche.
Cousin of Margaret Beaufort

JOHN BEAUFORT
(House of Lancaster)
Descended from Edward III
through his son John,
Duke of Lancaster (John of Gaunt)
and his third wife, Katherine Swinford.
Earl and Duke of Somerset
Died 1445

m.

Margaret Beauchamp

MARGARET BEAUFORT
(House of Lancaster)
Cousin of Henry VI

m.

EDMUND TUDOR
Earl of Richmond
(d. 1456)
son of Owen Tudor and Catherine of Valois,
the widow of Henry V.
Half-brother of Henry VI.
Descended from the ancient Welsh family Tewdwr

HENRY TUDOR
(HENRY VII)
(d. 1509)
m.
Elizabeth of York

HENRY VIII
(d. 1547)

JAMES VI of Scotland   *m.*   Anne of Denmark
JAMES I of England and Ireland
(d. 1625)

Elisabeth Stuart
m. Frederick V
Elector Palatine of the Rhine,
King of Bohemia

Mary
m. William II
of Orange

CHARLES II
(d. 1685)
m. Catherine of Braganza

SOPHIA
(d. June 1714)
(11 other siblings predeceased her)
Princess Palatine of the Rhine.
Cousin of Queen Anne.
Heiress presumptive of Great Britain
(being closest Protestant relative to Queen Anne)
m. Ernst Augustus,
Elector of Hanover

MARY II
m. **WILLIAM III**
Prince of Orange
(Mary d. 1694)
(William d. 1702)

GEORG LUDWIG
Elector of Hanover
Duke of Brunswick-Lüneburg.
Heir presumptive of Great Britain
(succeeded his mother Sophie to this title).
On death of his remote relative Queen Anne became
GEORGE I of Great Britain
(d. 1727)
m. Sophia of Celle
(div. 1694)

GEORGE II
Elector of Hanover
Duke of Brunswick-Lüneburg
King of Great Britain
m. Caroline of Ansbach
(d. 1760)

Frederick, Prince of Wales
(eldest of 8 children)
m. Augusta
of Saxe-Gotha-Altenberg
(d. 1751)

GEORGE III
King of Hanover (from 1814)
Duke of Brunswick-Lüneburg
King of Great Britain
(From 1811 his son
George Prince of Wales acted as Regent)
m. Charlotte
of Mecklenburg-Strelitz
(d. 1820)

GEORGE IV
King of Hanover
King of Great Britain
m. Caroline
of Brunswick, cousin
(div. 1795)

Frederick
Duke of York
(d. 1827)

William, Duke of Clarence
WILLIAM IV
King of Hanover
King of Great Britain
m. Adelaide of Saxe-Meiningen
(d. 1837)

THE HOUSE OF STUART AND THE HANOVERIANS

CHARLES I
(Executed 1661)
m. Henrietta Maria of France

JAMES II
(Enforced abdication and exile, d. 1701)
m. (1) Anne Hyde   *m.* (2) Mary of Modena
                                              (Catholic)

ANNE   James Francis Edward Stuart•
(d. August 1714)   (Catholic)
m. Prince George   The Old Pretender
of Denmark

                                       Charles Edward Stuart•
                                              (Catholic)
                                       The Young Pretender

• The Protestant Act of Settlement 1701
restricts the British throne to
the Protestant heirs of
Sophia, Electress of Hanover,
who have never been Catholic
and who have never married a Catholic

•• Under Salic Law
the Kingdom of Hanover could not descend
through the female line. Therefore the title went to
Prince Ernest Augustus, Duke of Cumberland,
younger brother of William IV

Edward,   *m.*   Victoria   and other issue
Duke of Kent   of Saxe-
                                    Coburg-Saalfeld

VICTORIA••   *m.*   Albert
Princess of Kent   of Saxe-
Queen of Great Britain   Coburg-Gotha
Empress of India
(d. 1901)

INTRODUCTION

THE IMPERIAL CROWN

In late 1487, King Henry VII had much to celebrate. In the space of only two years he had won the crown in battle; married the heiress of the rival royal house; fathered a son and heir; and defeated a dangerous rebellion. Secure at last on the throne, he decided to commemorate the fact in the most dramatic way possible by commissioning a new crown. And he would first wear it on the Feast of the Epiphany, 6 January 1488, at the climax of the Twelve Days of Christmas, when the monarch re-enacted the part of the Three Kings who had presented their gifts of gold, frankincense and myrrh to the Christ Child.

The new 'rich crown of gold set with full many precious stones' caused a sensation. As well it might. The circlet was thickly encrusted with rubies, sapphires and diamonds, highlighted with large and milky pearls. From the circlet there rose five tall crosses alternating with the same number of similarly proportioned *fleur-de-lis*. These too were thickly set with stones and pearls, with each *fleur-de-lis* in addition having on its upper petal a cameo carved with an image of sacred kingship. The crown was surmounted by two jewelled arches, with, at their crossing, a plain gold orb and cross, and it weighed a crushing seven pounds.

It was the Imperial Crown of England. As such it sits on the table at the right hand of Charles I in his family portrait by van Dyck as the symbol of his kingly power.

This book is the story of the Imperial Crown and of those who wore it, intrigued for it and, like Charles I himself, died for it. They include some of the most notable figures of English and British history: Henry VIII, whose mere presence could strike men dumb with fear; Elizabeth I, who remains as much a seductive enigma as she did to her contemporaries; and Charles I, who redeemed a disastrous reign with a noble, sacrificial death as he humbled himself, Christ-like and self-consciously so, to the executioner's axe.

Such figures leap from the page of mere history into myth and romance. And they do so, not least, because of the genius of their court painters, such as Holbein and van Dyck, who enable us to see them as contemporaries saw them – or, at least, as they wanted to be seen.

I have painted these great royal characters – and a dozen or so other monarchs, who, rightly or wrongly, have left less of a memory behind – with as much skill as I can. But this is not a history of kings and queens. And its approach is not biographical either. Instead, it is the history of an institution: the monarchy. Institutions – and monarchy most of all – are built of memory and inherited traditions, of heirlooms, historic buildings and rituals that are age-old (or at least pretend to be). All these are here, and, since I have devoted much of my academic career to what are now called court studies, they are treated in some detail.

But the institution of monarchy, and I think this fact has been too little appreciated, is also about ideas. Indeed, it is on ideas that I have primarily depended to shape the structure of the book and drive its narrative. But these are not the disembodied, abstract ideas of old-fashioned history. Instead, I present them through the lives of those who formulated them. Sometimes these were monarchs; more usually they were their advisers and publicists. Such men – at least as much as soldiers and sailors – were the shock-troops of monarchy. They shaped its reaction to events; even, at times, enabled it to seize the initiative. When they were talented and imaginative, monarchy flourished; when they were not, the Crown lost its sheen and the throne tottered.

I have already sketched this ideas-based approach in my earlier *The Monarchy of England: The Beginnings*, which deals with the Anglo-Saxon and Norman kings. In it, I argue that Wessex, round which the unitary kingdom of England coalesced in the ninth and tenth centuries, was a participatory society, which balanced an effective monarchy at the centre with institutions of local government which required – and got – the active involvement of most free men. It was this combination which enabled Wessex to survive and absorb the Viking invasions and finally to thrive. It is also why, after the destructive violence of the Norman Conquest and its immediate aftermath, the Norman kings decided that both the ethos and the methods of Anglo-Saxon government were too useful to be abandoned. Instead, the great law-giver kings of the Middle Ages, such as Henry II and Edward I, embodied them in an elaborate framework of institutions: the Common Law, the Exchequer and Parliament.

But, by the late fifteenth century, when I pick up the story, much of this was played out. The sense of mutual responsibility between Crown and people, which was the great legacy of the Anglo-Saxon nation-state, had eroded, and Parliament was flatly refusing to impose adequate taxation. The result was that the English kings, who had been the great military and imperial power of western Europe for much of the Middle Ages, found themselves outclassed by rulers who could raise more or less what revenues they wanted without the awkward business of getting their subjects' agreement first.

The young Henry VIII tried to breathe life into the embers. But even he had to admit defeat. Instead, the English monarchy took a radically different tack. And it did so purely by accident. Because he wanted a son – and because he wanted Anne Boleyn even more – Henry decided to divorce his first wife, Catherine of Aragon. But Continental power politics meant that the Pope refused. To get Anne, therefore, Henry had to do the hitherto unthinkable and displace the Pope by making himself head of the Church. The result fused politics with religion, first strengthening the monarchy beyond limits, then presenting it with the novel challenge of ideological opposition as the king-cum-Supreme Head of the Church found himself caught up in the vicious doctrinal disputes of the Reformation.

And all of this came to focus on Henry VII's Imperial Crown. Forged in an earlier age and for utterly different purposes, it came to symbolize the monarchy's inflated claims to rule Church as well as state, and, with the Stuart accession, Scotland as well as England.

But the very scale of the crown's claims triggered an equal and opposite reaction, and a century later a king was beheaded, the monarchy abolished and the Crown Imperial itself smashed and melted down.

This book tells the story of how and why this happened: of the Tudors, who carried the Crown of England to its peak; of the Stuarts, who united England and Scotland but eventually mishandled both; of the revolution that tried to extirpate monarchy in Britain. And, finally, of the monarchy's apotheosis – its extraordinary transformation from a priest-ridden absolutism to a limited, constitutional power in the state and the figurehead of the most extensive empire in the history of the world.

PART I

THE MAN WHO
WOULD BE KING

HENRY VII

I

THE MAN WHO ordered the Crown Imperial to be made was the founder of the Tudor dynasty, Henry Tudor. But Henry was a man who should never have been king at all. He seized the throne against the odds, amid bloodshed and murderous family feuds. But behind the beheadings and the gore was the fundamental question of how England should be ruled. Henry thought he knew the answer. But his cure proved as bad as the disease.

The story begins five years before Henry Tudor's birth, when a nine-year-old girl was summoned to court. Her name was Margaret Beaufort, and with her fortune of £1000 a year, she was the richest heiress in England. Even more importantly, as the direct descendant of John of Gaunt, Duke of Lancaster, Margaret was of the blood royal. Her cousin, the Lancastrian

King Henry VI, had decided that she should marry his own half-brother, Edmund Tudor – a man more than twice her age. It was a sordid mixture of money and power, with the technicalities fixed by a venal and accommodating Church.

King Henry VI was weak. He had failed in war; was incapacitated by long bouts of madness, and had fathered just one child, thus leaving the succession dangerously in doubt in an age of civil war and rival kings. The union of Margaret and Edmund would, Henry hoped, strengthen the weakened royal family. It would surely produce children, and therefore fulfil the Lancastrian dynasty's duty to provide a line of potential successors to the crown should anything happen to the sole heir. For what was the monarchy for if it could not guarantee the continuity of effective rule long into the future?

When Margaret was barely twelve, the earliest legally permissible age for sexual intercourse, Edmund brought her to Wales, where they lived together as man and wife. Shortly before Margaret's thirteenth birthday she became pregnant, but six months later, weakened by imprisonment during a Welsh feud and finished off by the plague, Edmund died on 1 November 1456. His child bride, widowed and heavily pregnant, sought refuge with her brother-in-law at Pembroke Castle.

And it was in a tower chamber at that castle that Margaret gave birth to the future Henry VII on 28 January 1457. Actually, it was a miracle that both mother and child survived. It was the depths of winter and the plague still raged, while Margaret, short and slightly built even as an adult, was not yet fully grown. The birth probably did severe damage to her immature body because, despite two further marriages, Margaret was to have no more children. Yet out of this traumatic birth an extraordinary bond was forged between the teenage mother and her son.

Margaret would need to be the strong woman behind her son; Henry was born into an England that was being torn apart by civil war. For their family, the Lancastrians, were not the only ones with a claim to the throne. Their opponents were the three brothers of the House of York. Also descended from Edward III, they had at least as good a claim to the throne, one which they determined to make good by force. The resulting conflict later became known as the Wars of the Roses, after the emblems of the two sides: the red rose of Lancaster and the white rose of York.

Such emblems, known as badges, were worn not only by the followers of the two rival royal houses, but by all the servants of the nobility and greater gentry. And the more land you had, the bigger the private army of badge-wearing retainers (as they were called) you could afford. The forces of York and Lancaster and their noble allies were evenly balanced, with the result that after fifteen years of fighting, the crown had changed hands twice between the Lancastrian King Henry VI and his rival Edward of York, who had declared himself Edward IV.

Their final showdown came at Tewkesbury in Gloucestershire, in May 1471. Edward – young, warlike, charismatic and supported by both his brothers, the twenty-one-year-old George, Duke of Clarence, and Richard, Duke of Gloucester, who was eighteen – was determined to annihilate the House of Lancaster once and for all. The battle soon turned into a massacre, leaving thousands dead on the field. It was a decisive victory for York; a disaster for Lancaster.

After the battle, many of the Lancastrians fled to Tewkesbury Abbey, where they took refuge in the church. The victorious Edward and his men then burst in. There are two different versions of what happened next.

According to the official account, Edward behaved with exemplary decorum, pardoning the fugitives and offering up solemn thanks at the high altar for his victory. But the unofficial accounts tell a different and much more shocking story. Edward and his men, rather than turning their thoughts to God and mercy, began to slaughter the Lancastrians. A lucky few were saved by the intervention of a priest, vested and holding the holy sacrament in his hands, in front of whom even the bloodthirsty Yorkists felt some shame. Edward then recovered control of the situation by issuing pardons to his defeated enemies. But already enough blood had been spilt to pollute the church and to require its reconsecration.

The Yorkists also claimed that the Prince of Wales had died in the carnage of the battlefield. But darker rumours had it that he had been taken prisoner and brought before Edward, who accused him of treason, pushed the boy away and struck him with a gauntlet. He was then murdered by Clarence and Richard. A day or two later, despite his solemn pardon, Edward ordered the beheading of most of the remaining Lancastrian leaders. Now only the life of the feeble Lancastrian king, Henry VI, stood between Edward and an unchallenged grasp of the throne.

On 21 May Edward entered the City of London in triumph. That night, between the hours of eleven and midnight, Henry VI was murdered in the Tower of London, probably with a heavy blow to the back of the head. Only one man is named as being present in the Tower at the time: Edward's youngest brother, Richard, Duke of Gloucester, who already, at the age of only eighteen, was emerging as the most effective hatchet man of the Yorkist regime. As he struck the fatal blow, he is supposed to have said, 'Now there is no heir male of King Edward the Third but we of the House of York!' Now, surely, the Wars of the Roses were over.

No one, a Yorkist chronicle exulted, of 'the stock of Lancaster remained among the living' who could claim the throne. But one Lancastrian claimant — however remote — did remain: Henry Tudor. Fourteen years had passed since Margaret had had her son. Now the teenage Henry was in danger of his life. Not even the massive walls of Pembroke Castle could protect the boy against the vengeful power of Edward of York, and his mother urged him to flee. He took ship at Tenby, and crossed the Channel to Brittany. And there Henry had to endure a decade and a half of politically fraught exile before he would see either England or his mother again.

II

Having annihilated his Lancastrian enemies, Edward of York was now King Edward IV of England indeed. But the problem of nobles who were almost as rich and powerful as the king himself remained. And richest and most powerful of all was Edward's middle brother George, Duke of Clarence, the man Shakespeare described as 'False, fleeting, purjur'd Clarence'.

The phrase is memorable. But it is misleading. It suggests that the key to Clarence's story lies in his character defects. It doesn't. It lies instead in his position. For Clarence was what Queen Elizabeth I, who would occupy the same unenviable place herself, called 'second person'. His title, Duke of Clarence, was the one that was given in the Middle Ages to the king's second son. As such, he was endowed with vast estates and many grand castles like Tutbury and Warwick. Here he kept what he called his 'court' with a state that was indeed royal. Only the life of Edward himself, and in time Edward's two sons, stood between Clarence and the throne itself. Some second persons were content to remain merely loyal lieutenants. Clarence was not one of them. He had a power over the king that was at once malicious and deeply harmful to the peace of England. Clarence's knowledge, should he choose to reveal it, concerned the future of the House of York itself and all that the brothers had fought for. It related to his sister-in-law, Elizabeth.

Elizabeth Woodville was one of the most controversial women ever to have been Queen of England, with a past that could provide plenty of ammunition for a man as unscrupulous as Clarence. She was beautiful, ambitious, greedy and a widow of modest family background, on her father's side at least. Edward first met her when she petitioned him about a problem with her late husband's estate. Edward, young, handsome and sensual, immediately propositioned his pretty supplicant, but Elizabeth defended herself, it is said, with a knife. Edward, as seems then to have been his habit when women resisted his advances, offered her marriage. But this time it was not an empty promise to ensure a seedy seduction and the two were married secretly at her father's house.

Perhaps Edward had intended to repudiate this clandestine marriage to an attractive but nonetheless obviously unsuitable wife once he had got what he wanted. But he did not. Had the marriage turned out to be valid after all? Had Edward the playboy fallen in love? At any rate, six months later the marriage was made public and Elizabeth acknowledged as queen. By the mid-1470s, Elizabeth had presented Edward with five daughters and, crucially, two sons. Immortalized in stained glass at Canterbury Cathedral, they look like the perfect royal family. Edward had what every king desired: an heir and a spare and a collection of marriageable daughters.

The elder son was called Edward; the younger, Richard. History would know them as the Princes in the Tower. But if their parents' marriage proved to be invalid, the serene image of a happy royal family that would carry on the Yorkist line long into the future would be shattered. The boys would become bastards, and Clarence would be heir once more. So the ambitious second person revived an old rumour. It was said that the libidinous king had been married to another woman at the time he married Elizabeth, thus making the present union bigamous and therefore illegal.

The rumour of a previous marriage may well have been true – certainly, bearing in mind Edward's notorious way with women, it was plausible. That only made it the more dangerous, and by throwing his weight behind it Clarence had tested his brother's patience too far. Clarence was arrested and put on trial before a specially convened parliament in January 1478. Edward had packed the parliament with his own supporters. He was himself both judge and prosecutor, and no one dared to speak on behalf of the accused but Clarence himself.

The verdict of guilty was a foregone conclusion, and on 18 January 1476 Clarence was executed in the Tower, famously by drowning in a butt of malmsey. The middle brother of York was gone. But the problem he represented was not. The monarchy had been weakened by the Wars of the Roses. Much royal land had been given away to buy support from the nobles, some of whom, like Clarence, had threatened to become mightier than the king. Such overweening subjects were difficult to manage at the best of times. But when there were rival claims to the throne, they became a dangerous source of visibility as Clarence's own career had shown.

To guard against the possibility of future Clarences, Edward needed to strengthen his own position and that of the Crown. To help him do it, he enlisted a surprising ally: a man who had spent thirty years working for the enemy. Sir John Fortescue had served as the Lancastrian Lord Chief Justice; had spent years in exile with the Lancastrian Prince of Wales, and had been captured after the Battle of Tewkesbury. But the king not only pardoned him; he placed him on his council.

At first sight, it's rather surprising that Edward decided to spare Fortescue. An enthusiastic hanging judge, Fortescue had planned the judicial murder of the young Edward and the whole Yorkist family. He had also written powerfully and learnedly against Edward's claim to the throne. But Edward set these personal grievances aside. He had work for the old man to do. Fortescue, the leading intellectual of Lancastrian England, would play an important part in the construction of the new, reformed Yorkist monarchy of England.

Fortescue could be called England's first constitutional analyst, his key ideas shaped by the years he had spent in exile in Scotland and France. For his experience of how other countries were governed led him to reflect on his own, and to ask a series of fundamental questions. What was unique and valuable about the English system of government? What had gone wrong with it to breed the dreadful malaise of the Wars of the Roses? And how could the disease be cured without killing the very benefits that made England what it was?

Fortescue set out his answers in a short but remarkable book. It is usually called *The Governance of England*, but its full title, as it appears in the early printed edition, is *The Difference between an Absolute and a Limited Monarchy*. Or in Fortescue's own lawyerly Latin terminology, between a '*dominium regale*' and '*dominium politicum et regale*'.

France, Fortescue says, is the supreme exemplar of absolute monarchy – *dominium regale* – and England of limited, or mixed, monarchy – *dominium politicum et regale*. And the key to the difference between the two lies in the rules governing taxation. In France, the king could tax the common people at will, a system Fortescue strongly disliked as it made the king rich, but kept the people poor. But in England the rule established since at least the thirteenth century was that the king could only tax with the agreement of Parliament. For the English had an inviolable right of private property, and in that lay their liberty.

This certainly made the English rich, with a standard of living that was the envy of foreign visitors and the boast of patriotic Englishmen like Fortescue. But did the rules limiting taxation make the English king poor, and because he was poor, weak and incapable of military conquest and enforcing the rule of law against a fractious and turbulent nobility? Fortescue thought that they did, and that this weakness was the explanation for the Wars of the Roses. For the administration of the laws – which guaranteed the property rights and liberty of Englishmen – worked only when the monarchy had the independence and authority to govern the powerful men of the kingdom. And that in turn depended on the relative balance of wealth and power between the king and his greatest subjects, the nobility. As it was, in the late fifteenth century the king was relatively poor, whereas a handful of the nobles were extremely rich, which made them in Fortescue's vivid phrase 'over-mighty' and potentially ungovernable.

One solution would have been for the King of England to follow the path of French absolutism and impose by force taxes that Parliament wouldn't vote by consent. But such a challenge to traditional English freedom – or more accurately to the rights of property owners – would be dangerously revolutionary. The question, therefore, was how to achieve the apparently impossible, and reconcile monarchical authority with the liberty of the subject. Fortescue's proposal was to strengthen the Crown *within* the existing system of limited monarchy. The king, he said, should acquire land, and rule by virtue of being the richest man in the kingdom. For if the king had an independent source of income, Fortescue argued, the English people would enjoy their wealth and liberty without being imposed upon by the monarch, who would in turn uphold the law because he would 'exceed in all lordship all the lords of his realm, and none of them would grow to be like him, which thing is most to be feared of all the world'. The execution of his brother allowed Edward to do just that, by keeping Clarence's vast estates for himself.

The royal revenues from land increased rapidly, which meant that Edward didn't need to call a parliament again for the unusually long period of almost five years. But land, Fortescue also understood, was about power as well as cash. And Edward took advantage of his new-found freedom to redraw the political map. He carved England up into territories, each controlled by a trusted member of his own household or family. It was all very cosy, but it depended to a dangerous extent on the force of Edward's own personality. It also loosened ties of loyalty, since it meant that those outside the charmed circle didn't care very much one way or another about who the king happened to be.

But as long as Edward remained alive and well, none of that mattered. Indeed, for the next five years the king grew rich; his Yorkist regime grew strong and it seemed that Lancastrian Henry Tudor, still sheltering in Brittany, would live out the rest of his life in exile. But at Easter 1483, disaster struck the House of York. Edward was taken ill with a fever after going fishing on the Thames. Within ten days he was dead. Only Richard, youngest of the brothers, remained of the generation of Yorkists that had defeated the Lancastrians at Tewkesbury. He was no more his brother's heir than Clarence, but true to family form he too would make his own brutal bid for power.

III

After the unexpected death of King Edward IV, all eyes turned west, towards Ludlow in the Welsh Marches, where Edward's son, heir and namesake – Prince Edward – was being brought up. But at twelve, was the boy old enough to rule in his own name? Much of the Yorkist clique, particularly the queen's family, who had become powerful after the secret marriage, staked their future on the premise that the child could reign in his own right. They had been responsible for his education and upbringing; they had much to gain in the new reign. But a faction emerged in favour of appointing the prince's uncle Richard as 'Protector' or regent until the boy was old enough to exercise power himself.

Queen Elizabeth, sensing danger, was determined to get her son crowned quickly, and the council agreed that the coronation should take place without delay. On 23 April, following the council's decision, Edward left Ludlow for London, his coronation and his reign. His escort, as his council insisted, was limited to 2000 men. It was enough to put on a fine show as the young king took possession of his kingdom. But the great lords of the kingdom were able to muster as many men or more. And unbeknown to the boy or his mother, Richard was summoning his own troops. He too was heading south.

Late on the night of 2 May, Queen Elizabeth Woodville, waiting in London for the arrival of her eldest son, received alarming news. Edward's cavalcade had been intercepted by his uncle, Richard, who had taken possession of his young nephew. The duke professed loyalty to the late king's son and heir, his own nephew after all. But Elizabeth, immediately suspicious of Richard's motives, fled that night with her younger son into the safe sanctuary of the abbey at Westminster. Richard entered London with his nephew a few days later. The council quickly ratified Richard's role as 'Protector'. Young Edward's coronation was 'postponed' until late June, and he was placed in 'lodgings' in the Tower.

What was Richard doing and why? Hitherto, he had had a reputation, in contrast to the flighty Clarence, for rock-solid loyalty to his brother Edward, who had rewarded him with the government of the whole of the north of England. There he had won golden opinions as a fine soldier and a fair judge, and the model of a king's younger brother. Nevertheless, his portrait suggests a man not entirely at ease with himself – or others. He is tight lipped, and he is fiddling nervously with the rings on his fingers; he also had the tic of biting hard on his lower lip and constantly pushing and pulling his dagger in and out of its sheath. Was he repressed, paranoid? A hypocrite with an iron grip on himself? Or did he genuinely believe, in view of Edward's tangled marital history, that he, Richard, was now rightful King of England?

On 10 June Richard, an over-mighty subject indeed, summoned his troops to London. His bid for the crown had begun in earnest. A week later, Queen Elizabeth was compelled to give up her younger son Richard into his uncle's charge. The young prince now joined his brother in the Tower.

Their uncle Richard now had both boys, first and second in

line to the throne, under lock and key. On 22 June a compliant parliament decreed that King Edward's marriage to Queen Elizabeth was invalid, and the princes bastards. Richard had succeeded where his brother Clarence had failed. He had robbed his nephews of their right to the crown and cleared his own path to the throne. He was crowned King Richard III at Westminster on 6 July, with the full blessing of Parliament.

During those frantic weeks, the two princes had been seen less and less around the Tower. Now they seemed to have disappeared altogether. By the late summer of 1483 everybody, including the princes' own mother, Elizabeth Woodville, took for granted that they were dead. They also took it as read that the responsibility for their deaths rested with Richard. For only Richard had the power, opportunity and above all the motive.

To this day, their exact fate remains a mystery. Writing thirty years later, Thomas More claimed that the Constable of the Tower was ordered to do them to death, but refused. Others, however, proved willing, and the two boys, More says, were smothered to death in their sleep with pillows, on the orders of their uncle.

His elder brothers were dead, the princes gone. The crown was his. But apparently doing away with the rightful heirs to the throne was a step too far, and opposition to Richard was now growing. Richard had been popular and might in theory have been a suitable king. But his sudden and bloody means of gaining power were seen as bringing a curse on England and perverting the sacred rule of succession. Soon he would be fight-ing to the death for the crown he had taken by fraud and force.

Opposition came to centre on a plot hatched between two

powerful and aggrieved mothers: Queen Elizabeth Woodville, whose sons were lost, and Margaret Beaufort – whose son Henry Tudor was in exile. Their machinations would prove Richard's undoing, and decide England's fate.

Some time in the late summer of 1483 Queen Elizabeth Woodville, still in sanctuary in the abbot's lodgings at Westminster, received a visit from a singular Welshman, Dr Lewis Caerleon. Dr Caerleon was a scientific jack-of-all-trades – mathematician, astronomer, astrologer and physician – and, unlike many polymaths, he was a master of all of them. The sanctuary, of course, was heavily guarded by the king's men, but Dr Caerleon was waved through because he was the queen's physician. He was also, not coincidentally, physician to Lady Margaret Beaufort, and in his doctor's bag he carried, on Lady Margaret's behalf, a remarkable proposal. The queen's eldest daughter – also called Elizabeth – should marry Margaret's son Henry. Thus the bloodlines would converge, and York, Woodville and Tudor should join together against the usurping Richard III. That Elizabeth accepted the proposal confirms that she was convinced that her sons were dead.

That Margaret made it shows that she had realized that Richard's murderous ambition had opened the way for her son to gain the throne of England. Margaret had been nursing her ambitions for her exiled son, Henry Tudor, for years. Now, thanks to Richard's murderous path to the throne, she could put them into practice.

His mother's plot under way, the thirty-year-old Henry set sail from Brittany, where he had lived in exile for the fifteen years of impregnable Yorkist rule, to make his bid for England's throne. On 7 August 1485, at Milford Haven, just a few miles from his birthplace at Pembroke, Henry Tudor's army made landfall in the evening. His years of exile were at an end.

As soon as he stepped ashore Henry knelt, overcome with emotion at his seemingly miraculous return, and began to recite the psalm 'Judge me Lord and fight my cause'. Then he kissed the sand and, making the sign of the cross, called on his troops in a loud voice to follow him in the name of God and St George. It was a magnificent beginning for a would-be King of England.

But only 400 of Henry's men were English. Most of the rest of his little army of 2000 or 3000 were French, and they had come in French ships with the aid of French money and the blessing of the French king. Indeed, most of Henry's own ideas about kingship were probably French as well. So just what kind of King of England would he be? That question was not asked for the moment. First, he had to wrench the crown from Richard's powerful grasp.

The two sides came face to face at Bosworth in the Midlands, where the fate of England's monarchy would be decided. The battle began when the vanguard of Richard's army, thinking to overwhelm Henry's much smaller force, charged down the hill. But instead of breaking and running, Henry's front line smartly reformed themselves into a dense wedge-shaped formation. Against this, the attack crumbled.

Richard, high up on Ambian Hill, now caught sight of Henry with only a small detachment of troops at the rear of his army. With courage or desperation, Richard decided that the battle would be settled by single combat – Richard against Henry, York against Lancaster. Wearing his battle crown, with a light robe with royal symbols over his armour, Richard led a charge with his heavily armed household knights down the hill. With magnificent courage he cut down Henry's standard-bearer and came within an inch of Henry himself. But once again, Henry's foot soldiers proved capable of assuming an effective defensive position. And Richard, isolated and unhorsed, was run through by an unknown Welsh pikeman, mutilated and stripped naked, more like a dishonoured outlaw than a vanquished King of England.

The third and last of the brothers of the house of York was dead. By his reckless ambition Richard had split the Yorkist party and handed victory and the crown to Henry Tudor. The symbolic union of York and Lancaster was made flesh in January 1486, when Henry Tudor married Elizabeth of York, just as their respective mothers had planned. A new iconography of union was created, merging the two once warring roses, red and white, into one – the Tudor Rose. A new dynasty was born.

But two years after the wedding, Henry ordered a new, ostentatious crown to be made, one that hinted at political ambitions that went well beyond Fortescue's limited monarchy. The crown was soon known as the Crown Imperial. Its unusual size, weight and splendour symbolized the recovery of the monarchy from the degradation of the Wars of the Roses and the expurgation of the foul crimes of Richard, which had brought down a curse upon the kingdom. The French fleur-de-lis, alternating with the traditional English cross round the band of the crown, looked back nostalgically to England's lost conquests in France. But might there be more to it than that? Henry had witnessed at first hand the powers of the absolute monarchy in

France and, some said, he had liked what he had seen. Might the Crown Imperial be the means by which these ideas could, as Fortescue had feared, be smuggled back into England?

IV

At Winchester Cathedral in 1486 it seemed that the new Tudor dynasty had set the seal on its triumphant beginnings. The queen had borne King Henry VII a son and heir. He was named Arthur, and his christening was designed to signal the start of a new Arthurian age. The baby's godmother was the Yorkist Dowager Queen Elizabeth Woodville, whose kinsmen also played a prominent part.

King Henry really had, it seemed, ushered in a new age of reconciliation. But it was to be short lived. Just six months after the christening, Elizabeth Woodville was stripped of her lands and sent to a nunnery, effectively banishing her from court for ever.

What had happened? Events had been triggered, almost certainly, because there were too many queen mothers and would-be queen mothers around. For Elizabeth Woodville, in her moment of restored glory, had reckoned without her some-time fellow-conspirator, Lady Margaret Beaufort. Henry VII had already honoured Lady Margaret with the title of 'My Lady the King's Mother'. But, since she hadn't actually been crowned queen, she had to defer to Edward IV's widow Elizabeth Wood-ville, who had. Lady Margaret didn't like that one little bit. So

Elizabeth Woodville, she decided, had to go. Indeed, Margaret gave precedence only reluctantly to her daughter-in-law the queen herself. She wore the same robes; she signed herself 'Margaret R'; and she walked only half a pace behind the queen. Lady Margaret, in short, was proving to be the mother-in-law from hell.

Margaret's behaviour was a political disaster. She was the heiress of the House of Lancaster; the humiliated Elizabeth was the matriarch of the House of York, and the Yorkist nobility felt spurned too. Henry's dream of reconciliation was fading in the face of family feuds and sidelined aristocrats. And within a year he faced a major uprising by rebellious Yorkist nobles, which he only narrowly beat off.

But in 1491 foreign affairs intervened. The French invaded Brittany, where Henry had spent his exile. Hoping to strengthen his position at home through victory abroad, Henry followed the traditional path of declaring war on France. The result was a curiously half-hearted affair for a man who had fought his way to the throne. A reluctant parliament made part of its grant conditional on the duration of the war; while Henry himself delayed setting sail for France until almost the end of the campaigning season in October 1492. Three weeks later the French offered terms, and on 3 November Henry agreed to withdraw in return for an annual payment of £12,500. The English soothed their injured pride by calling the payment a tribute. But the world knew better. Once the English armies had aroused terror throughout France. Now they were a mere nuisance to be got rid of by the payment of a cheap bribe.

It was a sharp lesson for Henry – England's limited

monarchy had let him down; it couldn't match the financial and military might of French absolutism. Now he had failed to achieve glory in war, just as he failed to unite York and Lancaster. There was nothing left but to lower his sights and return to the financial methods previously advocated by Fortescue and implemented by Edward IV. He did so with a novel degree of personal involvement, as each surviving account book of the Treasurer of the Chamber shows.

Like a diligent accountant Henry checked every single entry in it and, to confirm the fact, he put his initials, HR – known as the sign manual – alongside each one. It was not entirely regal behaviour. Rather than lead Englishmen in battle, Henry distinguished himself as an unusually scrupulous auditor. It was privatized government, medieval-style, with England run as the king's personal landed estate and the monarchy as a family business. It would make Henry rich, but would it make him secure?

Events showed not. In the autumn of 1496 he faced another rebellion. This one nearly cost him his throne. The uprising was led by a ghost from the past, a man claiming to be Richard, Duke of York, the younger of the Princes in the Tower, who had apparently and miraculously survived his uncle's bloody purge and had at last returned from exile to claim his crown.

He was a fraud, a Fleming called Perkin Warbeck, but he had powerful backers, the Scots, who threatened to invade England. A reluctant parliament ratified a substantial grant to the king of £120,000, and the royal army began to move north. But the tax sparked a rebellion in Cornwall. The rebels could see no reason why they should pay to fight the 400-mile-distant Scots.

And with the South empty of troops, a rebel Cornish army marched unopposed across the breadth of England.

As the Cornish rebels approached dangerously near London, Queen Elizabeth of York collected her second and beloved son, Prince Henry, from Eltham and took refuge with the boy in the Tower. It was a close-run thing. If his father were defeated, Prince Henry would share the fate of his Yorkist uncles – the Princes in the Tower – and be done to death in the grim London fortress. Instead, on 17 June 1497, Henry VII defeated the Cornish rebels at Blackheath, and on 5 October Perkin Warbeck himself was captured. But Henry VII had learnt his lesson. In the remaining dozen years of his reign he would summon only a single brief parliament, and he would impose no more direct parliamentary taxation.

Without parliaments, contact between king and people was weakened, and the narrowing of government was further intensified by a series of personal tragedies. In 1502 Arthur, Henry's son and heir, died, perhaps of tuberculosis, aged fifteen. Worse was to come. Two years later, Henry's much-loved wife Elizabeth died in childbirth. She was only thirty-seven, and her funeral saw an outpouring of public grief.

Most grief stricken of all was Henry VII himself, and the deaths in quick succession of his son and wife changed him greatly. His character became harder, his style of government more authoritarian. The sole purpose of Henry's kingship now became the soulless accumulation of riches. Racking up rents on royal lands was no longer enough; instead – in direct defiance of Magna Carta – he resorted to selling justice. The law was rigorously and indiscriminately enforced not according to strict principles of justice but as a means of drawing people into Henry's net of financial coercion. The usual punishments for crimes could be avoided by bribing the king, or, put more politely, paying a fine. The nobility bore the brunt, for they were fined large sums of money for feuding or retaining large private armies. The once powerful great men of the kingdom had finally been brought to heel, but as part of Henry's obsessive quest for revenue.

He had ceased to be a king and become, so his disgruntled subjects thought, a money-grubbing miser. He had crushed his over-mighty subjects, subduing the turbulent and lawless passions of the nobility, and avoided the trap of weak kingship; but along the way he had become a tyrant, an absolute monarch who manipulated the law at his pleasure. Was Sir John Fortescue turning in the grave, where he had rested for the last thirty years since his death in 1479? For Fortescue had believed passionately that a monarchy richly endowed with land and independent of faction would be a guarantor of English freedom and property rights. But it hadn't quite turned out like that. Henry had acquired the land and the money, getting his hands on more of both than any other king since the Norman Conquest. What he hadn't delivered on, however, were Fortescue's twin ideals of freedom and property. Instead, by the end of his reign they both seemed as dead and buried as the old Chief Justice himself.

Henry died on 21 April 1509, after a reign of almost twenty-four years. He was buried, next to his beloved wife, in the magnificent Lady Chapel which he had commissioned in Westminster Abbey. A few feet away would soon lie the other significant woman in his life, but for whom he might never have been king – his mother.

Henry died in his bed and he died rich. But if the last forty years had proved anything at all, it was that the traditional English limited monarchy had, in an age of Continental absolutism and increasingly professional armies, ceased to work. Henry's successor would give it one last try. And then, to his surprise and everyone else's, he would create a new and revolutionary imperial monarchy, different alike from that of his medieval predecessors and his authoritarian father. This successor was Henry's second son and namesake and, reigning as King Henry VIII, he would change the face of England for ever.

KING AND EMPEROR

HENRY VIII

ON 24 JUNE 1509, Henry VIII was crowned in front of the high
altar at Westminster Abbey. The supreme symbol of the Tudor
monarchy, the Crown Imperial, was now his.

But despite the myths and hopes embodied in the crown
that sat on the seventeen-year-old boy's head, it was a debased
inheritance. All Henry VII's dreams of an imperial English monarchy that ruled Scotland, Ireland and France and was a dominant power in Europe had ended in frustration. The old king,
in his last inglorious years, was regarded as a miser and a tyrant
hardly worthy of the crown he had designed. Instead, Henry VII
ruled his 'empire' like a private landlord – strictly and with a beady
eye on his rent. For those who knew anything of history, this
was not how the ruler of a great nation was supposed to behave.

The son agreed, and his subjects knew it. His personality –
sunny, gregarious and romantic – was the opposite of his
father's, and it promised a fresh start – although no one could
have guessed how radical, even revolutionary, it would prove to
be. Naturally, the young king was greeted with an outburst of

joy after so many years of repugnant rule. 'Heaven and earth rejoice,' wrote Lord Mountjoy; 'everything is full of milk and honey and nectar ... Avarice has fled the country, our king is not after gold, or gems, or precious metals, but virtue, glory, immortality.'

He was right and Henry's reign turned into a quest for fame as obsessive as that of any modern celebrity. It took many different forms. At first, Henry would try to breathe new life into the old monarchy. But it would essentially be a last gasp of traditional medieval kingship. Thereafter, the search for glory would eventually lead Henry into territory where no English king had ever dared to venture before. But it came at a price. Above all, it threatened to upset the traditional balance between freedom and authority and to turn English kingship into an untrammelled despotism that claimed power over men's souls as well as their bodies.

<h1 style="text-align:center">I</h1>

At the time of Henry's birth in 1491, the Tudors were a new, not very secure dynasty. His father had failed to reconcile the defeated Yorkist nobility and was about to embark on an unsuccessful war in France. Threats of rebellion and civil war stalked in the background, and the once hopeful king retreated ever more into privacy; ever more into the role of a greedy landlord.

And, in any case, the future of the Tudor dynasty was not

destined for Henry himself, but for his elder brother Arthur, Prince of Wales. Henry, as the second son, wasn't expected to be king, and as a result he received a rather modern, unkingly kind of upbringing. Instead of having the rigorous demands of kingship knocked into him by male tutors and role models, he was brought up at Eltham Palace by his mother and with his sisters, who idolized the robust and self-confident boy.

This early experience of women's love made Henry a romantic, and paved the way to the great passions and crimes of his adult life. Yet he was no mere pampered prince. Instead, Henry would always combine his romantic passions with sincere, if second-rate, intellectual ambitions. Once again it went back to his mother. She made sure that his education was of the best and a succession of distinguished tutors gave him a thorough grounding in the latest Latin scholarship. Even the super-learned Erasmus was impressed, and when he met Henry, aged only eight, he was bowled over by the boy's confidence, precocious learning and star quality.

In 1502, when he was eleven, Henry's life was struck by family tragedy. His brother Arthur died suddenly of a fever, followed soon after by their beloved mother. Henry was now the sole heir to the Tudor dynasty.

For the boy, his new status was a double-edged sword. He might be the Prince of Wales, but the carefree life that he had known as a boy was gone for ever. Quickly brought to court, he learnt at first hand the uncertain and inglorious reality of Tudor monarchy. Nor was there much love lost between Prince Henry and the king. Henry was growing up fast and he was already taller and broader than his father. But the king, aware that the whole future of the Tudor dynasty depended on the life of his only surviving son, was fiercely protective.

A chief source of the conflict came over participation in extreme sports. Henry wanted to take part in the manly, aristocratic sport of jousting. But, because it was so dangerous, his father allowed him to ride only in unarmed training exercises: the inheritance of Bosworth was too precious to be risked in mere games. So, when the real thing took place, Henry had to sit it out, chafing on the sidelines while his friends slugged it out like men. The result was a clash, not of arms, but of the conflicting values between father and son about what it meant to be an English king.

But on 21 April 1509, after twenty-four years on the throne, Henry VII died, and Henry VIII was proclaimed king amidst wild scenes of popular rejoicing. The most impressive tribute came from Thomas More, the great scholar and lawyer, whose life and death were to be inextricably linked with Henry's. 'This day', he wrote of the new king's coronation, 'is the end of our slavery, the fount of liberty; the end of sadness, the beginning of joy.'

Fired with the idealism of youth, Henry had strong ideas about kingship. He had been brought up on the myths of King Arthur and the exploits of his ancestor Henry V, and like them he believed that a great king should be a great warrior. When he was fourteen, Henry first saw what was then believed to be Arthur's Round Table at Winchester. The great visual and literary myths that surrounded the new Tudor dynasty might have been mere political contrivances for Henry VII; but for Henry VIII they were real. Now he was king, he was determined to take Arthur and Henry V as his models of kingship. Like them, he would be a great jouster, he would have a brilliant court, and above all he would follow in their footsteps and conquer France.

Funded by the large inheritance left to him by his father, and benefiting from the first peaceful transition of power since the Wars of the Roses, Henry's court took on the feel of a magnificently armed camp, with an endless round of tournaments and jousts. There was an insatiable appetite for martial entertainments and courtly splendour. All Europe was dazzled by the English court's new-found glamour and extraordinary pageantry. A Spaniard reported home that the courtiers had instituted a twice-weekly foot combat with javelin and spear 'in imitation of . . . knights of olden time, of whom so much is written in books'. Many young nobles participated: 'But the most conspicuous . . . the most assiduous and the most interested . . . is the king himself.' It satisfied the longing for a splendid monarchy. It also signalled Henry's intention: the conquest of France.

To that end, one of Henry's first acts as king was to marry his brother's widow, the Spanish Princess Catherine of Aragon, who was six years his senior. The marriage would sow the seeds of upheaval and revolutionary change in the English monarchy. At the time, however, it was much simpler. Henry loved Catherine, but the marriage also cemented England's alliance with Spain against France. In 1510 peace with France was renewed, but when the ambassador came to thank Henry, he angrily retorted to an unwisely phrased French sentence, 'I ask peace of the King of France, who dare not look me in the face let alone make war on me!' Henry was rearming England, and in 1511 he got both the council's agreement and a moral justification for war. The French king had committed the most mortal sin as far as Henry was concerned: he threatened to depose Pope Julius II and he had insulted the English ambassadors. On 28 June 1513, the English army crossed the Channel to France with Henry's banners intertwined with those of the Pope. For the first time in almost a century, Parliament had proved willing to vote serious war taxation. The result was the largest and best-organized English army since Agincourt. This was a holy war, and Henry was the Pope's greatest ally against schismatic France. The French king was stripped of the title 'Most Christian King', and it was given to Henry.

Henry, like his great hero Henry V, led the English army in person. He even came under fire occasionally. He defeated the French in the Battle of the Spurs – so called because the French knights ran away so quickly; captured important prisoners; and took two French cities after set-piece sieges. Henry hadn't conquered all France, of course, but he had restored the reputation of English arms. He had made England once more one of the big three European powers alongside France and the Habsburg Empire. Above all he had covered himself in glory.

At the same time, however, Henry – or rather Catherine, since it was always the woman who was blamed – had failed to produce an heir. She gave birth to a short-lived son in 1511, but then followed miscarriage after miscarriage. Henry was surprisingly understanding, but how long could he wait for a son?

II

King Henry VIII had triumphed in France, and had covered himself in glory, but he hadn't done it alone. The architect of his victories was Thomas Wolsey, a butcher's son from Ipswich. Wolsey had risen from nothing through his intelligence, drive and ambition. Though nominally only a royal chaplain, it was he who had organized the whole French campaign. Wolsey had an affinity with the king; they were both pleasure-seekers and men of broad vision. He flattered the young monarch, provided him with royal pleasures and relieved the king of the irksome, inglorious, pleasure-denying day-to-day business of ruling a country.

His rewards were commensurate with his usefulness: in quick succession he became bishop, archbishop and cardinal. Abroad his power and international standing added to the dignity of the English monarchy. At home, by virtue of his role as papal legate and a Prince of the Church, he was *de facto* Pope in England: so long as Wolsey held his personal supremacy there was no possibility of a foreigner interfering in the internal affairs of the kingdom or of the spiritual power of the Church challenging the temporal power of the Crown. He was also a territorial magnate and dominated the ecclesiastical establishment. And as Lord Chancellor, he held executive and judicial power.

Thus, by 1515, Wolsey was supreme in Church and state. But as much as his power, contemporaries were impressed by his overweeningly flamboyant character, by his taste, his magnificence and his sense of display. His supreme monument is his great palace at Hampton Court, where he kept a court every bit as lavish as Henry's own and demonstrated with his every move that the levers of power were in the hands of the cardinal legate. But we should not let this outward display deceive us about the reality of Wolsey's power. He had risen only because he was able to deliver what Henry yearned for – glory and war – and he would survive only if he were able to continue to deliver what Henry wanted, whatever it might be.

But it was becoming harder to see how Henry's lust for power could continue to be satisfied. For the gains of the war proved fleeting, and by 1516 Henry was no longer the teenage star of Europe. There was a new, young, warlike King of France, Francis I, and a new, even younger Habsburg emperor, Charles V, Queen Catherine's nephew, who ruled in his own right Spain, Germany, the Netherlands, and most of Italy.

Since both commanded much larger resources than Henry; glory in war was no longer a possibility. But peace, he was told, could be as noble and religious; it was also realistic. Henry was still only twenty-seven and the same ambitions to reclaim the throne of France burnt within him. How had he become the peace broker of Europe? Just as Wolsey fixed the king's wandering attention to mundane business with a rich gift or a relishing dish, so he made peace attractive. It was not merely peace with honour: it was peace with glory. England's military and material weakness had been transmuted into nobler metal. She was now, it seemed, the leader of Europe and Henry truly the Most Christian of Kings.

The change was also underpinned by material considerations.

For the moment, England seemed to hold the balance of power between Francis and Charles, and was courted by both sides. But could it last when the great rulers of Europe eyed each other with hostility? Wolsey, dextrous and inventive as usual, turned the situation to England's advantage by organizing a magnificent peace conference, the Field of Cloth of Gold, which took place on a dusty, windswept plain in the north-east of France on 6 June 1520. It centred on a personal meeting between Henry VIII and Francis I. And, in another first for Wolsey, it was one of the earliest modern summit conferences. But the jamboree was much more than that. Wolsey had pulled off the seemingly impossible: English and French aristocrats met in peace and friendship. Centuries-old conflict had been replaced by martial sports. Wolsey sought to overawe Henry, the aristocracy and the people with something so grand that it made up for what many believed to be a shameful peace. It had all the ritual of war, but none of the blood. It was an Olympic Games with international jousting and wrestling competitions; there were displays of lavish cloth-of-gold tents, fantastic pavilions and almost competitive feasting. The English were generally reckoned to have won.

But it proved to be a mirage. England's role as arbiter of Europe depended on the continuing balance of power between Francis and Charles. Sooner or later Francis and Charles would fight, and one of them would win. What would Henry and Wolsey do then? Still with Arthur and Henry V on his mind, Henry renewed his determination to defeat France. For all the posturing on the Field of Cloth of Gold and the rhetoric about the glories of peace, Henry was edging closer to Charles and

The Royal Supremacy: (1) Holbein's dynastic mural (in the surviving copy of the lost original) groups the first two Tudor kings and their wives round a monument inscribed with their claims to greatness: Henry's VII's for ending the Wars of the Roses, and Henry VIII's for making himself Supreme Head of the Church. (2) The title-page of the first official English translation of the Bible, in which an enthroned Henry VIII distributes the Bible to both his clergy and lay-folk, shows what the Royal Supremacy meant in practice.

3

4

(5) The Field of Cloth of Gold, the lavish summit conference between Henry VIII and Francis I of France, was typical of the showy foreign policy of Henry's early years.

5

(1) Henry VII, founder of the House of Tudor and maker of the Imperial Crown and (2) his wife, Queen Elizabeth of York.

(3) Henry VIII and an ageing Catherine of Aragon (4), painted on the eve of their divorce.

1

2

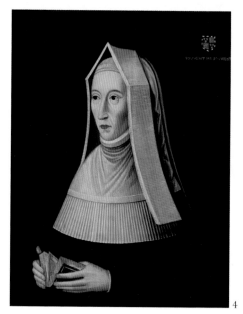

The Wars of the Roses: (1) Edward IV, who fought his way to the throne and (3) his younger brother, Richard III, whose murderous ambition destroyed Edward's legacy. (2) Elizabeth Woodville, Edward's widow and (4) Margaret Beaufort, mother of the future Henry VII, whose ladies' conspiracy brought down Richard III.

(1) Elizabeth I in her coronation robes. As Henry's daughter by Anne Boleyn, Elizabeth restored a Protestant religious settlement that, since it made some attempt to win over waverers, eventually won wide acceptance. But her childlessness triggered a succession crisis since her most obvious heir, her cousin, (2) Mary, Queen of Scots was a Catholic.

Mary's execution in 1587 paved the way to the smooth accession of her Protestant son, (3) James VI of Scotland in 1603.

1

2   3

1

2

(1) The Family of Henry VIII.
Henry's decision to leave the
throne to each of his children in
turn condemned England to
wild religious swings.
(3) The regime of his son,
the Boy-King Edward VI,
supported Archbishop Thomas
Cranmer (2) in introducing
radical Protestantism.

4

But his eldest daughter,
(5) Mary, used the Royal
Supremacy to return to a
persecuting Catholicism,
which created 500
martyrs (4) and left an
indelible impression.

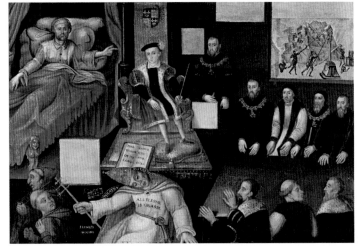

3

¶ The newe Te=
stament in Englyshe translated
after the Greke cōtaynynge
these bookes.

The Gospelles.
Mathew.   Luke.
Marke.   John.
The Actes.
The Epistles of S. Paul.
To the Romaynes   The.i.Thessalonyans.
The.i.Corinthyans.   The.ij.Thessalonyans.
The.ij.Corinthyans.   The.i.Timothe.
To the Galathyans.   The.ij.Timothe.
To the Ephesians.   To Titus.
To the Philippians.   To Philemon.
To the Colossyans.   To the Hebrues.
The Epistle of Saint James.
The.i.of S.Peter.   The.i.of S.John.
The.ij.of S.Peter.   The.ij.of S.John.
The Pistle of Jude.   The.iij.of S.John.
The reuelacyon of S.John.

the Holy Roman Empire. Together, they plotted to violate the sacred peace and vanquish Francis. Henry and Charles wanted to fight immediately, but Wolsey knew that England wasn't ready. With all his skills as a diplomatist, he continued to play both sides off against each other.

Henry had cast aside his humanist pretensions, and was animated by what the cardinal (with typical flourish) called the 'Great Enterprise' against France. By 1523, they seemed ready. But in reality the aims of Charles and Henry were very different. A tentative English invasion of France failed before it got farther south than Agincourt. But where was Charles? The allies were far from accord. In the autumn of 1523, a revolt by the leading French nobleman, the duc de Bourbon, provided the perfect opportunity for an invasion. But Henry's army invaded and fought on its own; what was supposed to be a multi-pronged invasion by England and the empire ended in farce. The Duke of Suffolk led the English army deep into France and it was poised to besiege Paris. But with winter coming on and no allies in the field, he was forced to abandon the campaign. The essential food supplies promised by Charles never arrived. England's best chance to defeat France came to nothing.

On 9 March 1525 Henry was woken by the arrival of a messenger come from Charles's army in Italy. He reported that the French had been crushed at Pavia, the capital of Lombardy; leading French nobles had been killed and Francis himself was a prisoner. Henry was elated. The Great Enterprise must surely enter its final phase, when England would reclaim her inheritance. He sent ambassadors to Spain to arrange the final destruction of France. Charles and Henry should launch an immediate invasion and take Paris, where Henry would be crowned king.

But the victory, which had promised so fair, was to be the final blow to Henry's great ambitions. For Charles had no intention of setting up Henry as the most powerful monarch in Europe. Instead he called Henry's bluff: if Henry wanted his share of France, he must conquer it himself. That required money. Parliament was unlikely to vote new taxes. In their place, Wolsey suggested an extra-parliamentary levy, to which, as spin doctor in chief, he gave the emollient name of 'Amicable Grant'.

It made no difference. All taxes are unpopular. This one caused riots, and the worst one took place at Lavenham in Suffolk, which was then a prosperous wool-weaving town. On 4 May, 4000 protesters poured through the streets, the church bells rang the alarms and the rioters swore that they would die for their cause. Other smaller protests took place throughout the South-East. In Lavenham, the rioters pleaded poverty. But in London, sophisticated constitutional objections were raised to a tax that hadn't been voted in parliament.

In the face of the protest, the government abandoned the Amicable Grant and with it Henry's projected invasion of France. Both Wolsey and Henry put a brave face on the climb-down. But it was a terrible humiliation. To Henry, it seemed that he had failed in both peace and war, and his dreams of glory were dashed. After sixteen years of trying to emulate Arthur and Henry V, this Henry was no better, in his estimation, than his failure of a father. But there was a ray of sunshine; Henry had fallen in love again.

Henry had some years ago fallen *out* of love with his wife, Catherine of Aragon. Like most kings before him, he'd had mistresses and, even an acknowledged son by one of them. The real problem was not with his wandering eyes and hands, but instead came from Catherine's own situation.

She was the aunt of Henry's great betrayer, Charles V. She had urged the Anglo-Imperial alliance. Any advantage that should have come from their marriage in 1509 was, some sixteen years later, and after so many disappointments, hard to spot. Fatally for her, Catherine was identified with Henry's crushing international embarrassment. And there was scant compensation. The age difference between Henry and Catherine was now really beginning to tell, as the miniatures of the couple painted in 1525 show.

Henry himself, then aged thirty-four, has kept his youthful looks, but Catherine, already forty, was wearing badly. As the massive neck and shoulders in the portrait show, her once trim figure had run to fat, while her face, which used to be so pretty, had become round and blotched and bloated. The explanation of course was childbearing. Catherine had been more or less continuously pregnant in the first ten years of her marriage and it had played havoc with her figure. If the progeny had been sons, none of this would have mattered, but of all those pregnancies there was only a single child that survived – a daughter, Mary. And a woman who had lost her looks, was past childbearing age and hadn't produced an heir was vulnerable indeed.

Henry and Catherine's marriage wasn't the first royal union to get into difficulties. The man whose responsibility was to sort out such problems was the Pope in Rome, head of the Catholic Church to which England, like all the rest of western Europe, belonged.

But at just this moment, the Pope's position was under greater threat than ever before. The attack was led by a young German academic, Martin Luther, who in 1517 had launched the furious assault on the corruption of the Roman Church which began the Protestant Reformation. Henry and his minister Cardinal Wolsey were united in their horror at Luther's heretical attack on the Church. In May 1521, Wolsey condemned Luther's works in a great book-burning at St Paul's Cathedral while Henry – the would-be Most Christian King, after all – wrote a reply to Luther called the *Assertio Septum Sacramentorum* or 'Defence of the Seven Sacraments'. It was the first book to be written by an English king since Alfred the Great. Composed in Latin, it was set in the latest Roman type for circulation to a sophisticated, select European audience.

Above all, Henry's book was loud in its defence of the papal monarchy over the Church. So much so that Thomas More, then Henry's friend and intimate counsellor, warned the king that since his present good relations with Rome might change in the course of time, he should 'leave that point out or else touch it more slenderly'. But Henry was adamant in his championship of Rome and his reward was the title of 'Defender of the Faith' from a grateful Pope.

Henry never wavered in his detestation of Luther and all his works. But his attitude to Rome, just as Thomas More predicted, underwent a revolution. The reasons were Henry's need for a son and heir – and love.

The woman he'd fallen in love with was Anne Boleyn, sister of one of his former mistresses. Sexy rather than beautiful, Anne behaved as no mistress had dared to before, and with consequences that no one could have imagined.

III

By the mid-1520s, Henry's reign had hit the buffers. He'd failed in his quest for glory in both peace and war. He'd failed to father a son and heir. He'd even failed to persuade Anne to sleep with him.

For Anne, supremely confident in her hold over Henry, refused him sexual relations unless he agreed to marry her. The difficulty, of course, was that Henry was already married to Catherine, who would never agree to a divorce. So Henry and Anne tried to find legal grounds for dissolving Henry's marriage.

Their best hope lay in the Bible, where the Book of Leviticus forbade a man to marry his dead brother's widow, on pain of childlessness. It was for this reason that Henry had received a special dispensation from Pope Julius II to permit him to marry Catherine, the widow of his late brother, Arthur. But now Henry's lawyers argued that, since the marriage broke biblical law, Rome had exceeded its powers, and the marriage was invalid. The case was submitted for decision to the man who was both the Pope's personal representative in England and Henry's own chief minister, Cardinal Wolsey.

In the subterranean bowels of the Ministry of Defence building in Whitehall in London, amidst the ducting, the central heating pipes and the civil servants, there is an extraordinary survivor of the Tudor world. It is the wine cellar of Cardinal Wolsey's town palace, known as York Place, which once stood on this site. On the first floor there was the principal reception room of the palace, known as the great chamber. It was, almost certainly, in this room on 17 May 1527 that the first trial of the marriage of Henry VIII opened.

It was known as the secret trial, since Catherine was kept in the dark to let Wolsey move as quickly as possible. For Henry was confident that the Cardinal, armed with his formidable spiritual authority, would rule his marriage invalid. Instead, to enormous surprise, on 31 May Wolsey adjourned the court indefinitely, on grounds of the difficulty of the case.

Why did Wolsey, who owed everything to Henry, defy the king's wishes? Did he fear Anne Boleyn's power as queen? Were his legal doubts genuine? Or was it, above all, because he knew that without the Pope's agreement, no one else could hope to adjudicate in so delicate a matter? Whatever his reasons, the delay was crucial.

For, at exactly the same moment, events were unfolding in Rome which would make it impossible for the Pope to come down on Henry's side, even if he had so wished. Two days after Wolsey adjourned the court, news reached England that troops of the Emperor Charles V had taken Rome, sacked and pillaged the city, and driven Pope Clement VII to take refuge in the Castel Sant'Angelo. The Pope was now in the power of Catherine's nephew and Henry's enemy, and he would remain so for the foreseeable future. Henry's hopes of a quick divorce were at an end.

Wolsey knew that his power and his life were at stake. Desperate to find his way back into Henry's favour, he wrote the king a long letter, setting out the case for his own approach to the divorce. He sat down at his desk at four in the morning, 'never', his valet noted, 'rising once to piss, nor yet to eat any meat, but continually wrote his letters with his own hand'. But not even Wolsey could change the reality of European power politics.

But he could and did disguise them from the King. Back in early 1527 Henry and Anne had thought to be married in months. Instead, the months stretched into years as the Pope, with Wolsey's connivance, strung out Henry with legal man-oeuvres and diplomatic subtleties. It was not a personal affair. Given Catherine's relationship to Charles, it was the empire and its vassal Pope against England. But the crunch came with the second divorce trial in 1529 – for Henry and for Wolsey most of all.

Getting the trial underway at all was something of a triumph for Wolsey. But it soon became clear that, faced with the brute fact of Charles V's power, Wolsey, for all his cleverness and confidence, and for all his claims of supremacy over the Church in England, had been unable to persuade the Pope to disavow his predecessor's dispensation. Henry's patience was at an end. So, just as importantly, was Anne's. Without that, all the formal-ities of the trial were empty and the court, once again, was adjourned without a verdict.

As the second divorce trial neared its abortive end, the Duke of Suffolk had expressed contempt at Wolsey's powerlessness to do the king's bidding. Wolsey replied that he was but a 'simple cardinal'. It was a humbling admission. Henry had no time for such creatures. Throughout his reign, Henry had been able to maintain his independence from Rome and even be seen as superior to it. Had he not taken the moral leadership of Christendom as the bringer of peace? If the Pope was supposedly an equal partner and Henry supreme in his own kingdom, Wolsey's weakness had exposed it all as a sham. This failure cost him his job as the king's minister, and it would have cost him his head, if he had lived longer. Wolsey died cursing Anne for causing his downfall, and predicting the ruin of the Church.

Before he fell, Wolsey warned the Pope that if the divorce was blocked, Henry would be forced 'to adopt those remedies which are injurious to the Pope, and are frequently instilled into the King's mind'. The refusal of Rome to deal with Henry honourably meant that 'the sparks of that opposition here, which have been extinguished with such care and vigilance, will blaze forth to the utmost danger of all'. This was an allusion to the Lutheran heresy, which was flourishing in Germany and the Low Countries and creeping into England, despite government repression of heretics and the public turning of heretical books. And there was no secret as to who had 'instilled' such radical ideas in Henry's mind. Blocked in Rome, Anne Boleyn, who was a Lutheran sympathizer, encouraged Henry to turn to Rome's English opponents.

Anne was an avid reader of heretical books that had been banned by the orthodox and loyal Catholic king. But these blasphemous books became increasingly appealing to Henry. When a radical clergyman was arrested for distributing Lutheran tracts and William Tyndale's English translation of the Bible, Anne stepped in to save him. It was a crucial moment. For not only did Anne protect heretics, but she brought their books to her lover's attention. One of them, Tyndale's *Obedience of the Christian Man*, had a particular relevance for him. As the books of Kings and Romans in the Bible made clear, it was kings whom God ordained with His power, not priests. Kings had rights as spiritual leaders. Such an argument flattered Henry's ambition. Kingship gave him a special place in Christendom, but that God-given authority had been usurped through the centuries by others. 'This is a book for me and all kings to read,' he declared, animated by this new vision of kingship. That might be true, but Henry needed more: he needed to find a way round the long-acknowledged authority of the Pope, an authority that, a few years earlier, he had defended to the hilt.

It's not what you know but who you know, we're told. In the case of Thomas Cranmer it was both. When the divorce crisis began, Cranmer was an obscure theology don at Cambridge. But in the summer of 1529, a chance meeting with two Cambridge acquaintances brought Cranmer to the notice of Henry and Anne. The consequences transformed Cranmer, his world and ours.

For Henry, Cranmer insisted, had been going about the divorce in the wrong way. He had been treating it as a legal matter. But it wasn't: it was moral. And in morals the Bible supplied absolute answers as to what was right and what was wrong. And there were experts who knew which was which – they were university theologians, like Cranmer himself.

Let Henry only consult the universities, therefore, and he

would have a clear, unambiguous verdict in favour of the divorce which even Rome and the Pope would have to recognize.

'That man hath the sow by the right ear,' the king exclaimed. Henry was already coming to believe that the Pope was not the sole judge in Christendom. Now Cranmer had confirmed it with all the weight of his theological scholarship. Immediately, the canvas of university opinion began, starting, like so many new ideas, in Cambridge itself. Cranmer had thought that it would be high minded and straightforward. In fact both sides played dirty and used every device known to the academic politician: rigged committees, selected terms of reference and straightforward bullying and bribing. But after two days toing and froing, the university delivered the verdict that Henry wanted. Cambridge would be on the side of the winners in Tudor England.

With Cambridge and (more reluctantly) Oxford secured, Henry's envoys set out for the Continent to pit the arguments of the King of England against the authority of the Pope. In universities across Europe they bribed, cajoled and threatened theologians to give a verdict in Henry's favour.

Over the next few years the whole power of the Tudor state was to be thrown against Rome and Catherine. But Catherine wasn't without her defenders. One of the boldest was her chaplain, Thomas Abell, who combined the very different roles of scholar and man of action.

In the winter of 1528 Henry sent Abell on a mission to Catherine's nephew, the Emperor Charles V, in Spain, where Abell played the desperately dangerous game of double agent. Outwardly he was working for Henry – secretly he was undermining the king's whole strategy on Catherine's behalf. Mission accomplished, Abell returned to England, where he quickly emerged as Catherine's most effective and outspoken scholarly propagandist.

Abell called his principal work, with magnificent defiance, *Invicta Veritas* – 'truth unconquered and unconquerable'. In it he attacked the verdict of the universities which provided the whole intellectual basis of Henry's case. The attack struck home, as the king's infuriated scribbles throughout the book show. At one point, Henry's irritation actually overcomes his scholarship and he scribbles in the margin in mere English: 'it is false'. But by the time he'd finished, Henry's composure had recovered sufficiently for him to deliver his damning verdict on the book in portentous Latin, on the title page. 'The whole basis of this book is false. Therefore the papal authority is empty save in its own seat.'

Not even that magisterial royal rebuke was enough to shut Abell up. Instead, it took the full weight of the law. He was twice imprisoned in the Tower, where he carved his name and bell symbol on the wall of his cell, and was eventually executed as a traitor in 1540. Even so, Abell's courage proved fruitless. As learned opinion in England swung in his direction, Henry became bolder. He now asserted that, by virtue of his God-given office, the King of England was an 'Emperor'. As such, he was subject to no authority on earth – not even that of the Pope. When the papal nuncio came to Hampton Court to protest, the Dukes of Norfolk and Suffolk and the Earl of Wiltshire told him that 'They cared neither for Pope nor Popes in this kingdom, not even if St Peter should come to life again; that the king was absolute both as Emperor and Pope in his own kingdom'.

Once Henry had been the stoutest defender of papal authority. But that had changed with the divorce, which had blown open the ambiguities of the monarchy's relationship with Rome. Now the achievement of his most fervent hopes for Anne and for an heir depended on the idea that religious truth was to be found not in Rome but in the Bible. Rome instead was the obstacle that had delayed his divorce for five long years. It was the enemy that stood between him and Anne.

But what of the Pope himself? Here again, the Bible spoke. For there were no popes in scripture, but there were kings. And it was kings, Cranmer and his radical colleagues argued, who were God's anointed, ordained by Him to rule His Church on Earth. The idea appealed to Henry's thirst for glory. It offered a means to cut the Gordian knot of the divorce, and it even promised to make Henry, not the Pope, heir to the power and status of ancient Roman emperors.

It was intoxicating. Henry now stood on the threshold of a decision that would transform the monarchy and England utterly, and for ever.

IV

On 19 January 1531, Convocation, the parliament of the English Church, met in the Chapter House of Westminster Abbey. It faced an unprecedented charge – of exceeding its spiritual authority. Henry offered it pardon, in return for £100,000. Fatally,

the clerics agreed to pay. Having forced them to admit their error, Henry increased his price: the clergy must acknowledge that the king was 'sole protector and also supreme head of the Church in England' with responsibility for the 'cure of souls' of his subjects. Over the next two weeks they fought that demand word by word and letter by letter.

Finally, subject to overwhelming royal pressure, the Archbishop of Canterbury proposed that Henry should be accepted as Supreme Head in Earth of the Church of England 'as far as the law of Christ would allow'. His announcement was greeted with a stunned silence, which the archbishop ingeniously took to mean consent. The weasel words 'as far as the law of Christ allows' meant what anybody wanted it to mean, and the next year they were dropped. Until then, the Pope had still been acknowledged as nominal head of the international Church. But Henry's new direction was radical. The Pope was left as a sort of figurehead, but kings in their realms held a power directly from God. Also, in 1532, the House of Commons, having been given the green light by Henry's council, submitted a provocatively-worded position against the Church's remaining independent legislative power. This was a step too far and Convocation repudiated the arguments of the position with outrage.

Their reply was brought before the king who reacted by screwing up the pressure. On 10 May he ordered the clergy to submit to royal authority: all new clerical legislation would in future be subject to royal assent and existing law would be examined and annulled by a royal commission. This was a direct order from the king. Nevertheless, the clergy persisted in their defiance, citing scripture in defence of their rights and privileges against secular interference. The king's response was a hammer-blow. He summoned a delegation from Parliament and uttered those famous and emotive words: 'well beloved subjects, we thought that the clergy of our realm had been our subjects wholly, but now we have well perceived that they be but half our subjects, yea, and scarce our subjects: for all the prelates at their consecration make an oath to the Pope clean contrary to the oath they make to us.'

In effect, Henry was accusing the clergy in its entirety of treason for giving oaths of loyalty to someone other than the king. In the face of this, convocation had little choice but to surrender. On 15 May, it caved in, and gave up its independence. Parliamentary statute would dot the i's on Henry's new title of Supreme Head. But all the crucial stops had been taken. Henry had also broken Magna Charta and the first clause of his own coronation oath, by which he had sworn that the Church in England should be free.

And he had become a bigamist as well. In October 1532, Anne finally gave in and slept with Henry. By Christmas she was pregnant, and in January 1533, in strictest secrecy, Henry married her, despite the fact that Catherine was still legally his wife. A solution was now urgent. If Henry's second marriage was not declared valid, then the child (a boy if all was well) would be a bastard. The future of the Tudor dynasty would once again be in danger. The next month, Cranmer was made Archbishop of Canterbury. He was placed in the uncomfortable position of having to swear loyalty to the Pope, even though his purpose, as archbishop, was to implement the divorce and complete the break with Rome. 'I did not acknowledge [the

Pope's] authority', he swore in a secret disclaimer, 'any further than as it is agreed with the express word of God, and that it might be lawful for me at all times to speak against him, and so impugn his errors, when time and occasion should serve me.'

Time and occasion arrived very soon. Cramner derived his authority from Henry – God's representative in England – not the Pope, despite the oath he had made. It was Henry, in this capacity, who gave him permission to determine the validity of his marriage to Catherine, 'because ye be, under us, by God's calling and ours, the most principal minister of our spiritual jurisdiction within this our realm'.

A new trial was held at Dunstable Priory in Bedfordshire. Catherine was not represented, and crucial documents were missing. This did not matter. Using the verdict of the universities, Cramner ruled the first marriage void and upheld Henry's marriage to Anne. There would be no appeal to Rome. After seven years, Henry had the woman and queen he wanted. The London crowds grumbled, Charles V was furious and the Pope eventually excommunicated the king. But Henry and Anne defied them all.

Henry's second marriage and its intellectual foundation in the Act of Royal Supremacy, which finally passed into statute in November 1534, were profoundly divisive. Some opposed them viscerally because they hated Anne or loved the old Church. Others were more nuanced and, subtlest of all, as befits the man who warned Henry about exaggerating the Pope's powers when the king wrote the *Assertio*, was Henry's old friend and counsellor, Sir Thomas More. Opponents of whatever sort were whipped into line by laws, which required them to swear oaths upholding the new settlement. They had to swear an oath of allegiance to the Royal Supremacy. They also had to swear to the Act of Succession, which declared that Henry and Anne's baby daughter Elizabeth was the true heir. The implications went deeper than merely ratifying the king's marital and dynastic decisions. By agreeing, the country was being made to acknowledge that the break with Rome was permanent, and to assent to it. To refuse the oath meant treason and death. Thomas More was still loyal to the papacy, and he knew that his conscience forbade him to take the oath.

Thomas More was imprisoned in steadily worsening conditions in a cell in the Tower for over a year. But when, on 1 July 1535, he was removed for his trial at Westminster Hall, it looked as though he might escape with his life. More now did what he hitherto steadfastly refused to do and spoke his mind. He could not be guilty, he said, because the English Parliament could not make Henry VIII Supreme Head of the Church, for the common consent of Christendom, of which England was a tiny part, gave that title to the Pope and had done for over a thousand years. The judges reacted with consternation to the force of More's argument. But the Lord Chief Justice recovered the situation with a characteristic piece of English legal positivism. English law was what the English Parliament said it was, he asserted. More was condemned and beheaded on 6 July.

Working *with* Parliament rather than against it, Henry had hugely outdone his father. He had invested the so-called Imperial Crown with a truly imperial authority over Church and state. He would even get his hands on more land and money than the ravenous Henry VII could have dreamt of, and he got it by plundering the wealth of the Church.

Henry's personal authority over the Church gave him access to incredible riches. There were about five hundred monasteries scattered over England, some desperately poor but many rich and well run, and maintaining a thousand-year-old tradition of prayer, work and learning. But a change of intellectual fashion away from monasticism made them vulnerable, and their collective wealth made them tempting. So in 1536, the process of dissolving the monasteries began. At first, the objective was presented as reform. The habits of the religious community were investigated and vices and irregularities were found, many petty and some serious. In the guise of enforcing the rules, all the smaller monasteries and abbeys were dissolved and ransacked. But it soon turned to outright abolition: the zeal of the investigators ensured that abuses were found in every aspect of monastic life. By 1540 the last abbey had gone and the Crown had accrued a fortune. The monks were pensioned off and their lands, buildings and treasures confiscated. A few abbeys were retained as parish churches or cathedrals, but most were not. They were stripped of the lead on their roofs, the gold and jewels on their shrines, and left to rot. It was desecration and sacrilege on the grandest scale.

It provoked shock, outrage and, finally, open revolt. If the full implications of the Supremacy were not fully appreciated at the time, the spoliation of the monasteries made real the break with Rome and the change in the nation's religious life. And it was too much for many. The result was that in the autumn of 1536 Henry faced the worst crisis of his reign, the rebellion known as 'The Pilgrimage of Grace'. The first uprising was in Lincolnshire, and spread quickly across the North of England. Under their banner of the Five Wounds of Christ, noblemen and peasants joined together, demanding the restoration of the monasteries and the return of the old religion. Monks and priests played a leading part in the revolt, preaching incendiary sermons and even wearing armour. Adam Sedbar, abbot at Jervaulx Abbey, wasn't one of them. Instead, when the rebel hordes turned up at the gates of his monastery, he fled to the surrounding moorland. But the threat to burn down his monastery forced him to return, however reluctantly, and join the revolt.

Secure in their control of the North, the formidable, well-disciplined rebel army marched south. By the time they reached Doncaster, only the king's much smaller forces stood between them and London and, perhaps, Henry's throne.

Scawsby Leys, now an unprepossessing track, was once the line of the Great North Road where it crosses the broad plain of the northern bank of the River Don. And it was here at dawn on the morning of 26 October that the rebels called a general muster of their troops. The flower of the North was there, and when the final count was taken they numbered 30,000 men with another 12,000 in reserve at Pontefract. It was the largest army that England had seen since the Wars of the Roses, and it wasn't the king's. But even though the rebels faced only 8000 of Henry's forces, they chose to negotiate. They persuaded themselves that the attack on the Church was the work not of the king but of his wicked advisers like Cranmer. They were also double-crossed by the king's representative. He promised them pardon and, believing him, the huge rebel army dispersed.

But a few months later, a new minor revolt in the North gave Henry the excuse he needed to break his promises and exact revenge. The leaders of the revolt were arrested and sent to London for trial. Henry was especially severe on clerics who had been involved, even when, like Abbot Sedbar of Jervaulx, they had been coerced into joining the revolt. Sedbar was arrested with the rest and sent to the Tower. Then he was tried, condemned and saw Jervaulx Abbey confiscated. The aristocratic leaders of the revolt were beheaded, but the rest, including Sedbar himself, suffered the full horrors of hanging, drawing and quartering. Henry's supreme headship of the Church, which had begun in the name of freeing England from the papal yoke, was turning into a new royal tyranny, to be enforced in blood.

No one was exempt. In May 1536, after only three years of marriage, Anne was executed on trumped-up charges of adultery, incest and sexual perversion. But her real crimes were less exotic. She had failed to adjust from the dominant role of mistress to the submissive role of wife and, above all, like Catherine before her, she had failed to give Henry a son.

Within twenty-four hours of Anne's execution Henry was betrothed again, and on 30 May he married his third wife, Jane Seymour. Demure and submissive, conservative in religion, Jane was everything that Anne was not. And in October 1537 she did what Anne and Catherine had both failed to do, and gave birth to a healthy son and heir, Edward. Jane died a few days later of puerperal fever, but the boy lived and became Henry's pride and joy.

All the problems that had led to the break with Rome – the

king's first two disputed marriages, his lack of a male heir –
were now solved. With the occasions of the dispute out of the
way, why didn't the naturally conservative Henry return to the
bosom of the Roman Church?

The answer lies in Hans Holbein's great dynastic mural of
Henry VIII (page 6 of plate section). The original, of which only
a copy survives, was sited in the king's private apartments and
as such takes us into his very mind. The date, 1537, is the
year of Prince Edward's birth. In the foreground is the proud
father, Henry VIII, together with the recently deceased mother,
Jane Seymour. Behind are Henry's own parents, Henry VII and
Elizabeth of York, while in the middle there are inscribed
Latin verses which explain the meaning of the painting. 'Which
is the Greater,' the verses ask, 'the father or the son?' 'Henry
VII was great,' they reply, 'for he brought to an end the Wars
of the Roses. But Henry VIII was greater, indeed the greatest
for while he was King true religion was restored and the power
of Popes trodden under foot.'

This, then, is why Henry refused to return to Rome. The
Supremacy may have begun as a mere convenient device to
facilitate his marriage to Anne Boleyn. But it had quickly taken
on a life of its own as Henry had persuaded himself that it was
his birthright, *raison d'être* and above all his passport to fame,
not only in relation to Henry VII and all the other Kings of
England, but in the eyes of posterity as well.

Henry had got what he wanted. But to do so he'd had to use
ideas based on Lutheranism, which he detested. The symbol of
these compromises was the new English translation of the Bible.
The title page shows how literally Henry took his new grand

title of 'Supreme Head in Earth of the Church of England'. At the top of the page, of course, appears Christ as God the Son, but he's very small. Instead, the composition is dominated by the huge fleshly presence of Henry VIII. As king *and* Supreme Head, he sits enthroned in the centre with, on the left, the bishops representing the clergy and Church and, on the right, the Privy Council representing the laity and the state. Below there are the people, who all join together in the grateful, obedient acclamation of '*Vivat, vivat Rex*': Long live the King, God Save the King.

The title page of the Great Bible represents in microcosm the extraordinary achievement of Henry's reign. He had broken the power of the Pope, dissolved the monasteries, defeated rebellion, beheaded traitors and made himself supreme over Church and state. All the powers and all the passions of a ferocious nationalism were contained in his person and at his command. No other monarch had ever been so powerful. Fortescue believed that the liberties of Englishmen consisted of the independence and power that nobles and yeomen had in relation to the Crown. But that balance had been upset by the Royal Supremacy. The monarchy, rich in land, money and spiritual authority, had no competition in the kingdom – not from over-mighty subjects, not from freeborn yeomen. Henry had been seeking glory all his life. At last he had found it.

But the Royal Supremacy also contained the seeds of its own destruction. For in employing the new biblically based theology, Henry had allowed into England those very subversive religious ideas he had once tried so hard to suppress. The genie of Protestantism was out of the bottle.

And it was Protestantism which, only a hundred years later, would first challenge the powers of the monarchy, and finally dethrone and behead a King of England.

SHADOW OF THE KING

EDWARD VI, MARY I, ELIZABETH I

IN 1544 KING HENRY VIII, now in the third decade of his reign, bestrode England like an ageing colossus. By making himself Supreme Head of the Church of England he had taken the monarchy to the peak of its power. But at a huge personal cost.

For the supremacy had been born out of Henry's desperate search for an heir and love. The turmoil of six marriages, two divorces, two executions and a tragic bereavement had produced three children by these different and mutually hostile mothers. It was a fractured and unhappy royal family. Now the king felt it was time for reconciliation.

Henry's reunion with his family is commemorated in a famous painting, known as 'The Family of Henry VIII'. The painting shows Henry enthroned between his son and heir, the seven-year-old Edward, and, to emphasize the line of dynastic succession, Edward's long-dead mother Jane Seymour. Standing farther off to the right is Henry's elder daughter Mary, whom he bastardized when he divorced her mother, and to the left his younger daughter Elizabeth, whom he also bastardized when he had her mother beheaded.

But this is more than a family portrait. It also symbolizes the political settlement by which Henry hoped to preserve and prolong his legacy.

To secure the Tudor succession, he decided that all three of his children would be named as his heirs. His son Edward would, of course, succeed him. But if Edward died childless, the throne would pass to his elder daughter, Mary. If she had no heir then her half-sister Elizabeth would become queen. The arrangement was embodied both in the king's own will and in an Act of Parliament.

Henry's provisions for the succession held, and, through the rule of a minor and two women, gave England a sort of stability. But they also ushered in profound political turmoil as well, since – it turned out – each of Henry's three children was determined to use the Royal Supremacy to impose a radically different form of religion on England.

First, there would be the zealous Protestantism of Edward; then the passionate Catholicism of Mary. Finally, it would be left to Elizabeth to try to reconcile the opposing forces unleashed by her siblings.

The divisions within Henry's family reflected the religious confusion in the country as a whole. The Reformation of the Church had been radical at times, cautiously conservative at others. In some parts of the country, people had embraced Protestantism and stripped their local churches of icons and Catholic ceremonies. In others, the people cleaved to the old ways, afraid of the radical change that had been unleashed. Like the royal family, Henry's subjects were divided among themselves, unsure of the full implications of the Supremacy.

Containing this combustible situation was Henry VIII, with all his indomitable personality. On Christmas Eve 1545, Henry made his last speech to Parliament. It was an emotional appeal for reconciliation between conservatives who hankered after a return to Rome and radical Protestants who wished to press on to a complete reform of the Church. Henry sought a middle way which would both preserve the Royal Supremacy and prevent their quarrel from tearing England apart. It was also an expression of his personal views: he held on to the old ceremonies of the religion he had known from his youth; at the same time, he had repudiated the papacy that was their bedrock. And, as he was determined that his people should continue to tread the same narrow path, he made no secret of his contempt for the extremes in the religious disputes. Both were unyielding and zealous. Both were in some way flouting royal spiritual authority. Radicals and conservatives alike were under notice that unseemly disputes in the religious life of the country would not be tolerated.

I

Just over a year later, on 28 January 1547, Henry was dead, aged fifty-five, and with him died any prospect that the Royal Supremacy would be used to save England from religious conflict. Three weeks later, Henry's nine-year-old son was crowned

King Edward VI at Westminster Abbey. The ceremony was conducted by Thomas Cranmer, England's first Protestant Archbishop of Canterbury, who, sixteen years earlier, had helped Henry VIII to achieve supreme authority over Church and state. But the Supremacy had not taken the Church as far as he had wanted down the road of reform. Now Cranmer used Edward's coronation to spell out fully the Supremacy's awe-inspiring claims.

During the ceremony no fewer than three crowns were placed successively on the boy king's head. The second was the Imperial Crown itself – the symbol of the imperial monarchy to which Edward's grandfather Henry VII had aspired and which his father, Henry VIII, had achieved.

And it wasn't only the crown. Instead, Cranmer turned the whole ceremony into a parable of the limitless power of the new imperial monarchy. First, he administered the coronation oath to the king. But then, in a moment that was unique in the thousand-year history of the coronation, he turned directly to the king and congregation to explain, or rather to explain away, what he had done. He had just administered the oath to the king, he said, but, he continued, it was a mere ceremony. God had conferred the crown on Edward and no human could prescribe conditions or make him abide by an oath. Neither he nor any other earthly man had the right to hold Edward to account during his reign. Instead, the chosen of God, the king, was answerable only to God. 'Your Majesty is God's Vice-regent, and Christ's Vicar within your own dominions,' Cranmer told the little boy, 'and to see, with your predecessor Josiah, God truly worshipped, and idolatry destroyed, the tyranny of the

Bishops of Rome banished from your subjects, and images removed.'

The full nakedness of the absolutism established by Henry VIII now stood revealed. And both those who ruled in Edward's name – and in the fullness of time Edward himself – were determined to use its powers to the uttermost.

For Edward was being tutored by thoroughgoing Protestants, and he learnt his lessons well, writing in an essay at the age of twelve that the Pope was 'the true son of the devil, a bad man, an Antichrist'. Edward and his councillors now determined to use the Supremacy to force religious reform, and make England a fully Protestant, godly nation. It was a resort to one of the extremes that Henry had warned against in his last speech.

And there was much to reform. For, as part of Henry's cautious middle way, most English churches and much ceremony had remained unchanged. But thanks to Edward's education in advanced Protestantism, *he* believed that his father's reign had been marred by undue caution in religious reform. So now Edward and his council ordered the culmination of the Reformation, or, in other words, a revolution in the spiritual life of the country. Stained-glass windows, the crosses over the choir screens and the crucifixes on the altars were torn down and burnt. The pictures of saints were whitewashed, and the Latin mass replaced by the English of the 1549 Book of Common Prayer, written by Cranmer himself. England had had a Reformation; now, many said as bonfires raged through the country and statues were vandalized, it was going through a 'Deformation'. Where once the crucifix hung high above the heads of the congregation for veneration, there was now just one image: the royal coat of arms.

A highly emotional religion of ritual and imagery gave way to an austere one of words, as Protestantism, for the first time, definitively replaced Catholicism. And it was not just a cosmetic reform. The old Easter processionals, saints' days and pilgrimages of the unreformed religion allowed lay people to participate in religious life. But Protestants saw them as blasphemous ceremonies that took the mind away from true devotion, and they were abolished. The new religion was one where the people should receive the word of God intellectually, not take an active, passionate part in the colourful rituals of Catholic worship.

And with the icons and processions also went charitable institutions like hospitals, colleges and schools, town guilds and chantries, which had been part of the old religion. These institutions were paid for by people who believed that good works on Earth would speed their souls to Paradise when they died. But Protestants didn't believe in Purgatory; therefore there was no need for these charitable institutions designed to help the soul through the intermediary stage of the afterlife. They also believed that the soul would be saved by faith alone, not good works. And so a way of life was brought to an abrupt end. The effect was devastating. The fabric of religious life was torn to pieces, and many were left fearing that they would be condemned to hellfire. The popular reaction was riots and uprisings, especially in the South-West, protesting against the Act of Uniformity and the introduction of the Book of Common Prayer.

In 1549, in their camp outside Exeter, the rebels drew up

their list of demands for concessions from Edward's government. It survives in the government's printed counter-propaganda, and it is remarkable both for the bluntness of its language – 'we will', the rebels state repeatedly – and for the picture that it presents of their religious beliefs.

For what the rebels wanted was the restoration of a whole series of religious ceremonies: 'We will', the seventh article reads, 'have holy bread and holy water made every Sunday, psalms and ashes at the times accustomed, images to be set up again in every church, and all other ancient, old ceremonies used heretofore by our Holy Mother Church.'

Religion, in other words, was a matter of belief made real by ritual. And it was the abolition of these time-honoured and well-loved rituals which had so outraged the common man and common woman and driven them to rebel. They believed that if the artefacts and practices of their religious life – the candles and rosaries, holy water and Easter processions, relics and icons, pilgrimages and prayers – were taken away, their souls would be damned. But Cranmer disregarded the sincerity of their rebellion and responded in the language of self-confident nationalism. It was not, he said, an issue of traditional forms of worship. The rebels' demands amounted to a treacherous call for the country to submit to the laws of the Pope and 'to make our most undoubted and natural king his vile subject and slave!'. The protesters were a fifth column – they had demanded the mass to be said in Latin: 'And be you such enemies to your own country, that you will not suffer us to laud God, to thank Him, to use His sacraments in our own tongue?' Protestantism was England's *national* religion. Moreover, Edward was God's

Vice-regent. To oppose his reforms was heresy and treason combined.

In fact, the rebellion was easily defeated. But Edward soon found a more dangerous opponent in his own half-sister Mary. It was to divorce her mother, Catherine of Aragon, and marry Anne Boleyn, that Henry had broken with Rome, and so for Mary the Supremacy had always been a personal as well as a religious affront. Now, faced with the radical reforms of her brother and his council, she discovered her true vocation – to be the beacon of the old, true religion in England. In defiance of the law, therefore, she openly continued to hear mass in the traditional Latin liturgy.

The clash between Mary and Edward, who was as stridently Protestant as Mary was Catholic, began at Christmas 1550. It was a family reunion, with Mary, Edward and Elizabeth all gathered together under one roof for the festivities. But, as so often, Christmas turned into a time for family quarrels, as the thirteen-year-old Edward upbraided his thirty-four-year-old sister for daring to break his laws and hear mass. Humiliated, Mary burst into tears. She replied: 'I have offended no law, unless it be a late law of your own making for the altering of matters in religion, which, in my conscience, is not worthy to have the name of law.' The law that she recognized was that which had been laid down by Henry VIII. He had retained at least the outward essentials of the old religion. She would not accept that Edward, a child, could have any kind of authority, especially not *spiritual* authority, to change the religion of the country. She believed instead that the country should be pre-served as it was in 1547. But Edward was capable of holding his own opinion, and defend it he would. He truly believed what he had been told at his coronation. He was God's anointed, and he would purge Catholic blasphemy from his realm.

When she was next summoned to court a few weeks later, Mary came with a large retinue, all of them conspicuously carrying officially banned rosaries as a badge of their Catholicism.

Mary had arrived in force for what she knew would be a confrontation with the full weight of Edward's government. But when she was summoned before the king and council and taxed with disobedience, she played her trump card. Her cousin on her mother's side was the Holy Roman Emperor Charles V, the most powerful ruler in Europe. Mary now invoked his mighty protection, and the imperial ambassador hurried to court to threaten war if Mary were not given freedom of religion. Faced with the combination of foreign war and Catholic insurrection at home, the council backed off. It was Edward's turn to weep tears of frustration.

And there was worse to come. In the winter of 1552, Edward started to cough blood, and by the following spring it was obvious to everyone that the young king was dying.

In the same year the Reformation reached its high point. What little there remained of Henry's moderation was abandoned as Protestant reform reached its climax. The real presence of Christ in the sacrifice of Eucharist during mass was rejected by Cranmer's second Book of Common Prayer. Altars – which symbolized the sacrifice of Christ during the Eucharistic rites – were stripped from churches throughout the country and replaced with rough communion tables. It was a complete rejection of the old faith and the end of the compromise between

Catholicism and Protestantism that Henry had advocated. Reform was hurtling in one direction. But Mary's intransigent Catholicism now became more than an obstacle to the progress of reform – it threatened the very survival of Protestantism itself. For Mary, her father had declared, was Edward's heir. She would succeed as queen and Supreme Head of the Church, and like her father and brother before her, she would be able to remake the religion of England according to her own lights. It was clear to everyone, even Edward, that this was only a matter of time.

The thought of Mary as his Catholic successor was intolerable to the hotly Protestant Edward. So, with a confidence that was breathtaking in a dying fifteen-year-old boy, he decided unilaterally to change the rules.

He set down his commands in an extraordinary document. It is headed in his bold schoolboy hand 'My Device for the succession'. It was against statute law and drawn up without parliamentary consent. But the sickly king believed that his God-given authority would extend beyond the grave. First, he excluded Elizabeth as well as Mary from the succession on the grounds that both his half-sisters were bastards. Second, he transferred the throne to the family of his cousins the Greys; and third, he decided that women were unfit to rule in their own right, though they could transmit their claim to their sons, or, in legal jargon, their 'heirs male'.

The problem was that all his Grey cousins were women, and though they had been married off at breakneck speed, none of them had yet had children. In the course of time, no doubt, the problem would have solved itself, but in view of Edward's rapidly declining health there wasn't time. Instead Edward swallowed his misogyny and called for his 'Device'. With two or three deft strokes of the pen he altered the rules one last time. Originally he had left the crown to the sons of the eldest Grey sister, the Lady Jane: 'the Lady Jane's heirs male'. One crossing out and two words inserted over a caret changed this to: 'the Lady Jane and her heirs male'. If Edward could make his choice stick, the impeccably Protestant and deeply learned Lady Jane Grey would be his successor as queen.

On 6 July 1553 Edward died. On the tenth the sixteen-year-old Lady Jane Grey was brought to the Tower to be proclaimed queen. The Tower was the traditional location for such a declaration. The difference in this case was that Jane Grey would never leave its precincts again.

II

By leaving the throne to Lady Jane Grey, Edward had flouted both his father King Henry VIII's will and the Act of Succession. This flagrant disregard for the law was unacceptable even to many Protestants. It would have given the Crown even greater powers, putting it above Parliament and the law. Moreover, Lady Grey's supporters had made a fatal mistake – they had failed to arrest Edward's Catholic sister Mary, who was, according to Henry's will, the legitimate heir to the throne.

Instead, forewarned by friends at court, Mary fled out of reach to the depths of East Anglia, were she had vast estates and a loyal following. On 10 July she proclaimed herself rightful Queen of England, and two days later she took up residence at the great castle of Framlingham, which she made her head-quarters for armed assault on the throne of England. Troops flooded in and Mary inspected her army in front of the castle in true royal style.

But no blow needed to be struck. Faced with Mary's over-whelming strength the Grey faction threw in the towel and Queen Jane was deposed after reigning for less than a fortnight. It was legality, legitimacy and the sense that she was Henry VIII's daughter which had won the day for Mary, but she herself didn't see it like that. 'In thee O Lord I trust, that I be not confounded forever,' Mary said; 'if God be for us; who can be against us?' She was convinced that her accession against all the odds was a miracle brought about by God for His own purposes; it was a sign, and she was now a woman with a mission to restore England to the Catholic faith.

In public, Mary promised to return to something like the consensus of her father's last years: there would be no forced conversions, her propaganda implied. In private she was more candid: 'she boasted herself a virgin sent of God to ride and tame the people of England.' The contrast was reflected in the hesitant start to reconversion: to begin with people were 'en-couraged' to return to the old faith after nearly twenty years of Protestant reforms and Edward's policies were assaulted only slowly. But it would not be long before Mary increased the pace of bringing England back to true religion.

First, however, to prevent the country ever returning to the heresy of Protestantism, Mary must marry and produce an heir.

For otherwise her father's will left the throne to her Protestant half-sister, Elizabeth. Long ago in her youth, Mary had been briefly betrothed to the Emperor Charles V. Now Charles offered her his own son and heir, Philip, who had been brought up in Spain and was imbued with that country's passionate Catholicism. More importantly, his father had dedicated the empire's resources to stamping out Protestantism throughout Europe. Now England would be brought back to due obedience to the Pope. But the idea of a Spanish king ruling in England was wildly unpopular. Even though a yearning for Catholicism remained wiedespread in England, decades of anti-papal, nationalistic propaganda had also done their work. The papacy was looked upon as foreign and unEnglish. Thus, when the Spanish embassy arrived, boys threw snowballs at them, and the rest of the crowd, 'nothing rejoicing, held down their heads sorrowfully'. More seriously, an uprising in Kent in 1554, led by Sir Thomas Wyatt, fought its way to London, and for a while Mary's throne was in jeopardy.

Mary rose to the occasion, won over Londoners with a magnificent speech in Guildhall and crushed the revolt. She then exacted a terrible revenge, executing all the leaders of the conspiracy, and Lady Jane Grey herself, whom she had hitherto spared. Elizabeth was implicated in the rebellion and sent to the Tower. With the rebellion defeated, and with Parliament's reluctant acquiescence, there was now no barrier to Mary's marriage to Philip.

Philip landed in Southampton on 20 July 1554. It was close to the first anniversary of Mary's accession. Five days later Philip and Mary were married at Winchester Cathedral. The couple processed through the west doors along an elevated walkway to a high platform in the centre of the nave where the ceremony took place. It deliberately invoked an older and better world. Mary used an old-fashioned wedding ring made of a band of plain gold, and she swore the woman's old oath, to be 'Bonny and buxom in bed and at board'. If the couple were able to have children, that older, better Catholic world would live again.

Mary was thirty-seven and prematurely aged. But she sincerely believed that God would once again favour her and England with a miracle. A few months later, Mary, like her namesake the Blessed Virgin, declared that the 'babe had stirred in her womb'. The prospect of a Catholic heir greatly strengthened Mary's hand, and Parliament voted to return the Church of England to the obedience of the Pope. The Royal Supremacy, which Henry VIII had forced on the English people, seemed to be over.

In early April 1555, Mary moved to Hampton Court for the birth of the child that would crown her life and reign, and guarantee the future of Catholic England. Her confinement, as customary, began with the ceremony of 'taking to her chamber', in which she bade farewell to the male-dominated world of the court and withdrew instead to the purely female realm of her birthing chamber. There, etiquette required she remain secluded and invisible until the birth. But Mary couldn't keep her joy to herself. Instead, on St George's Day, she appeared at a window to watch her husband Philip lead the Garter celebrations, and she turned side-on to show off her big belly to the crowd below.

Good Catholics rejoiced with the queen, as they did when the serious business of enforcing Catholicism began. Part of the return to Rome was the restoration of heresy laws that punished those who denied the Catholic faith with the terrible death of burning alive.

The burnings began in February 1555. Over the following three years more than three hundred men and women died in agony at the stake. Faced with such persecution, many other leading Protestants fled into exile. One of the exiles was the Protestant cleric John Foxe, who decided to write a history of the persecution. Using the trial records, eyewitness accounts and the writing of the martyrs themselves, he compiled his *Acts and Monuments*. Soon known as *Foxe's Book of Martyrs*, it became, after the Bible, the second-most widely read book in English and it damned Mary's reputation for ever as Bloody Mary – especially the gruesome woodcuts (see first plate section, page 7).

But Foxe's propaganda would have amounted to very little if it hadn't quickly become obvious that Mary's condition was a phantom pregnancy. By early summer she was a public laughing stock, with stories circulating that she was pregnant with a lapdog or a monkey. By August even Mary herself had abandoned hope. Moreover, at thirty-nine, it seemed unlikely she would ever conceive again.

With her pregnancy exposed as a delusion, power started to ebb away from the queen. Philip, now with no long-term interest in England, abandoned his wife to return to his Continental possessions. Still worse, her failure to produce an heir, and with it the guarantee of a Catholic future, broke Mary's hold on Parliament.

Crucial to the government's plans for the final suppression of Protestantism was a Bill to confiscate the landed estates of the

Protestant exiles. If the Bill passed, the economic foundations of their resistance would be destroyed. The government strained every nerve, but so too did the opposition, led by Sir Anthony Kingston. With the connivance of the sergeant-at-arms the doors of the House were locked from the inside. Kingston thundered his protests and the Bill was defeated. Such scenes would not be seen again in Parliament until the seventeenth century.

Despite the loss of the political initiative, Mary grimly persisted with the persecution of Protestants. Her most illustrious victim was Archbishop Thomas Cranmer. But Cranmer was caught on the horns of a dilemma. In creating the Royal Supremacy, he had argued that monarchs were God's agents on Earth and were owed obedience as an absolute religious duty.

But what to do when the monarch was of the wrong religion? Obey the queen? Or Christ? Cranmer's prosecutors at his trial for heresy probed the dilemma ruthlessly, and Cranmer, old, worn out and terrified of the fire, recanted his Protestantism. It was a huge propaganda coup for Mary. But foolishly, she wasn't satisfied. She bore Cranmer a deep and personal grudge for divorcing her mother and, even though Church law said that a repentant heretic should be pardoned, she was determined that he would burn.

Cranmer's execution was to take place in Oxford, preceded by a public repetition of his recantation. After a good supper, Cranmer slept well and early on a rainy morning he was brought to the University Church. It is still possible to see where sections of the pillars of the church were cut away to build a high platform to give maximum publicity to what the authorities were confident would be a repetition of his recantation and confession.

Instead, in an astonishing theatrical coup, Cranmer repudiated his recantation, and as the hubbub rose through the church he managed to shout out a final denunciation of the Pope as Antichrist. He was pulled down from the scaffold and hurried to the stake.

But Cranmer hadn't finished. As the flame rose he stuck out his right hand, which had signed his recantation, and pushed it deep into the heart of the fire. It had sinned, he said, so it should first be punished. It was a magnificent gesture which vindicated Cranmer's personal integrity, and saved the good faith of Protestantism. Mary's vengefulness had turned the propaganda coup of Cranmer's recantation into a PR disaster, which fired her opponents with a new zeal to resist Bloody Mary.

Among them was John Ponet, a Protestant bishop who'd fled into exile in Strasbourg when the burnings began. He was an old friend of Cranmer's. But, unlike Cranmer, Ponet's experience of Mary's tyranny led him to question the intellectual foundations of the Supremacy, and reject outright the idea that the king was God's anointed, ordained by Him to rule His church on Earth.

In 1556 he published a revolutionary book – *A Shorte Treatise of Politike Power*. Its title page, with the motto taken from Psalm 118, says it all: 'it is better to trust in the Lord than to trust in princes.' This meant that kings, far from being the God-like figures of Cranmer's and Henry VIII's imaginations, were human at best and subhuman at their all-too-frequent worst. And this meant in turn that kings were human creations and had to be subject to human control.

If, therefore, Ponet went on to argue, a king or queen broke human or divine law they should be reproved or even deposed. And if, like Mary, they were cruel and persecuting idolaters then it was a virtuous act to assassinate them as a tyrant. Henry VIII had realized that the Royal Supremacy could survive only if the monarchy kept to a middle way in religion. But Edward and Mary had ignored his warnings, and now, in Ponet's ground-breaking work, had provoked a head-on challenge to the authority and legitimacy of kingship itself.

Mary was soon beyond the reach of Ponet's seditious theorizing. In 1558 she became seriously ill, although she fondly imagined she was pregnant again. She even wrote her will, leaving the throne to her unborn Catholic child.

But six months later, with her health rapidly fading, even Mary had to face reality, and she added a codicil to her will. In it, she finally acknowledged that it was likely that she would have 'no issue or heir of her body', and that she would be succeeded instead 'by her next heir and successor, by the laws and statutes of this realm'. That of course was her half-sister Elizabeth, though Mary couldn't even bring herself to write her name. Seeing visions of heavenly children to the last, she died on the night of 16 November 1558. She was forty-two.

Two of Henry's three children had succeeded to the throne and, by their contrasting religious extremism, had imperilled both the Supremacy and the Crown. Would his last surviving heir, Elizabeth, do any better?

III

After years of danger and uncertainty, Henry VIII's last heir, his daughter Elizabeth, stood on the verge of becoming Queen of England.

A portrait of Elizabeth aged fourteen, painted in the last weeks of her father's life, shows her as the very model of a religious, learned princess. But the reality of Elizabeth's life under the reigns of her brother and sister was to be very different from the studious calm suggested by this picture – especially under her sister Mary.

During Mary's reign, Elizabeth occupied the impossible position that she would later call 'second person'. By their father's will, she was Mary's heir presumptive; she was also, as a covert Protestant, guaranteed to undo everything that Mary held dear. This made her both the focus of every conspiracy against Mary, and the target of her sister's fear and rage.

Mary had sent her to the Tower after the Wyatt rebellion in 1554 on charges of treason, and would certainly have had her beheaded if she had been able to scrape enough evidence together. Such experiences left Elizabeth with a set of indelible memories, which meant she took a very different view of policy from either her brother or her sister.

News of Mary's death was brought to Elizabeth at Hatfield. The story has it that she fell on her knees, impulsively exclaiming with the psalmist: 'This is the Lord's doing; it is marvellous in our eyes.' Actually, Elizabeth had been preparing herself for this moment for weeks. Her right-hand man in her preparations for power had been Sir William Cecil. It was to be the beginning of a lifelong partnership.

Cecil, born the son of a Tudor courtier some thirteen years before Elizabeth, had shared many of her experiences and, as a Protestant, suffered the same fears under Mary when he too had saved his skin by conforming to Catholicism. But there was a difference. Cecil, unlike Elizabeth, responded to the fears he had experienced under Mary by hardening his opinions: never again must there be a Catholic monarch or heir, and if by mischance one appeared then people, council and Parliament together could – and should – remove them.

These were Ponet's arguments, though Cecil was a moderate in comparison. Nevertheless, it would make for an interesting relationship between Cecil and his imperious, headstrong young queen, with her high view of royal power and her moderate line in religion. And indeed, establishing a new religious settlement was Elizabeth's first task as queen. Mary's parliament had made Catholicism once more the religion of England and only another parliament could change it. But to what?

Elizabeth's first parliament met in January 1559. It was opened with a speech by the acting Lord Chancellor. He spoke in Elizabeth's name but his phraseology deliberately invoked her father's great speech on religion to the parliament of 1545. Since then, England had been to the extremes of religion. It had been, as Henry predicted, bloody and destructive. Most had tried to avoid being caught up in the conflict between Protestants and Catholics. The people, clergy, many of the council and Elizabeth herself had compromised with Mary and outwardly conformed to Catholicism. Elizabeth herself had heard mass in Latin and professed loyalty to her sister's faith. She, like the majority, had dissembled her true religious views. For she was never a Protestant in the mould of Edward. Like her father, she appreciated religious ceremony and deplored the name-calling of bigots from both sides of the divide. And so, like Henry, Elizabeth wanted the middle way in religion – partly because she believed in it, and partly because she too saw it as the best defence of the Royal Supremacy, which she was determined to revive as her God-given right. Only once the explosive passions of religion were contained would the throne and Elizabeth's life be secure.

But Elizabeth's plans for a moderate religious settlement came under fire from both extremes – from Catholics in the Lords and Protestants in the Commons and council. Which group offered the best chance of pacifying England with a workable religious settlement? Extreme Protestantism was a danger for Elizabeth. It had gained a new, radical way of thinking during the dark days of Mary's reign. It saw those who had hidden their beliefs as enemies of true religion. It had its martyrs, Cranmer foremost among them. And there were many who thought that even the Edwardian Reformation had not gone far enough and that Cranmer had been cut down before the Church had become fully reformed, leaving it stranded midway between mild, watered-down Protestantism and Catholicism. Moreover, these enthusiastic Protestants did not like female rule and had worked out a theory of justifiable resistance to monarchs during Mary's reign. They were politically and personally offensive to Elizabeth. But, just the same, they were a bulwark against the Catholics, who opposed the Supremacy.

Finally, to overcome her Catholic peers and bishops, Elizabeth had to join forces with her Protestant Commons and councillors. She duly got the settlement and the Supremacy, though with the narrowest of majorities in the Lords of three votes. The price, however, was her acceptance of Cranmer's second, much more radically Protestant Book of Common Prayer of 1552. In the infighting between the religious extremes, it seemed that Elizabeth's hope for moderate settlement had been lost.

The outcome of the parliament of 1559 had been a triumph for Cecil. He had outmanoeuvred and strong-armed the Catholics to restore the Royal Supremacy, and he had, so it seemed, outmanoeuvred Elizabeth as well, to bring back the full-bloodied Protestantism of her brother Edward. Elizabeth was equal to the challenge, however. She insisted, against fierce opposition, on inserting the so-called Ornaments Rubric into the legislation. This empowered her, on her sole authority, as Supreme Governor of the Church, to retain traditional ceremonies, such as making the sign of the Cross in baptism, and to require the clergy to wear traditional vestments, like the surplice and the cope. These vestiges of Catholicism were offensive to radical Protestants. If they had had their own way, they would have sped the Church of England on the road to extreme Protestantism of the kind that existed in Europe and Scotland – a Church without bishops and ceremonies. It was only the queen's personal supremacy which prevented this. Far from hurtling along the road of reform in the way that Edward and his supporters had envisioned, the Church of England was frozen in time. The result was a Church that was Protestant in doctrine,

Catholic in appearance and which would, Elizabeth hoped, satisfy all but a handful of extremists on both sides.

And Elizabeth's hopes would almost certainly have been fulfilled but for the issue of the succession. It was the succession which had driven the giddy switch back course from Protestantism to Catholicism and back again, and it had the potential to do it again. It was clear to Cecil that the best way to secure the succession was for the queen to marry and produce an heir. But Elizabeth was less sure. She had seen how her half-sister's choice of a husband had sparked dissent and rebellion. Elizabeth determined that England would 'have one mistress and no master'.

But if Elizabeth could not and would not marry, who should succeed her? Her father's will had an answer for that too, for, if Elizabeth died childless, a clause prescribed that she should be succeeded by the descendants of her Aunt Mary, Henry's younger sister, the Greys.

But Elizabeth hated the Grey family, because they had helped put Jane Grey on the throne. Then Elizabeth had been publicly branded a bastard and barred from the succession. In revenge, she would never allow the throne to pass to a Grey. But what to do about her father's will? Her brother and her sister, to whom its terms were equally unacceptable, had challenged it head-on and failed. Elizabeth was subtler. The will was given one last public outing in the second parliament of the reign and then it was returned to the safe deposit of the treasury and put in an iron chest. And the key to the chest in effect was thrown away. It was a case of out of sight, out of mind.

With the lightest of touches Elizabeth had nudged her

father's will into oblivion. This left as her most obvious heir her cousin Mary, the granddaughter of Henry's eldest sister Margaret. Mary was Queen Consort of France and Queen of Scots in her own right. She was also a Catholic.

In August 1561, after the death of her husband, the French king, Mary, having spent most of her young life on the other side of the Channel, returned to Scotland as queen. Brought up among the splendours of the French court, Mary was far more interested in her claim to the English throne than her paltry Scottish inheritance, and in September she sent her personal emissary, Sir William Maitland, to negotiate directly with Elizabeth. His mission was to secure formal recognition of Mary's status as Elizabeth's heir.

Elizabeth was all graciousness in her private, face-to-face interviews with Maitland. She acknowledged that Mary was of the blood royal of England, was her cousin and her nearest living kinswoman, and that she loved her dearly. And she also, under Maitland's subtle prodding, went farther. She knew, she said, no one with a better claim to be her successor than Mary, nor any that she preferred to her. She even swore that she would do nothing to impede Mary's claim. But the final step – declaring Mary her heir – Elizabeth told a crestfallen Maitland plainly, she would never, ever take. But Elizabeth had already gone far too far for Cecil. He had lived through the reign of one Mary and her attempt to re-Catholicize England, and he was determined never to suffer another one.

Matters came to a head in the parliament of 1566, which attempted to force Elizabeth to name a successor, and by implication to exclude the claim of Mary Queen of Scots. Furious,

Elizabeth summoned thirty members of each House to her palace in Whitehall, where she delivered an extraordinary speech.

Elizabeth was at her fiery, brilliant best. She would never name an heir, she said, because he or she would become 'second person'. And Elizabeth, better than anyone else, knew the danger of that position, since, as Mary's legally appointed heir, she had been 'second person' herself. As such, her own life had been in constant danger and she had been the focus of plots and treason. At this point Elizabeth became sharply personal. Many of the MPs, she said, turning to the Commons delegation, had been among the plotters, and only her own honour prevented her from naming names. Similarly, turning now to the Lords, she proclaimed that many of the bishops, under Jane Grey, had preached treasonably that she, Elizabeth, was a bastard. 'Well, I wish not for the death of any man,' she said, not altogether convincingly. No head can have felt too secure on its shoulders by the time the queen had finished.

The issue of the succession would bedevil Elizabeth's entire reign. Parliament was terrified that they would be faced withan interregnum on the queen's death. As history made clear, a throne with no known heir guaranteed civil war and bloodshed when the monarch died. What would become of the monarchy? Would the absence of a known heir turn England into an elective monarchy? Would the religion of the country have to change once more depending on who emerged as the successor? But Elizabeth knew equally well that the 'second person', however convenient for Parliament and the country, would be her worst enemy. If Mary was named as successor, her accession was a knife blow away – a tempting prospect for a foreign power or a Catholic.

But however much it was ignored or passed over as too dangerous to discuss openly, the problem of the succession wouldn't go away, and it was brought into sharp focus when a rebellion brought about by disgust at her scandalous personal life forced Mary to flee Scotland in May 1568 and seek Elizabeth's protection in England. The presence of Mary Queen of Scots in England would force Elizabeth into the very actions that she had tried so hard to avoid.

IV

Mary Queen of Scots' flight to England was a disaster for Elizabeth. In Scotland, Mary, despite her Catholicism, had been lukewarm to religion. She had lived with a Protestant government, and she had even taken a Protestant as her third husband. But in England it was a different story. Here Mary played up her Catholicism, and Catholics in turn identified with her.

The issue for both Mary and the English Catholics was the succession. Mary was Elizabeth's obvious heir because she was her closest relation, but Elizabeth steadfastly refused to recognize her as such. The implications for the monarchy were vast. If not Mary, then who would inherit the crown? For if the succession was not determined by unalterable descent of blood, what gave the monarchy its legitimacy and divine right to rule? Mary played on this sensitive issue. By bidding for Catholic support, she was hoping to force Elizabeth's hand, and, in turn, the prospect of an heir of their own faith gave English Catholics, who had almost lost hope, stomach for the fight once more. The spectre, which Elizabeth had striven so hard to lay to rest, of a 'second person' who differed in religion from the monarch was about to rise once more. And its baleful effects were to be quickly felt.

For the next twenty years Elizabeth was to keep Mary prisoner, moving her from one secure castle to another. In all that time the two queens never met. And as Elizabeth had foreseen, the plots soon began. Catholics saw Mary as a means back to power, and used her as a focus for rebellion. Despite her precarious position, Mary was naive enough to allow herself to be implicated in several of these plots. But Elizabeth refused to take action against Mary. Her instinct was to try to defuse the conflict, and above all she did not want Mary to become a martyr.

But Elizabeth's hopes of avoiding conflict were dashed when her middle way came under attack from both extremes. First to move was Rome with a papal edict or Bull, issued by the Pope in 1570. Known by its opening words as *Regnans in Excelsis*, 'reigning on high', it sets out the most extreme version of the papal claim to rule 'all people and all kingdoms'. Then, for her defiance of this claim, it condemns Elizabeth; deposes and excommunicates her, and absolves all her subjects from their oath of allegiance.

The Bull was the Catholic version of the arguments of the Protestant Ponet, and, as with Ponet, its logical outcome was tyrannicide, the assassination or murder of the errant ruler. The

Pope had, in effect, declared war on Elizabeth by calling for her death. But two could play at that game, and Elizabeth's council responded in kind.

Violent times breed violent measures and few have been more violent than the Bond of Association. Drawn up by the Privy Council in 1584, the bond is a kind of licensed lynch law. If Elizabeth were to be assassinated in favour of any possible claimant to the throne, then those who took the bond swore to band together to 'prosecute such person or persons to the death' and 'to take the uttermost revenge upon them by any possible means'. Furthermore, the bond would forbid anyone on whose behalf such an assassination took place from succeeding to the English throne. Finally for any Catholic rebel or foreign power that thought that Mary would automatically succeed if Elizabeth met an untimely end, the bond made clear that the right of nominating an heir belonged to 'Elizabeth, the Queen's Majesty that now is, with and by the authority of the Parliament of England'. The Protestant nobility and gentry flocked to subscribe to the bond in their hundreds, as the masses of signed and sealed copies that survive at the Public Record Office show.

Mary wasn't mentioned by name in the bond but everybody knew she was the target. The bond was subsequently legalized by an Act of Parliament, which also set up a tribunal to determine her guilt or innocence. But Cecil had wanted to go much, much farther and establish a Great Council to rule England in the event of an assassination and the inevitable interregnum that would follow. The Great Council would exercise all the royal powers and together with a recalled Parliament would choose the next monarch. This was a radical constitutional innovation. If a council in alliance with Parliament had the authority to choose monarchs, it would also have the authority to set conditions on them and challenge their subsequent actions. This was Ponet translated into a parliamentary statute, and Elizabeth was having none of it.

For Elizabeth saw the bond as being as offensive as *Regnans in Excelsis*, since it too set religion above the Crown, and permitted subjects to judge a sovereign and elect a new one. But not even Elizabeth could protect Mary from her own folly or Cecil's vendetta. In 1586, Mary was lured into giving her explicit endorsement to a plot to assassinate Elizabeth. Faced with incontrovertible evidence of her guilt, Elizabeth was forced to agree to her trial and condemnation. She even signed the death warrant. But she gave instructions that the execution wasn't to be carried out without her further command. For once, Cecil did not obey his queen.

Instead, a secret meeting of the council was convened in his private rooms at court and, acting on their own authority, and in defiance of the queen's express command, the councillors dispatched the death warrant to Mary's prison at Fotheringhay castle. There, in the Great Hall, Mary was publicly beheaded. She died magnificently, clutching the crucifix and wearing a scarlet petticoat as a martyr to her Catholic faith.

But the removal of a threat to the monarchy and the Church of England had serious implications. Queen Regnant anointed by God though she was, Mary had been publicly executed like any other common criminal. The 'divinity that doth hedge a King', which Elizabeth had fought so hard to preserve, had evaporated, never to return.

The execution of Mary was a watershed. Henry and his three children had sought to reshape the religion of England according to their own preferences. But as a fierce, nationalistic Protestantism took root in England, it was becoming clear that a monarch – or an heir – who fell too far out of step with the religious prejudices of the nation would do so at their peril. The dangerous liaison between monarchy and religion had claimed its first royal victim in Mary Queen of Scots. She would not be the last.

REBELLION

ELIZABETH I, JAMES VI & I, CHARLES I

In August 1588 Europe was convulsed by religious war, and Protestant England faced the world's foremost Catholic power. With the Spanish Armada in the Channel and a large and fearsomely professional Spanish army in the Low Countries, England was under dire threat.

On 18 August Queen Elizabeth came to review her troops at Tilbury. She wore a breastplate and carried a sword and addressed them in words that have echoed down the centuries: 'I know I have the body of a weak and feeble woman, but I have the heart and stomach of a King, and of a King of England too; and think foul scorn that Parma or Spain or any Prince of Europe should dare invade the border of my realm.'

But even as the queen spoke, the moment of danger had passed. The English fireships had broken up the Armada's 'invincible' formation off Calais, and coastal storms would do the rest. Nevertheless, despite the defeat of the Spanish Armada, England would not escape the horrors of religious war, and some of those who had heard Elizabeth at Tilbury might live long enough to see another English monarch raise his banner in defiance on English soil. But this time the king's enemies would not be foreign princes, but his own people.

I

Within a generation the monarchy was to move from a position of strength under the Tudors to abject weakness under the Stuart succession. With the defeat of the Spanish Armada, Elizabeth's reputation stood at a zenith at home and abroad. Even Pope Sixtus V, who had helped finance the Armada expedition, expressed his admiration of her and regretted only that they were unable to have children together! Inheriting their combined talents, he said, their offspring would rule the world.

Defending the realm was the most fundamental duty of an English monarch and Elizabeth had acquitted herself admirably. But, by virtue of the Crown Imperial, she had a further responsibility. She also had different opponents – and they were at home. As time moved on from the dizzying religious convulsions that had engulfed England since Henry took the momentous step of assuming the Supremacy, it was becoming increasingly clear that the monarchy's power over religion was a double-edged sword. The problem was not now simply Protestant against Catholic but also Protestant against different kinds of Protestants. As queen, Elizabeth presided over a national Protestant Church and, as Supreme Governor, she made religion in her own image. It was a right that she affirmed came direct from God. Could Elizabeth, mere woman that she was, maintain this lofty claim? And how could she as Supreme Head of the Church, avoid being drawn into the religious conflict, which threatened to turn quarrels about religion into disputes with the Crown?

Elizabeth did her best in establishing a Church of England that was Protestant in its doctrines but Catholic in the appearance of its ceremonies and clerical dress. Elizabeth's policy was successful in heading off much Catholic opposition, but it had the opposite effect of opening up divisions on the Protestant side – between those who wanted the rigorous, stripped-down Protestantism of the Continent and Scotland, and those who followed Elizabeth in her attachment to bishops and ceremonies.

This was not a struggle between government and opposition; rather it was a schism within the highest ranks of the Elizabethan establishment, with Elizabeth's chief minister and eldest confidant, William Cecil, on one side, and her Archbishop of Canterbury, William Whitgift, on the other. The bad feeling between the two men burst into the open in the queen's own presence, and Elizabeth came down publicly and heavily on Whitgift's side.

Matters of religion, she insisted, were for her and her bishops alone. Neither the council nor Parliament had any say in the matter. Instead, since her Supremacy over the Church came to her from God alone, she was answerable only to God in how she chose to exercise it. This was Henry VIII's high view of the Royal Supremacy, and in sticking to it Elizabeth showed herself every inch her father's daughter.

But this version of the Church would, as everyone knew, last only as long as the queen's life. Would the next monarch continue the difficult but necessary balancing act as the middle way in religion after the ageing Elizabeth died? Or would he or she impose a new version of Protestantism on the Church? Her nearest blood relation was King James VI of Scotland. Son of a Catholic mother, but brought up in the rigorous and austere Protestant Kirk, the possibility of James's accession aroused wildly contrasting hopes. While he was still only a claimant, he could flatter them all. But when – *if* – he became a King of England, he would have to choose which way the Church of England would go.

Born in 1566, James was the only child of Mary Queen of Scots' disastrous marriage to Lord Darnley. His mother, widely suspected of murdering his father, had been forced to flee to England by a Protestant revolt. James would never see her again. Instead, the Scottish nobility and Kirk saw the baby as a king they could mould into a monarch of their own choosing. They intended that, king from the cradle, he would have none of the absolutist pretensions of other monarchs and none of his mother's Catholicism. The very first coins of James's reign showed him carrying an oversized sword; the motto read, in reference to the sword, *pro me si mereor in me* – 'for me, but against me if I deserve it'. James was crowned at the parish kirk at Stirling on 29 July 1567, when he was just thirteen months old. He was King of Scotland in his own right, despite the fact that his mother was still alive. He was also heir to Mary's claims to the English throne.

This boy, of great rank and greater prospects still, was

largely brought up at Stirling Castle. It was a strange, insecure kind of childhood. A series of regents who ruled Scotland on his behalf were murdered in quick succession, and the boy's own life was more than once in danger. On his fourth birthday, a tutor arrived at Stirling Castle, charged with the responsibilities of creating a king in his own image. George Buchanan was a scholar known throughout Europe (and through him) James would have one of the most rigorous and academic educations possible. Dour and self-opinionated, Buchanan was also a leading figure in the Scottish Presbyterian Kirk. He and his fellow Presbyterians believed that the supreme authority in the state was *not* the king, as it was in England, but the General Assembly of clergy.

Kings also, Buchanan believed, were mere servants of their people, who could and should be punished if they misbehaved. Indeed, his hatred of monarchy was not even disguised and, in his little pupil, he had a convenient target to hand. Like many sixteenth-century teachers, Buchanan thought that sparing the rod spoiled the child, especially if that child was a king, and he set about beating and birching his beliefs and learning into King James with gusto. It was a kind of pre-emptive punishment of a ruling monarch, intended to beat out any residual monarchical pretensions. Buchanan was charged with creating a Scottish monarch from the small boy, one who would submit to the authority of the Kirk and the dominant Scottish lords and learn that kings were not absolute or possessed of divine powers, but weak-minded mortals. And, as James would in all probability be King of England one day, zealous Protestantism would be immeasurably strengthened there as well.

This treatment indeed succeeded in making James a considerable scholar. But in terms of religion and politics, it produced only an equal and opposite reaction to which James was able to give expression with unusual force and clarity when he grew up.

And the result was a work of scholarship that rejected every aspect of Buchanan's anti-monarchical lessons. It is called *The Trew Law of Free Monarchies*, which James wrote and published in 1598. In it, he says succinctly: 'Kings are called Gods; they are appointed by God and answerable only to God.' James grounded these assertions, just as Henry VIII had his claim to the Royal Supremacy, in the biblical story of Old Testament kings. But James went beyond even Henry VIII by claiming that kings were accountable to no human law at all – born in affairs of state. They were bound by God's laws, and were answerable to Him only. This was what he meant by a 'free monarchy'. Subjects, for their part, had the obligation to treat kings as if they were God's representatives and judges on Earth. To act against the king was to rebel against God.

But all this was fantasy in Scotland, where James had neither money nor following with which to challenge the dominance of the Kirk and the aristocracy. Here his grandiose claim of divine majesty was a reaction to a situation in which he was one of many competing powers in the kingdom. Only in England, where kings were indeed supreme, could he hope to realize his vision of monarchy. But his claim to the English throne was not secure. Just as Elizabeth had refused to name Mary Queen of Scots as her heir, so she refused to name James, terrified that if the succession were known an attempt would be made on her life. James was, for her, a 'false Scotch urchin', and he was left waiting.

But matters were taken out of her hands. In 1601, with the ageing queen's health beginning to fail, Elizabeth's leading ministers began to make moves to secure James's path to the throne. A successor had to be established before the queen's death, or else there would be an interregnum, perhaps a violent one. James was closest in blood to Elizabeth. He had to succeed to keep intact the claims of the monarchy to be a divine institution for which God provided a known line of successors. Worried Englishmen looked back wistfully to Henry VIII, who had left a will and an Act of Parliament ensuring that the crown would pass peacefully through the generations. But that certainty was at an end while Elizabeth retained the authority to nominate a successor but kept silent. Indubitable succession by the closest relative was historically the most peaceful method. The alternatives were horrifying. In the past kings had taken the crown by conquest, civil war or election when the succession was in dispute. The spectre of ambitious families jostling for supreme power brought to mind the Wars of the Roses.

The matter became pressing during the Christmas holidays of 1603, when both Elizabeth's health and her temper suddenly worsened. In mid-January she moved to Richmond for a change of air, but within a few weeks she was clearly dying. She lay on a pile of cushions on the floor of her privy chamber refusing to eat and unable to sleep. Finally she was carried to her bed, became speechless and died in the small hours of the morning of 24 March after Archbishop Whitgift had lulled her into her last sleep with his impassioned prayers.

Elizabeth had restored Protestantism, preserved the Royal Supremacy, protected her country from invasion, and allowed nothing to challenge either her crown or her popularity. Above all, her studiously broad religious settlement had brought peace – though at the inevitable price of alienating extremes of all forms. With the Great Queen dead, all eyes now turned to Scotland – and to James.

II

James VI of Scotland was proclaimed King of England within eight hours of Elizabeth's death. And his first parliament proclaimed that he was by 'inherent birth right and undoubted and lawful succession' the successor to the Imperial Crown of England and Scotland. It sounded good because it retained the monarchy's constitutional position. But it was a dangerous doctrine since it implied that James's title to the throne was above and beyond the law, as of course James himself, as the author of *The Trew Law of Free Monarchies*, firmly believed.

In April 1603, James arrived in London in triumph, the undoubted heir of his great-great-grandfather, Henry VII. Henry VII had commissioned the Imperial Crown as the symbol of the recovery of the monarchy from the degradation of the Wars of the Roses. Now James, the first ruler of all Britain, would endow it with a larger significance still. James's aim was to be *rex pacificus*, the peacemaker king. He had ensured the smooth passage of the crown without bloodshed. He would reconcile Catholic and Protestant, thus re-establishing Christian unity at home and abroad. He would end England's debilitating war with Spain, and above all he would terminate the ancient feud between England and Scotland, and fuse instead the two warring kingdoms into a new, greater united realm of Britain. It was an enormously ambitious programme, and to realize it James, in a strikingly modern gesture, summoned three major conferences on peace, religion and union with Scotland.

The peace conference and ensuing treaty at Somerset House were commemorated in a notable painting, which shows the English and Spanish delegates confronting each other across a richly carpeted table. Through its successful outcome James ended the twenty-year war with Catholic Spain. It was an auspicious start for James the international peacemaker. But the result, paradoxically, was trouble at home. On the one hand, the Somerset House treaty meant that the hotter Protestants were shocked to discover that England, now at peace with the leading Catholic power, would no longer be the champion of their fellow Protestants in Europe. And, on the other hand, the more extreme Catholics were equally dismayed to find out that Spain had not exacted toleration for Catholics as a price of the peace. Abandoned by their allies abroad, such Catholics turned in desperation to direct action at home.

At the beginning of November 1605, James was shown a tip-off letter warning that the political establishment of England would receive a 'terrible blow' in the parliament he was due to open on 5 November. James immediately appreciated that the wording of the letter pointed to an explosion. But in order to catch the plotters red-handed it was decided not to search the vaults under the Parliament Chamber until the night of the fourth.

At 11 p.m. the search party entered and found a man standing guard over a pile of firewood, thirty-five barrels of gunpowder and with a fuse in his pocket. His name was Guy Fawkes. If the gunpowder had exploded as planned it would have been the ultimate terrorist bombing, wiping out most of the British royal family and the entire English political establishment.

Nevertheless, the immediate political consequences were small. To James's credit there was no widespread persecution of Catholics in England and the peace with Spain held. But in the longer term the plot played an important part in the development of the anti-Catholic myth in England. At this early stage of the seventeenth century the reality was that English Catholicism was a beleaguered minority faith. But in the fevered imagination of the hotter sort of Protestants it became instead the fifth column of a vast international politico-religious conspiracy masterminded by the Pope in Rome and aiming not only at the conversion of England but at the subversion of English Protantism and English freedoms by the foulest possible means.

And so, at the second of James's great conferences, held at Hampton Court in January 1604 to determine the nature of religious settlement under James, those hot Protestants, known pejoratively as Puritans, demanded that the English Church be purged of what they regarded as its damnable Popish elements, which had been retained by Elizabeth. But they reckoned without the seductive powers of the English monarchy and the English Royal Supremacy.

In Scotland, James VI had sat in the body of a church as the preacher 'bore down upon him, calling the king but God's silly vassal'. Another time the minister of St Andrews said that 'all kings are devils' children'. He was lectured that as far as the General Assembly of the Presbyterian Kirk went, he was not a king or master, but a member equal with all the rest. But in England it was the same man, now known as King James I, who sat on high in the Chapel Royal, enthroned in a magnificent royal pew while the preacher, under correction, went about his humbler task far below. It was the most graphic possible illustration of the power of the Royal Supremacy, which James was determined to keep in England and, if he could, extend to Scotland.

Instead of making the Church of England more like the Scottish Kirk, therefore – as the Puritans had hoped – James used the Hampton Court conference to proclaim that he was satisfied with the Elizabethan religious settlement, and was resolved to keep it, as it stood. Beaten by Buchanan and hectored by zealous Presbyterians, James associated Puritanism with disloyalty to monarchy. He would not, any more than Elizabeth, soften Whitgift's hard line in enforcing ceremonies and vestments, which the Puritans thought scandalously Catholic. And, above all, he would allow not an inch of movement by bishops away from the English government of the Church towards a role for assemblies of presbyteries or clergy as in Scotland. 'No Bishop, No King,' he summed up memorably.

He even managed to subvert the Puritans' demands for a new translation of the Bible. James eagerly agreed, since he detested the so-called Geneva version of the Bible, which was then used by Presbyterians in Scotland and Puritans in England, because of its marginal notes, which show typically hot Protestant disrespect for kings and queens. The King James version of the Bible, on the other hand, as the large and learned team of translators explained in the preface, was to tread soberly the middle way between 'popish persons' on one hand and 'self-conceited brethren' – that is the Puritans – on the other. Thus this monument of the English language was born out of a long-dead politico-theological dispute, and it is the only classic to have been written by committee. Nevertheless, the King James Bible became the book which, more than any other, shaped the English language and formed the English mind.

James's other lasting legacy was to be the union of the crowns of England and Scotland, and he set out his case in a speech from the throne at the opening of his first English Parliament in March 1604. His succession had united the kingdoms of England and Scotland, ending the ancient divisions of the island of Britain. It was, said James, impossible to rule two countries, 'the one great, the other a less'. It would be easier 'for one head to govern two bodies, or one man to be husband of two wives'. Moreover, the king claimed, these divisions were largely in the mind. Were not England and Scotland already united by a common language, the Protestant religion and similar customs and manners? Was not the border practically indistinguishable on the ground? It was as though God had always intended the union to happen.

To resist union, therefore, James concluded, was not simply impolitic but impious: it was to put asunder kingdoms that God himself had joined together. But the English Parliament,

1

...ames VI and I made peace with Spain at the (1) Somerset House Conference; rode out
...he Catholic terrorist threat of the (2) Gunpowder Plot and tried but failed to turn his
...ual kingship of England and Scotland, shown in the Royal Coat of Arms on the
...3) Great Seal, into the unified state of Great Britain.

2

3

(1) Charles 1 and his Catholic Queen Henrietta Maria, with their two eldest children, Charles, Prince of Wales and the Princess Royal Mary, who married William II, Prince of Orange and was mother to William III of England. On the table is the massive, jewel-encrusted Imperial Crown of the Tudors and in the background a view of the royal palaces of Whitehall and Westminster.

Charles's Catholic wife and the supposedly Catholicizing policies of his (2) Arch-bishop of Canterbury, William Laud, provoked a parliamentary attack on royal government, which turned into civil war when the King tried to arrest the leaders of the (3) House of Commons.

THE DESCRIPTION OF THE ARMIES OF HORSE AND FOOT OF HIS MAJESTIES, AND
Sᵗ Thomas Fairefax his Excellency, as they were drawne into severall bodies, at the Battayle at NASBYE
the Fowerteenth day of June 1645

NASBYE

2

Charles II's government faced threats at home and abroad. It was humiliated in 1667, during the Anglo-Dutch war, when the Dutch sailed up the Medway and captured the flagship of the English Navy, the *Royal Charles*, (1) seen here being towed into Dutch waters. At home, the anti Catholic hysteria, provoked by the 'revelations' of the liar and fantasist, (2) Titus Oates, threatened to lead to the exclusion of Charles's brother and heir presumptive James, Duke of York, who had converted to Catholicism himself, from the succession. But, thanks to his own cunning and the extremism and divisions of his opponents, Charles saw off the threat.

The restored monarchy of (2) Charles II, seen here crowned and enthroned in state robes, tried to efface the memory of the Interregnum by putting on a fine show: the (1) Coronation Procession was magnificent and the regalia (including the crown), which had been destroyed by the Parliamentarians, was remade as closely as possible after the old models.

Rather against Charles's better judgement, the old monarchy's claim (3) to cure scrofula by the king's sacred touch was also revived, along with the fusion of political and religious power inherent in the Royal Supremacy.

3

4

The (1) Battle of Nasby, fought on 14 June 1645, was the first major test of the reorganized parliamentary forces, known as the New Model Army and their cavalry general, (2) Oliver Cromwell. Both were triumphantly vindicated when they inflicted a shattering defeat on Charles I which broke the royalist war effort. The battle also turned Cromwell and the New Model Army into a new force in English politics. It was the army which forced through the (3) Execution of Charles I on 30 January 1649, the abolition of kingship and the elevation of Cromwell to power as military dictator with the title of Lord Protector. But, in order to legitimate his rule, Cromwell more and more surrounded himself with the trappings of royalty and his funeral effigy (4) was actually crowned.

impoliticly and impiously, decided to look the gift horse of union in the mouth. Partly their decision was governed by straight-forward anti-Scottish xenophobia. But more fundamental causes were involved as well. These centred on James's appar-ently innocuous wish to rename the Anglo-Scottish kingdom 'Britain'.

A new name meant a new kingdom. It would, one MP said, be like a freshly conquered territory in the New World. There would be no laws and no customs and James, by his own rules in *The Trew Law of Free Monarchies*, would be free to set himself up as an absolute, supra-national Emperor of Great Britain. The English Parliament, in contrast, would be left as a mere provincial assembly. It was not an enticing prospect for MPs, who saw themselves as the Great Council of the realm.

James's reaction to their opposition was to try to enact the union symbolically, using his own powers under the royal pre-rogative. By proclamation he assumed the title of King of Great Britain. He restyled the royal coat of arms, with the lion of England balanced by the unicorn of Scotland, and he insisted on a British flag, known as the Jack after the Latin form of the name James, again by proclamation. But not content with symbols, James also practised a kind of union by stealth. The English political elite had prevented him from establishing an evenly balanced Anglo-Scots council. But a king could do what he liked with his own court. So, in revenge, James filled his bedchamber, the inner ring of his court, almost exclusively with Scots. It was a pleasure, since James took a more than fatherly interest in braw Scots lads with well-turned legs and firm but-tocks. But it also suited him politically since it compelled proud

Englishmen to sue for patronage to his Scots favourites and to bribe them as well.

But James's policy of union by stealth had a fatal flaw. He had inherited a substantial debt from Elizabeth. He had a large family to maintain, and he wanted to continue pouring money, and, to his eyes, his new-found wealth, on his favourites and his pleasures. For all this, the Crown's so-called 'ordinary income' from land and custom duties was hopelessly inadequate. There was no choice but to ask Parliament to vote money. The English Parliament, however, saw no reason why taxpayers' money – their money – should end up in the pockets of Scots favourites, and they said so rather crudely. How, asked one MP, could the cistern of the Treasury ever be filled up if money continued to 'flow thence by private Cocks'? 'Cocks' meant taps and, well, what it means now . . .

So James's project for British union remained an unfulfilled dream, while his relations with Parliament, which he thought he could master, turned into a disaster. The king was forced to fall back on his scriptural argument about the divine rights of kings. And, mundanely enough, the issue was tax. Blocked by Parliament in his pursuit of an adequate income, James used his prerogative to levy money from indirect taxation. Many saw this as unconstitutional, but, backed by the opinions of judges, James got his own way. But it meant a head-on collision with Parliament. If ever an English king managed to raise enough money by indirect means without consent, MPs reasoned, he would be able to dispense with parliaments altogether and reign as a tyrant.

Addressing Parliament in 1610, James went far beyond all

his predecessors in arguing for his rights as king. Although he would respect Parliament, he said, MPs had no right to question his prerogative of taxing without consent. It may have been a constitutional or legal matter, but James went one step farther. 'The state of monarchy is the supremest thing upon earth,' he told Parliament; 'for kings are not only God's lieutenants upon earth, and sit upon God's throne, but even by God Himself they are called gods.' James had after all been brought up a scholar, and this was the intellectual justification for what he was doing. He would not turn the monarchy into quite the absolutist institution which many were coming to fear would be the ultimate outcome of the Stuart succession. But that was because of his moderation and not because of any limitation on his quasi-divine majesty.

But James's words fell on deaf or deliberately uncomprehending ears. And, faced by widespread obstruction, by the time of his death, in 1625, he had retreated into a sort of internal exile, abandoning the task of government, and secluding himself with his favourites and horses at Newmarket. Nevertheless, he had managed, by a mixture of tact, duplicity and masterful inaction, to stick to the middle ground and hold together the warring extremes of the Church of England on the one hand and the differing religious policies of England and Scotland on the other. The result was a smooth succession on both sides of the border of James's son Charles to the glittering inheritance of the Imperial Crown of Great Britain. Within a decade and a half, Charles, by his intransigence and his ineptitude, had thrown it all away.

III

Charles was crowned King of England at Westminster Abbey on 2 February 1626. For James, divine right had been an intellectual position; for Charles it was an emotional and religious one. This was immediately made clear by his coronation service, which, meticulously organized by the up-and-coming cleric William Laud, lovingly reproduced all the splendour, solemnity and sacred mysteries of the medieval Catholic rite.

The ceremony is one of the best-documented as well as the best-organized of coronations thanks to the survival of two fascinating service books. One is Charles's own copy of the coronation service, which he used to follow the ceremony. The other is Laud's version of the same text, which he used as a kind of score to conduct the service. He also made notes in the margins in a different-coloured ink to record unusual features of the ceremony as it actually took place.

These notes take us into Charles's own mind. During the five-hour ceremony the king was invested with the carefully preserved robes and regalia of Edward the Confessor, the last sainted Anglo-Saxon king, and Charles's attitude to these ancient relics was unique. Laud notes that he insisted on placing his feet inside the sacred buskins or sandals which were normally only touched against the royal leg and that he actually used, apparently for the only time in the 1500-year history of the coronation, the Anglo-Saxon ivory comb to tidy his hair after he had been anointed on the head with the holy oil.

This wasn't mere idle curiosity or historical re-enactment for its own sake. Instead Charles was treating each and every item of the regalia as a holy sacrament of monarchy. With each touch of the precious oils and the ancient fabrics, jewels and comb God was washing away the merely human in him and leaving him purely, indefeasibly and absolutely a king. Or so Charles at least thought.

Charles, as his behaviour at his coronation would suggest, was an aesthete, a lover of beauty, elegance and order. His tutor had been chosen not for his scholarship but for his taste in fashion, and Charles himself grew up to be not only fastidious in dress and manners but also the greatest connoisseur ever to have sat on the throne of England. He built up a staggering collection of paintings and he commissioned portraits of himself and his family from the greatest contemporary artists, such as Sir Anthony van Dyck. And it is van Dyck above all who shows us Charles as he wanted to be, suggesting the grandeur of his kingship on the one hand and the Christ-like wisdom and self-sacrifice with which he hoped to rule on the other. It masked the reality. Charles was short of stature, weak and shy. Even when he was a teenager, his father nicknamed him 'Baby Charles'. The lustre of majesty with which Charles surrounded himself was intended to make up for his personal failings.

Like most royal heirs, Charles defined himself by espousing policies that were the opposite of his father's. Throughout his reign, James had been unfavourably compared with Elizabeth, the queen who had defeated the Armada. Throughout his reign, many had wanted a war to help the beleaguered and persecuted Protestants of France, Denmark, the Low Countries and Germany. Charles was pro-war, but Parliament, despite its vocal enthusiasm for a Protestant crusade in Europe, was never prepared to vote enough taxation to make war an affordable option. Frustrated by Parliament's unwillingness to put its money where its Protestant mouth was, Charles, instead of fighting the Catholic French, married the French, and of course Catholic, princess Henrietta Maria in 1626. On account of Henrietta Maria's religion the marriage was extremely unpopular with Parliament. It didn't even succeed in cementing an alliance with France.

The result was that Charles soon found himself in the worst of all possible worlds – without money, with a Catholic wife and fighting a hopeless war against both major Catholic powers, France and Spain. Charles, looking for a scapegoat for the debacle, found it in what he saw as Parliament's sullen obstructiveness. He decided that parliaments were more trouble than they were worth and that in future he would rule without them.

All over Europe, monarchs were dispensing with parliaments. So in attempting personal rule, Charles was simply following the European trend. But unlike his European counterparts, he lacked the legal ability to tax his subjects at will. Only Parliament could legislate new taxes. So, like his father before him, Charles's only recourse was to squeeze more revenue out of his customary rights and prerogatives. In order to launch a campaign to save the French Protestants persecuted by France, he asked for a 'Free Gift' from his subjects. In reality it was a forced loan, raised by threats. The subsequent campaign was a disaster, and much of the money, rather than being used to raise and support soldiers, was spent on the royal art collection.

Those who bravely refused the 'Free Gift' were sent to prison. As the 1630s continued, the unconstitutional methods of revenue-gathering, the threat to liberty and the flagrant waste of money on rash military adventures hardened parliamentary opinion against Charles. The king seemed to be augmenting his wealth at the expense of freedom. Parliament would not vote him money unless he gave guarantees that he would rule constitutionally. Parliament's attitude, in turn, hardened Charles. He resolved to rule regardless of its obstructiveness and belligerence. Fortunately, he had a crack team of lawyers to help him.

The most ingenious of Charles's lawyers was the Attorney General, William Noy. 'I moil in the law' was the anagram of his name, and he moiled – that is toiled or laboured – in the legal archives to great effect. His masterpiece was ship money.

Ship money was a traditional levy imposed on the port towns to raise vessels for the navy in times of war, as, for example, against the Spanish Armada in the heyday of Elizabethan England. This was uncontroversial, but Attorney General Noy said that the law allowed the king to extend ship money from the ports to the inland counties and to impose it in peacetime as well as in war. All this at the king's mere say-so. The extended ship money was first imposed in 1634, and within a year it was yielding over £200,000 annually and producing 90 per cent of what the king demanded. This was the Holy Grail of royal administration, which had eluded English kings ever since the Middle Ages: a large-scale permanent income which came in regularly, year by year, without the bother of consulting troublesome parliaments.

Those who refused to pay the tax on the grounds that it was unconstitutional soon found themselves confronted with the full force of royal government. The MP John Hampden was one of these people. His trial was a test case for Charles's new style of government by royal decree. Hampden was found guilty and the judge ruled that the king might levy money whenever he liked 'for the preservation of the safety of the commonwealth'. Without this power, one of the judges continued, 'I do not understand how the King's Majesty may be said to have the magisterial right and power of a free monarch'. But for a growing number of people, the king's actions marked the beginning of absolute royal government. It appeared that Charles had the right to confiscate private property and punish people at will. All legal and property rights were at his mercy. 'Grant him this,' wrote John Milton of extra-parliamentary levies, 'and the Parliament hath no more freedom than if it sat in his Noose, which when he pleased to draw together with one twitch of his Negative, shall throttle a whole Nation.'

The idea of taxing without any parliamentary consent was bound to cause grievances, as James I had found. But Charles exacerbated matters still further by attempting religious innovation at the same time.

Whatever the formal rules of the Church of England, many of the parish churches in the country had seen the development of a stripped-down fundamentalist Protestantism, very little different in practice from the Scottish Kirk. But a richer, more ceremonious vision had been preserved in a handful of places, in particular the Chapels Royal and the greater cathedrals. Here there were choirs, organs and music, candles and gold and silver plate on the communion tables, and rich vestments for the clergy. William Laud, now Charles's Archbishop of Canterbury, determined to use the Royal Supremacy to impose this opulent religious tradition on the whole country. He did so because he thought religion should be about sacraments as well as sermons, and appeal to the senses as well as to the mind. Above all he wanted to stamp out the menace of Puritanism that was gaining a hold on the Church.

In England some welcomed the new policy, but many more saw it as an assault on the very essence of their beliefs and a covert attempt to re-Catholicize the Church. Had not Charles married a Catholic? And had he not failed to help European Protestants? It all began to seem like a sinister conspiracy. But, despite some foot-dragging and grumbling, there was little overt resistance. Emboldened, Charles and Laud decided the policy should be extended to Scotland as well. Here the Reformation had been far more thoroughgoing and radical and the risks of change were correspondingly greater. But Charles, confident as ever in his God-given rightness, was undeterred. He decided that a barely modified version of the English Book of Common Prayer should be used throughout Scotland. And he did so on his own personal authority without consulting either the Scottish Parliament or the General Assembly of the Kirk. Charles was behaving as though he were the Supreme Governor of the Scottish Kirk. But would the Scottish Presbyterians accept his authority?

The answer came on Sunday, 28 July 1637, when the new prayer book was used for the first time in St Giles Cathedral in Edinburgh in the presence of the assembled Privy Council of

Scotland. As soon as the dean had begun the service a great shout erupted from the crowds at the back of the church. Heavy clasped Bibles and folding stools were hurled at the councillors and the clergy, and the rioters were ejected from the church by the guards only with difficulty. And even outside they continued pounding on the doors and pelting the windows, until the service was finished.

It was the same throughout Scotland wherever the prayer book was used. Then the protest turned political. And in Greyfriars Kirk in Edinburgh an influential group of citizens and noblemen drew up and signed an undertaking to resist Charles and 'the innovations and evils' he had introduced into the Kirk. Borrowing the name from God's solemn compact with the Jews in the Old Testament, the undertaking was known as the Covenant, and its adherents were called Covenanters.

The scene at Greyfriars was repeated in churches all over the Lowlands. It was now the Covenanters, not Charles, who controlled Scotland. Britain, which so far had escaped the wars of religion that had devastated much of the rest of Europe, now faced the horrors of sectarian conflict on its own soil. The Covenanters demanded that Charles withdraw what they saw as a Catholic prayer book and all the rituals and innovations. But Charles would not tolerate any challenge to his royal authority, in matters of money and especially in matters of religion. 'I *will rather die*,' he bluntly stated, 'than yield to their *impertinent* and *damnable* demands.'

IV

By 1640, Charles's religious policies had brought about a crisis throughout Britain. Scotland was in the hands of the Covenanters, while in England Charles's opponents drew strength north of the border. But it was the recall of Parliament after eleven years which brought things to a head.

Charles had no choice, since only Parliament could vote the money needed to suppress the Covenanters, but equally Parliament provided an unrivalled public forum for the king's opponents. Most dangerous and effective of these was the hitherto obscure lawyer and MP for Tavistock, John Pym. Like other Puritans, Pym believed that Charles's policies in Church and state were the result of a Catholic conspiracy to subvert the religion and liberties of England. But instead of wasting his time in fruitless opposition, he had used the eleven years without a parliament to build up a compelling dossier for his case.

During the 1630s Pym read voraciously; followed every detail of politics at home and abroad, and noted down useful headings and extracts in his book. This meant that, when Charles was forced to recall Parliament in April 1640, Pym was the best-informed and the best-prepared man in the House, ready with both a rhetoric of opposition to Charles's government and a plan of action for curbing royal power. Charles had hoped to prey on English xenophobia to persuade Parliament to impose an immediate and vast tax to crush the traitorous Scots. Pym countered by dragging up his list of political and religious grievances against Charles's government of the 1630s. Parliament was willing to listen and to support Pym's demand as well as to avenge itself after over a decade of neglect and unlimited royal government. Charles countered with a move designed to break the deadlock. He hinted at the surrender of ship money, but the hint only emboldened Pym.

Finally Charles lost patience with a parliament that had, once again, refused to deliver, and whose demands proved troublesome. The Short Parliament was dissolved after less than a month. Rather than help their king fight the rebellious Scots, most parliamentarians admired, in secret at last, their stand against Laud's offensive religious policies. In the face of their resistance, Charles resolved to fight the Scots without a parliamentary grant. It was a catastrophic decision.

The disaster happened at Berwick-on-Tweed, which Henry VIII had fortified with mighty ramparts as a border fortress to protect England from the Scots. Expensively refortified by Charles, it stood as a seemingly impregnable barrier between the two countries. But in August 1640 the Scots army, large, well armed, well disciplined and well provisioned, took the daring decision to outflank Berwick; cross the River Tweed farther upstream and head straight for Newcastle, which in contrast to Berwick was only lightly defended. Only the River Tyne now stood between the Scots and Newcastle. They forced a crossing at Newburn, and entered Newcastle in triumph on 30 August 1640. Never had so many run from so few, it was said, and never had Scotland won a greater victory on English soil or one with such momentous consequences.

With the Scottish army camped in England, Charles was forced to call Parliament again. Once again Charles faced Pym. And, once again, Pym cleverly focused on the financial, constitutional and religious grievances against Charles. Here Parliament was united in its opposition, and Charles was forced into a wholesale surrender of ship money and all the other objectionable aspects of his reign. His court was purged of the men Parliament regarded as 'evil counsellors', including Laud. Most humiliatingly, he was forbidden to dissolve Parliament without the consent of its members. It seemed as if opposition to the king would be permanent and that his powers would be stripped one by one in return for a dribble of cash. Charles believed that Parliament had 'taken the government all in pieces, and I may say it is almost off the hinges'.

But Charles would not accede to Pym's demand that he should abandon all his religious policies, to the extent of abolishing bishops. 'No Bishop, No King,' as his father had famously said. The parliamentarians also wanted to remove Catholics from Henrietta Maria's court and to appoint a 'well-affected person' to teach the Prince of Wales 'matters of religion and liberty' so that he would not repeat his father's mistakes when he came to the throne. Not only had Parliament taken away most of his powers, it now wanted to dictate the day-to-day running of the court and, worst of all, his family.

There was only one way out of this intolerable situation. Boxed in by his opponents in the English Parliament, Charles tried to break out by coming to terms with the Scots. In the summer of 1641 he journeyed to Edinburgh and in an astonishing change of front accepted the religious and political revolution of the last three years. He worshipped in the kirk; agreed to the abolition of bishops and filled the government of Scotland with the leading Covenanters and his own sworn enemies. The king also played several rounds of golf and, reasonably confident that he had solved one of his problems, returned in an excellent mood to England.

Events in England also seemed to be moving in Charles's direction. He was greeted with joy in London, as if nothing had happened over the last few years. And the parliamentary alliance that had exacted so many concessions was beginning to fracture. For, with Charles's surrender of ship money and other unconstitutional measures, the religious divisions in the Commons between Puritans like Pym and those who were sympathetic to Charles's ceremonious religion were opened up. Pym tried to whip his troops into line and put 'The Grand Remonstrance' to the vote. This was Pym's searing condemnation of Charles's conduct throughout his entire reign, and an explicit statement of dissatisfaction with his government, in particular in religious matters. These amounted, the Remonstrance claimed, to an all-embracing Catholic conspiracy to subvert the religion and liberties of England. The king himself, it was careful to point out, had been only the unwitting agent of the conspiracy. Nevertheless, Charles's gullibility meant that he could never be trusted to choose his own advisers or to command his own troops again. And, most importantly, after a hundred years the Royal Supremacy would be abolished in all but name. All Charles's and Laud's reforms would be reversed and Catholicism would be suppressed.

The Remonstrance was nominally addressed to the king.

But in fact it was a manifesto, for a constitutional revolution at the least, perhaps even for an armed revolt. The Remonstrance was also bitterly divisive and, after days of acrimonious debate, it was passed on 1 December 1641 by 159 votes to 148 – a bare majority of eleven. The vote showed that the broad-based opposition to Charles had broken up. And the more Pym pushed the Puritan attack on Charles's Church reforms, the more his majority risked disappearing entirely. But then Charles over-reached himself. Immediately, by dismissing Parliament's armed guard, there were dark rumours that he intended to restore his power by force. Plenty of Irish Catholic veterans from the Scottish war were skulking in London. Henrietta Maria was suspected of negotiating with a Catholic country to help her husband. Suddenly, all those conspiracy theories regarding a Catholic coup were revived, and Parliament' united hostility to Charles was renewed. Pym said that he had picked up on 'whispering intimation' that there was 'some great design in hand' to ensure that 'the necks of both the parliaments should be broken'.

As if to confirm the fears, Charles made his greatest blunder. Convinced, probably correctly, that among MPs there were traitors who had colluded with the invading Scots in 1640, Charles determined to bring five Members of Parliament, including John Pym and John Hampden, to trial on charges of high treason. He ordered Parliament to give them up, but instead they voted him in breach of parliamentary privilege.

Charles was unsure how to deal with this latest rebuff. His mind was made up for him. 'Go you coward!' Henrietta Maria shouted at him, 'and pull those rogues out by the ears, or never see my face more.' On 4 January 1642 King Charles strode into the chamber of the House of Commons to arrest his principal opponents. His guards stood outside, fingering their weapons as, to uneasy silence, the king sat himself in the Speaker's chair. 'Where are the five members?' the king demanded, calling them by name. In response, the Speaker fell on his knees, protesting that he could answer only as the House directed him.

In fact, the five members, forewarned of the king's movements, had made good their escape by boat from the back of the Palace of Westminster as Charles and his guards had entered on the landward side at the front. Instead, it was Charles himself who had walked into a trap. By trying to seize the five members by force, he had shown himself to be a violent tyrant. By failing, he had revealed himself to be impotent. As Charles left the chamber empty handed, he murmured disconsolately, 'All my birds have flown.' So too had most of his power.

Parliament exploited its advantage and took control of all aspects of government, including the militia. MPs claimed to be 'watchmen trusted for the good and welfare of the King, Church and State'. It was, they said, only temporary. They had been forced to act in this way because Charles had proved himself unfit to rule. The king could only complain that he was 'no idiot, nor infant, uncapable of understanding to command'.

Battle lines were now drawn up. Charles's violent, ill-thought-through gesture not only preserved Pym's parliamentary majority but also turned London decisively against the king. Throughout the rest of the country it was a different story as Pym's increasingly extreme Puritan attack on the Church won Charles a devoted following. But in fact Charles was no

longer really King of Great Britain or even of England. Instead
he was only the leader of a faction.

For history had come almost full circle. The attempt to
expand the powers of the Imperial Crown so that it ruled both
Church and state, and Scotland as well as England, had back-
fired. Instead England was about to return to the factional strife
of the Wars of the Roses and Britain to the national struggles
of the Anglo-Scottish wars. And it began at Nottingham in
August 1642 when Charles raised his standard in a war against
his Parliament and half his people. He had fewer than 4000 men
under his command.

NEW MODEL KINGDOM

CROMWELL

ON 23 NOVEMBER 1658 a solemn procession wended its way through the silent streets of London towards Westminster Abbey. It was the funeral cortège of the most powerful ruler the British Isles had known since the fall of Rome.

For this latter-day emperor had achieved what had eluded the greatest warrior-kings of the Middle Ages. He had welded the countries of England, Scotland and Ireland into one United Kingdom. He had bent Parliament to his will; levied taxes as he pleased; stilled the fratricidal religious conflict of the Reformation and created the most feared navy and army in Europe. He lay in his robe of state, a sceptre in one hand, an orb in the other, with an Imperial Crown laid on a velvet cushion a little above his head. Yet this ruler was not a king. He was in fact a regicide – a king-killer.

His name was Oliver Cromwell, and his story is the tale of how England abolished its age-old monarchy only to find that it couldn't do without it after all.

I

Just fourteen years before, in 1644, England had been embroiled in a bloody civil war. On one side was King Charles I, insisting on his supremacy over Church and state. And on the other parliamentary forces that believed the king's powers should be limited and that religion was a matter for individual conscience (providing it was Protestant), rather than royal decree.

Despite thousands of dead and an economy in tatters, neither side had been able to force a decisive victory. And Parliament's original war aims, which were, in essence, to limit Charles's authority in matters of state and religion, and to place his authority under the control of Parliament, were about to be replaced by the almost inconceivable notion of executing the king for treason. Playing with increasingly high stakes, Parliament fell to bickering.

Matters came to a head in November 1644 when Edward Montagu, Earl of Manchester and major general of the parliamentary forces, questioned how the war should be prosecuted. Were they fighting the king to crush him, or merely to bring him to the negotiating table? The latter was Manchester's view. Aristocrat that he was, he couldn't conceive of a kingless world. He also had a thoroughly realistic fear of Charles's residual authority. 'If we fight the King 100 times, and beat him 99, he will be King still,' he said. 'But if he beat us once or the last time, we shall be hanged, we shall lose our estates and our posterities will be undone.'

This was the paradox of Parliament's war aims. Parliamentarians saw themselves as 'watchmen' over the constitution, who wanted to preserve the essentials of the ancient monarchy. Indeed, in 1645 only one MP voted for a republic while the vast majority still saw kingly government as the best of all the possible alternatives. But there was no sign that Charles would ever compromise with them. As the king bluntly stated, 'There are three things I will not part with – the Church, my crown, and my friends; and you will have much ado to get them from me.' He would fight to the end. Where did that leave Parliament?

Confronted with these realities, the original aims of Parliament were coming under attack. John Pym and John Hampden, its earliest leaders, had both died in 1643, while their manifesto, The Grand Remonstrance, with more than two hundred demands offered no coherent, unifying war aim. But beneath the surface of the parliamentary armies were brewing new forces and Manchester's moderate conservatism was met with fierce resistance from one of his officers, General Oliver Cromwell. For Cromwell, a Puritan, a radical and now a rising parliamentarian, rejected not only the king's authority in religious matters but also any reconciliation with the Crown.

Cromwell, despite his rank, belonged to the wilder shores of religious belief. He and his fellows repudiated all human authority in religion and all fixed outward forms of belief. Instead they believed in their Christian liberty to seek after truth and to follow it where it led them personally and individually.

Born in 1599, Cromwell had Protestantism in his blood, and it was further drummed, indeed beaten, into him at school and university. Like many religious men, Cromwell experienced a crisis of faith in his thirties from which he emerged with a burning confidence in his own salvation. But there was nothing otherworldly about Cromwell's faith. He was a big, bony, practical, rather awkward man – hands-on, sporty, unscholarly despite his Cambridge days, but with the gift of the gab and a knack for popular leadership. Fearless, with no respect for persons however grand or institutions however venerable, Cromwell was a man waiting for God to reveal himself to him in actions. But as the war ground into stalemate, there were few obvious signs of divine favour. Cromwell noticed early in the Civil War that the royalists fought with fervour and almost religious conviction. They truly believed in kingly government and the righteousness of their cause. Parliamentarian soldiers, on the other hand, bogged down in constitutional quibbles, lacked inspiration.

The New Model Army, filled with men who were seekers like himself, proved to be the answer to his prayers. Created in February 1645 by a Parliament that was increasingly despairing of victory, the New Model Army was England's first truly professional fighting force: a meritocracy founded on strict discipline, thorough training and ability rather than social rank. It was said that they fought with a pike in one hand and a Bible in the other. Cromwell, for these men, seemed to epitomize the Christian warrior. As a contemporary said after one of Cromwell's early victories, 'It was observed God was with him, and he began to be renowned.'

The first great test of the New Model Army came at Naseby on 14 June 1645. On one side were the royalist forces led by King Charles himself in gilt armour and mounted on his beautiful Flemish horse. On the other a company of 'poor prayerful men', many of whom were new to battle but who nevertheless outnumbered the more experienced royalist forces. During the course of the day, the solid ranks of Cromwell's New Model cavalry and Cromwell's own generalship proved decisive. By one o'clock in the afternoon, Charles had lost his infantry, his artillery and in effect the kingdom. 'God would', Cromwell wrote after the battle, 'by things which are not bring to nothing things that are.' It was a biblically inspired, messianic confidence which Cromwell shared with his troops.

The New Model Army proved to be the decisive weapon in Parliament's struggle with the king. But in forging this weapon, Parliament had called into being a new power in the land, one whose strength would grow with each victory that it won. Indeed, Cromwell's victory with the New Model Army at Naseby was not only the beginning of the end for the royalist forces; it was also the beginning of new ideas about the role of the monarchy, indeed, of its very existence.

After the battle, the army was visited by a clergyman, Richard Baxter. Baxter was a noted Presbyterian who had preached against the king's religious policies. Instead, like all Presbyterians, Baxter believed in an austere authoritarian national Church run not by king and bishops but by committees of zealous clergy and laymen known as presbyteries. Nevertheless, like most Englishmen, he anticipated that the king would eventually agree to a negotiated settlement and consent to a reformation of the national Church.

But Baxter now encountered in the New Model Army a body of men among whom radical ideas were eagerly embraced. They were fed on a diet of tracts and pamphlets that cast Charles as an evil tyrant and godly MPs and soldiers as God's true 'Vice-regents' on Earth. They believed that kingly government was ordained by God, for they read in Deuteronomy: 'one from among thy brethren shalt thou set king over thee.' But if kings were ordained by God, it did not mean that all kings were godly. Some monarchs did God's work, while others, like Pharaoh, were scourges that the pious were charged with fighting as a religious duty. Charles, it was clear to them, was akin to an Old Testament tyrant who set up false idols and oppressed the people of God. Such a man must be resisted, lest Englishmen commit blasphemy themselves by acquiescing in the sacrilege of a latter-day King of Babylon. It was not that Charles was just a secular despot: he was a tyrant over Christianity itself. One writer described the Parliamentarian forces as a 'quiver so full of chosen and polished shafts for the Lord's work'. And another urged them: 'let us proceed to shed the blood of the ungodly.'

These tough, Bible-quoting, disputatious soldiers were agreed on two things – that the state had no right to interfere in their religion and that Charles was a tyrant and a traitor who must be defeated and brought to account for his crimes. For the Presbyterian Baxter, who believed in a God who ordained order and discipline, this was a nightmarish vision of unchristian anarchy. But it was also a vision, Baxter realized, that the men of the New Model Army were determined to turn into reality.

To Baxter's horror these religious extremists were to have no qualms in calling for the trial, and eventually the execution, of their monarch.

II

After his defeat in the Civil War, King Charles had been prisoner first of the Scots, who handed him over to Parliament for money in January 1647; then he was seized by the New Model Army in April 1647. For most parliamentarians, the thought that Charles should be put on trial, let alone executed, was abhorrent. Moreover, as Charles travelled through the country as Parliament's prisoner, he was met by cheering crowds everywhere, even in Puritan Cambridge, which was the constituency of Oliver Cromwell himself. The majority of the people, it was clear, were not ready for a revolution, and might even support the king if things were pushed too far. Sensibly, in view of this sentiment, Charles was offered a generous settlement to end the war.

But characteristically, Charles overplayed his hand, rejecting the astonishingly lenient political terms he was offered by Cromwell and the other army leaders in order to guarantee religious toleration. Instead, in a cynical *renversement d'alliance*, the king joined forces with his original enemies – the Scots Covenanters. In return for the king's promise to impose Presbyterianism throughout the British Isles – which he had no intention whatever of keeping – the Scots were to invade England to restore King Charles I and wipe out the New Model Army.

In 1648 the Scots army invaded England, initiating what became known as the Second Civil War, which was finally decided in a wet and bloody three-day-long battle at Preston in Lancashire. By a masterpiece of strategy, Cromwell and his New

Model Army turned the Scots' defeat into an annihilating rout. The parliamentarians were indeed victorious. But it was the New Model Army which had won the war and was now determined to dictate the terms of peace.

They were decided at a three-day prayer meeting in Windsor in April 1648, when the army claimed to be fighting 'in the name of the Lord only'. The ultimate war aim now was 'to call Charles Stuart, that man of blood, to account for the blood he had shed, and mischief he had done to his utmost, against the Lord's cause and people in these poor nations'. But they were at odds with Parliament, which was terrified by the army's radical religious views. In November, MPs rejected the 'Remonstrance of the Army', a demand that Charles be brought to trial for treason because he had started the war and called in the Scots. Parliament was prepared to make yet another deal with the king.

But the army wasn't prepared to concede again. Its officers now moved with lightning speed. On 1 December it seized the king, who had escaped into light, protective custody on the Isle of Wight; on 6 December Colonel Thomas Pride entered the House of Commons and purged it of the Presbyterian majority. One hundred and eighty-six members were turned away, forty-one were arrested and eighty-six didn't turn up. Cromwell left the North for London, making known his support for the purge. And on 4 January what remained of Parliament, a group known as the Rump consisting of 150 MPs, proclaimed itself the Supreme Power in the nation. It was a military coup fronted by a pseudo-parliamentary dictatorship.

The Second Civil War and his great victory at Preston now produced a marked hardening in Cromwell's attitudes, especially towards the king. Until Pride's Purge he had kept his opinions secret. Henceforward, he, too, saw Charles – who had engineered war on his own initiative and for his own selfish ends – as a man of blood who must be punished for his crimes. Convinced as always that God revealed Himself in events, he quickly shifted ground to take a leading part in the decision to put King Charles on trial for his life.

The army and remaining parliamentarians knew full well that Charles, for all his blunders and obstinacy, retained significant support in his kingdoms. Even some radical elements in the army were objecting that the purge of MPs was an act of tyranny. The officers and remaining MPs had to act quickly. A High Court of Justice comprising 135 Commissioners was set up to try Charles. Opposition was bulldozed, as were constitutional niceties. When one Commissioner said that there was no known, legal way to try a monarch, Cromwell shouted him down: 'I tell you we will cut off his head with the crown upon it!'

On 20 January 1649 King Charles was bought to Westminster Hall to be tried for high treason. According to the indictment, Charles was 'a tyrant, traitor, murderer and a public and implacable enemy to the commonwealth of England'. The unthinkable act of killing the king was drawing even closer. Charles's strategy, which he stuck to with remarkable persistence, was to refuse to recognize either the authority or the legality of the court, and throughout the week-long trial both the king and his judges sat with their hats firmly on their heads in a stand-off of mutual disrespect.

Charles laughed openly at the charges and questioned the right of a minority of Parliament to try him. 'Is this the bringing of the King to his Parliament?' he asked. '. . . Let me see a Legal Authority warranted by the Word of God, the Scriptures, or warranted by the Constitution of the Kingdom.' He warned that a parliamentary or military tyranny would be a disaster for England. After him there would be anarchy or oppression when the known constitutional landmarks were torn away.

Charles was correct in saying that he was not being tried by the parliament that had initiated opposition to his style of government. Under Cromwell's leadership, the radicals had grown from a fringe element to control not just the army but also the Parliament that now sat in judgement of the king, preparing for the almost inconceivable step of killing their anointed ruler. The death warrant of Charles I was signed and sealed by fifty-nine of his judges, ordering his execution by the severing of his head from his body on 30 January 1649, with the requirement that the execution should take place in the open street before Whitehall. It is a bold and brave document.

But it also highlights the titanic effort of will that was needed to bring even this panel of committed parliamentarians to take the terrible, irrevocable step of publicly executing the king. Both the date of the warrant itself and the date of the execution are inserted over erasures. The names of two of the men who were in charge of the execution had been changed following the refusal of the original nominees to act, and many of the signatures, we know, were obtained only after long, hard lobbying. Overseeing it all, driving it all and allegedly even guiding the pens of the reluctant signers was the third man to sign, Oliver Cromwell.

30 January was bitterly cold. Charles put on two shirts: he

did not want to be seen shivering lest onlookers mistake it as a sign of fear. At about noon the king drank a glass of claret and ate a little bread, and then he was escorted through the Banqueting House at Whitehall, the scene of the gaudy triumphs of the Stuart court, and stepped through one of the windows on to the high, black-draped scaffold in the street below. 'I go from a corruptible to an incorruptible crown,' the king said to his chaplain, Bishop Juxton, 'where no disturbance can be, no disturbance in the world.' And then the king removed the garter jewel of St George, made of a single onyx encircled with diamonds, from round his neck, and handed it to Juxton with the instruction that it was to be given to the Prince of Wales with the single word, 'remember'.

Charles's most valuable legacy to his son was the manner of his death. Sixty years before, Charles's grandmother, Mary Queen of Scots, had died flamboyantly as a passionate martyr to the Catholic faith. Charles instead offered himself up with quiet dignity as a sacrifice to his vision of Christian kingship.

Barely two months later, on 17 March 1649, the House of Commons passed an act stating 'That the Office of a King, in this nation ... is unnecessary, burthensome, and dangerous to the liberty, safety, and public interest of the people of this nation; and therefore ought to be abolished'. An attempt was made to eradicate the very word 'king' from the language, and all the images and icons of monarchy were removed. After almost two centuries, the supreme symbol of monarchy – the Imperial Crown itself – was smashed. The Commonwealth of England, ruled by the Rump Parliament, was established.

But getting rid of kings was easier said than done. There

had been kings in England since before England itself had existed. Kings had made England and had forged the Imperial Crown with its claim to rule Church as well as state, and Scotland as well as England. Could this king-made, king-centred country successfully become a kingless republic? In eleven years of audacious political experiment, the parliamentarians tried every means possible and every bold constitutional experiment to transform England into the kingless society of their dreams.

The parliamentarians' first problem was that in killing one king they had created another. Charles II, the eldest son of Charles I, had spent part of the war fighting for the royalist cause, most notably at the Battle of Edgehill. But defeat had forced him into exile in France. Monarchs and rulers throughout Europe all expressed their horror of the English regicide, but none was willing to supply a single soldier to help Charles regain his throne.

Only the Scots were ready for that, and then only on terms that Charles II found profoundly distasteful – both personally and politically. For, the Scots demanded, Charles must not only accept the Presbyterian Kirk in Scotland itself, he must also promise to impose the Presbyterian system in England and Ireland as well. For eighteen months Charles wriggled until finally he was forced to accept the inevitable, swear the Covenant and give the undertakings the Scots demanded. The result was that in 1650 a Stuart once again rode at the head of an army on British soil. But it was a Scots army dedicated to the imposition of a Scottish Presbyterian empire by force throughout the British Isles.

Convinced of the holiness of his cause, and that he would

find a large number of royalists who had been horrified by the murder of his father, Charles II took on the New Model Army once more. But as he travelled through Scotland and later England, he found a population eager to come out and cheer his ragged army, but reluctant to lay down their lives for the royalist cause. His plans of invasion and a glorious restoration of the Stuarts now ended in humiliation. Once again the Scots faced Cromwell's New Model Army. At Dunbar, despite mustering a force twice the size of Cromwell's, the Scots suffered a crushing defeat. And in 1651 Charles's invasion of England also ended in defeat at Worcester.

Charles, who had been crowned King of Scots on New Year's Day, became a fugitive, hunted throughout England for forty days. It was a remarkably long time, for Charles was unusually tall and had a dark complexion. The government had put out a description, but the young king was able to evade capture with the help of a few loyalists and his own play-acting skills. He fled the Commonwealth's troops under the name of Will Jackson, a servant. Stopping to reshoe a horse, he made pleasant conversation with the blacksmith. 'What news?' he asked. The man told him of the defeat at Worcester, adding that the king was still at large. Charles replied amiably 'that if the rogue were taken he deserved to be hanged, more than all the rest, for bringing in the Scots'. Charles said that the blacksmith replied 'that I spoke like an honest man'. As he continued through England, the king saw bonfires and heard church bells pealing in celebration of his defeat. At last the king was able to slip across the Channel in a fishing boat.

Otherwise Cromwell's victory was complete. The English,

as Charles II found, would not rebel against the Commonwealth in favour of the Stuart cause. Scotland, too, was conquered and occupied by the English army, and the General Assembly of the Kirk dissolved by force. It was Cromwell's last battle as an active commander. Now, leaving others to mop up in Scotland, he started the journey back to London.

Cromwell, like Julius Caesar before him, now bestrode the world like a colossus. He had outdone the greatest of the medieval kings and had succeeded where even King Edward I, the hammer of the Scots, had failed. He had conquered Ireland, Scotland and, in a series of coruscating victories, had forged a new united Britain. Except, curiously, in England. For the government of England remained in the limbo that had followed Charles's execution. The monarchy had gone, but it was unclear what would replace it.

Having won the war the new republic now had little idea what to do with the ensuing peace. By 1653 Britain had been without a king for nearly five years and a decade of war had left the country economically drained. But the remaining Rump Parliament proved incapable of producing a new reformed constitution or providing effective leadership. There were calls that every adult male should be given the vote, that land should be redistributed and that the government should adopt a fully republican constitution. But radical proposals such as these were fiercely rejected as the English Republic became increasingly conservative. Indeed, by refusing to stand for re-election and meeting in continuous session the members of the Rump threatened to become a permanent and self-perpetuating oligarchy. Was it for this that the army had brought down Charles I?

Parliament and the army were locked in mutual hatred, and only Cromwell was strong enough to hold power without the two coming to blows. But, after all, he owed his position to the army. As Parliament tried to take more power, his dominance was being challenged. The last straw came when the Rump began moves to deprive Cromwell of his position of Commander-in-Chief.

On 20 April 1653 Cromwell entered the Commons dressed as a mere citizen, in a plain black coat and grey worsted stockings. He rose to address the House, putting off his hat as was then customary and speaking moderately in praise of parliaments. But, as his passion and his confidence rose, he began to pace up and down, put his hat back on his head and thundered, 'You are no Parliament. I say, you are no Parliament. I will put an end to your sittings.' He looked down at the mace and said, 'What shall we do with this Bauble? here, take it away.' He then took the Speaker's chair and told the assembled members that 'some of them were Whoremasters. That others of them were Drunkards, and some corrupt and unjust men, and scandalous to the possession of the Gospel, and that it was not fit they should sit as a Parliament any longer.'

'Call them in,' he cried, 'call them in.' Members of Cromwell's regiment burst into the Commons, the Speaker was removed from his chair, the mace from the table and the members of the Rump dispersed. England had already lost her king; now it had lost its parliament. Cromwell managed to do what Charles I had so humiliatingly failed to do when he came in 1642 to arrest just five MPs. Power flowed unmitigated and undisguised from the barrel of a musket.

III

Now Cromwell, with the backing of the army, ruled England without Parliament as Commander-in-Chief. A portrait of him, painted shortly after Charles I's execution, shows how far Cromwell – the erstwhile gentleman farmer – had transmuted into a princely figure, in armour, attended by his faithful page, wielding the field marshal's baton and able to exercise supreme power in civil as well as military affairs (see second plate section, page 4).

But Cromwell was a reluctant revolutionary and eager to cloak his military dictatorship in decent constitutional garb. Surveying the post-war situation, he mused on what form of government was suitable for England now the Stuarts were gone. He admitted that for 'the preservation of our Rights, both as Englishmen, and as Christians ... a settlement, with somewhat of Monarchical Power in it, would be very effective'. But he would not say as much, in public at least. Neither Parliament nor the army wanted another king, but they did recognize the need for a new kind of authority – and so, under a new constitution, the office of king was renamed Lord Protector (the then usual English name for a Regent) and offered to Cromwell, who accepted it.

Cromwell then summoned a Parliament as provided for by the constitution. But the Parliament of Cromwell immediately picked up where the Parliaments of Charles I had left off, by arguing about the Lord Protector's control of the army, his income and his right to appoint advisers. And Cromwell responded by behaving like Charles I – first denouncing Parliament, then dissolving it.

As Lord Protector (and now untramelled by Parliament), Cromwell was invested with all the authority of a dictator. And, having come into power as the nominee of the army, he set himself to carry out that which the army had set forth in its petitions and manifestos. Cromwell's most dramatic concession to the army came in 1655 with his agreement to the appointment of eleven major generals as military governors of the English regions. The major generals were doubly unpopular. First, because they were responsible for the enforcement of the Protectorate's programme of social reform. This showed that the Puritans really were puritanical since it involved not only an assault on swearing, drunkenness, gaudy female fashions and fornication but also attempted abolition of such staples of English life as horse races, theatres, casinos and brothels. Not even pubs were exempt. Still worse, from the point of view of the constitutionally minded, was the fact that the major generals were to be paid for by a 10 per cent income tax on ex-royalists, known as the 'decimation' and levied purely on the authority of the Lord Protector.

But the decimation tax was seen as taxation levied without parliamentary consent, and it came under remorseless attack when a revised version of the Rump Parliament finally returned in September 1656. Concerned by what they saw as Cromwell's arbitrary use of power, and unable to recognize this new form of republican authority, Parliament now sought a return to the kind of constitutional government it had been used to in the past – working not with a Protector but a king.

They set out their claims in the 'The Humble Petition and

Advice', hoping that Cromwell would exchange the title of Protector for that of king. The title and office of a king, they argued, had been long received and approved by their ancestors. And had not Cromwell always wondered whether he might not be the Lord's anointed? What if a man, even a humble God-fearing man like himself, were king?

Cromwell was obviously fit to be king, but why should Parliament, which had just killed one king, now seek to create another? The reason was that the powers of the king, unlike those of the Lord Protector, were known and limited. A king had to respect ancient custom, and to seek the consent of Parliament to make law and to raise taxes. King Oliver would have been an altogether more circumscribed figure than Lord Protector Cromwell.

But the army was aghast that its godly revolution might amount to no more than the replacement of the House of Stuart by the House of Cromwell. So they lobbied hard against the title of king, and Cromwell himself, after weeks of agonized indecision, decided that God had 'blasted the title and the name of King'. He would accept the powers – and indeed more than the powers – of a king, but not the title. Cromwell, asserting that he was 'not scrupulous about words or names or such things', brushed over the implications of his decision.

Cromwell's second inauguration as Protector took place on 26 June 1657 in Westminster Hall. The first had been modest; this was virtually regal. Edward I's Coronation Chair was brought from Westminster Abbey. Cromwell was invested with an imperial robe of purple velvet lined with ermine. He was presented with a gilt-bound and embossed Bible, a golden-hilted sword and a massive solid gold sceptre. He swore a version of the Coronation Oath and finally, seated in majesty in the Coronation Chair, he was acclaimed three times to the sounds of trumpets and the cry 'God Save the Lord Protector'.

All that was missing was the crown itself, and that appeared on his coinage and Great Seal. Oliver was now indeed king in all but name. Cromwell had rid Britain of its king – but as Lord Protector he now held more power than any king of England had ever held. His achievements rivalled those of any English monarch.

But just one year after his investiture, Cromwell fell ill, and on 3 September 1658 he died at the royal palace of Whitehall. In Cromwell's magnificent funeral ceremonies, which stretched out over fifteen weeks, any coyness about his royal status was finally abandoned. Cromwell had ruled like a king. He was buried as a king with solemn ceremony, a vast cortège, which included no fewer than three state-salaried poets, and at enormous expense. Presiding over it all, as was traditional in royal funerals, was a lifelike effigy of Cromwell himself, which wore in death the remade Imperial Crown that he had first destroyed and then refused in life. Few British rulers have left a grander legacy or one that seemed more stable.

But if Cromwell had taken on the forms of a king without the name, one very important thing was missing. Did the laws and constitution die with him? Was the Protectorship hereditary or elective? These matters were never cleared up, despite pleas that Cromwell should make the office hereditary to preserve the good order and stability of the Commonwealth after his death. But Cromwell, as usual, refused to antagonize the regicidal army by restoring a full hereditary monarchy. He acted at the very end, however, when he was beyond the jealousy of the generals. On his deathbed Cromwell nominated his eldest surviving son Richard as his heir, and within three hours of his father's death Richard was, to the sound of trumpets, proclaimed Lord Protector by the Grace of God. Loyal addresses flooded in from the counties and towns, and messages of condolence and congratulations from foreign sovereigns. Few royal successions have been as smooth.

Richard was not without his personal qualities either. He had been brought up to be a simple country gentleman, spending part of his youth in Ely at his father's modest house. Perhaps fearing that if he were seen to be grooming an heir the army would object, Oliver had kept his son out of the way. Nonetheless, as Lord Protector Richard went on to display charm, dignity and even an unexpected eloquence. But he lacked the killer instinct for power on the one hand and a secure power base in the army on the other. Richard also inherited the unresolved political dispute between the army and Parliament. His father had been strong enough to control it, but it quickly threatened to overwhelm the son.

His first parliament met in January 1659, but by April the council of officers was calling on Richard to dissolve Parliament and entrust himself to the army. Their intention was to preserve the Protectorate under military rather than parliamentary control. Richard, unwilling that one drop of blood should be spilled to preserve his greatness, as he was supposed to have said, reluctantly agreed. He dissolved Parliament and threw himself on the mercy of the council of officers.

But dissension in the ranks quickly thwarted the council's plan, as junior officers and republicans joined together to call for the restoration of the Rump Parliament that Richard's father, Oliver Cromwell, had dismissed in 1653. The generals were forced to concede and the Rump, reassembled on 7 May 1659, immediately voted to abolish the Protectorate. Richard resigned from office just eight months after his investiture. The reign of Queen Dick, as Richard was derisively known, was over.

Once the army would have stepped decisively into the breach. But the army, for the first time, was divided. There was no unifying vision of how England should be governed and no recognized commander. In London its leadership was weak, self-interested and vacillating. In Scotland, however, General George Monck had power and influence enough to decide the situation. Monck was a canny politician who had fought on the royalist side in the Civil War until his capture and imprisonment by parliamentary forces. In exchange for his promise to command a parliamentary army, Monck was released. Now, as leader of the English army in Scotland, he took action.

But Monck was a restorer, not a revolutionary. He decided that Britain would never be at peace until the traditional forms of government were brought back. That certainly meant a new parliament; but might it also mean a king? On 26 December 1659, under pressure from Monck, the Rump Parliament was restored yet again and it appointed him commander-in-chief of the military forces. A week later, Monck and his army crossed the River Tweed and entered England.

For the first time events in England now offered Charles II, still in exile in the Low Countries, real hope. His advisers had been quick to spot the opportunity offered by the split in the army and the rise of Monck, and they put out secret feelers to him. But Monck had played a subtle game. So subtle indeed that his real motives still remain debatable. Was he resolved on the restoration of Charles II all along, or was he open minded about everything apart from the necessity for constitutional legitimacy? At any rate, Monck kept his contemporaries guessing and hoping long enough to head off the risk of renewed civil war and to let events acquire their own momentum. And it was a momentum, as irresistible as a force of nature, towards monarchy.

IV

By spring 1660 the English Parliament and its army were in disarray. England teetered on the brink of another civil war. It seemed to everyone, especially Monck, that the only authority that could rule England was a Stuart monarchy. Samuel Pepys recorded, 'Everybody now drinks the King's health without any fear, whereas before it was very private that a man may do it.'

On 4 April Charles II wrote formally to the Speaker of the House of Commons from exile in the Netherlands. It was a tactful letter, offering his help and stating how the presence of the monarch might give the country the stability it had been lacking since the death of Lord Protector Cromwell. His approach was a masterpiece of clemency and statecraft.

The Declaration of Breda was intended to serve both as a

manifesto for his restoration and as a blueprint for a comprehensive settlement after the turmoil of twenty years of civil war and unrest. And it shows that the lessons of those years had been well learnt. Its principal argument in favour of monarchy was that the proper rights and power of the king were the guarantor of the rights of everybody else, and without the king's rights nothing and no one was safe. As Cromwell had found, only monarchy could tame a fractious army and a power-hungry parliament. But as Charles now argued, only a Stuart monarchy had the legitimacy to guarantee known laws and a stable line of succession.

Most importantly, the Declaration stated that there would be no bloody reprisals or the restoration of the Stuart monarchy as it had existed under Charles I. Instead, the restoration would *not* be the victory of the royalist cause, but a continuation of strong government as it had existed under Cromwell. Finally, the Declaration of Breda promised to bind up the wounds of a bleeding nation. It offered pardon to all, save effectively those directly participating in the late king's execution. But most strikingly and unthinkably for the heir of Charles I, it also offered liberty of worship. 'We do Declare a Liberty to tender consciences; and that no Man shall be disquieted or called in question for Differences of Opinion in matter of Religion, which do not disturb the Peace of the Kingdom.' Was the genie of the Royal Supremacy, with its fatal harnessing of politics and religion, to be exorcized at last?

In April 1660 a new parliament, known as the Convention, was elected. Edward Montagu, Earl of Manchester, who a decade and a half earlier had opposed the king's trial and execution, was appointed Speaker of the House of Lords. Over-whelmingly pro-royalist, the Convention's first undertaking was to debate the question of the restoration of the monarchy. The parliament that only eleven years earlier had helped kill the king now debated the return of his son, Charles II.

On 30 April the Convention MPs processed to hear a sermon in St Margaret's, Westminster. Preached by the Presbyterian Richard Baxter, who, a few years previously, had been so shocked by the religious anarchy of the New Model Army, it was entitled 'A Sermon of Repentance'. It argued that both the Episcopalians and the Presbyterians had sinned by fighting each other to establish their exclusive vision of the Church. Instead they should unite in as comprehensive a national Church settle-ment as possible. His call was heeded, and the next day both sides joined together to vote for the recall of the king.

On 1 May 1660 Parliament declared that the government should be by king, Lords and Commons. A week later, Charles was proclaimed by both Houses. The king and his court made haste to return to England. He was greeted with joy in London, where he processed through the streets. The diarist John Evelyn recorded: 'I stood in the Strand, and beheld it, and blessed God: And all this without one drop of blood, and by that very army, which rebelled against him.'

On 23 April 1661, Charles II, who had already been crowned King of Scotland a decade earlier, processed to Westminster Abbey for his second coronation, this time as King of England, almost a year after his return. It was St George's Day, and everything was done to restore the traditional forms. The king had even revived the eve-of-coronation procession from the

Tower to Westminster that had been dispensed with by his father and grandfather. The procession took over five hours to pass and was of unparalleled magnificence, as was the coronation. All the ancient robes and regalia, which had been deliberately destroyed after the abolition of the kingship, were lovingly re-created as far as possible to the old dimensions and forms.

The service followed the text used for his father and grandfather, and at the ensuing coronation banquet held in Westminster Hall the King's Champion flung down his gauntlet in the traditional challenge to fight in single combat any who would deny the claim of Charles II to be the rightful heir to the Imperial Crown of England.

It was almost as though the Civil War, the Republic and the Protectorate had never been. But political clocks cannot be turned back so easily – as Charles II, his church and people, quickly discovered.

PART II

RESTORATION

CHARLES II, JAMES II

At Rochester on 23 December 1688, King James II of England, who had reigned less than four years, fled into exile. It was the second time in forty years that the English had dethroned a king.

There was to be none of the high tragedy of the trial and execution of Charles I, James's father, the last time the English rid themselves of a king. Instead, James's downfall was a pitiable farce. He had already tried – and somehow failed – to flee from his subjects a fortnight earlier on the 11th, when, after throwing the Great Seal in the Thames, he rode disguised as an ordinary country gentleman to the north Kent coast. There he embarked for France. But his boat was intercepted by suspicious and disrespectful fishermen and forced back to Faversham. And even his second attempt at flight succeeded only with the connivance of his son-in-law and usurper, William III, who sensibly wanted him out of the way.

But, despite these elements of black humour, James's dethronement brought about lasting change in a way which his father's hadn't. This, the second part of the book, tells the story of how this came about. It follows the resulting spread of the values of property, prosperity and freedom from these islands across the globe. And it shows that – despite some conspicuous exceptions – individual kings and queens tended to help rather than hinder the process.

But it begins at the monarchy's lowest point, by explaining how the House of Stuart lost the throne again only thirty years after James's elder brother, Charles II, had regained it in the Restoration of 1660. The old issues of religion and succession had arisen once more. But so too did a new question: which model of modernity should the British monarchy follow – the French or the Dutch? At stake were fundamental choices: between persecution and religious toleration, between absolutism and government by consent, and between success and failure.

I

Outside the Banqueting House in Westminster every Friday from June 1660 a huge crowd waited impatiently to be admitted into the presence of their newly restored sovereign, King Charles II. Many of them may well have remembered a very different scene at this same spot eleven years previously, when King Charles I had been publicly beheaded following his trial for treason.

But now England's experiment with republicanism was at an

end, and once more a son of the House of Stuart sat beneath the canopy of state to receive his people. But they were here not merely to pay their respects. They had come instead to be cured by the magical caress of their sovereign, for it was firmly believed that the king's hands could banish scrofula, a disfiguring tuberculosis of the lymph nodes. Every Friday Charles would touch for the King's Evil, and over the course of his reign he would lay his hands on more than 90,000 of his grateful subjects.

The ceremony of touching for the King's Evil was a sign of the divine nature of English kingship. But ever since the reign of Henry VIII, the connection between divinity and kingship had been more than mystical – it was political.

The assumption of religious authority was an enormous boost to royal power and prestige, but for Henry's successors the Supremacy had proved to be something of a poisoned chalice as inevitably, the monarchy had become the focus of the violent religious conflicts provoked by the Protestant Reformation. Charles II had grown up as these disputes reached their culmination in political meltdown, civil war and regicide. Now he had been swept back with popular rejoicing to take the crown that had been abolished with his father's execution. He would soon find, however, that the quarrels that had led England into civil war were far from settled.

At first sight, King Charles was well suited to pick his way through the political quagmire that followed Cromwell's death. Charles I had lost the throne by his unbending adherence to principle: to the authority of the king in the state and of the bishops in the Church. In contrast, the only rigid thing about Charles II was his male member. He fathered at least fourteen children by nine different mothers and more or less single-handedly repopulated the depleted ranks of the English nobility. When he was egregiously hailed as 'Father of his people', Charles laughed, replying that he had certainly fathered a great number of them.

Otherwise there was nothing to which he would not stoop his six-foot frame; no corner, however tight, which he could not turn; and no loyalty, however deep, which – once it ceased to be convenient – he recognized as binding.

Like many such men, he had an easy charm. He was affable, good humoured and witty, though his intelligence was practical rather than scholarly. But he was as lazy as he was treacherous, and only really applied himself when his back was to the wall. In short, Charles could ride almost any tide. But steering a consistent course was beyond him.

The first test of both Charles's resolution and his honesty came over religion. As one MP said, the principles of the restored monarchy were that Charles should 'not be king of this or that party, but to be king of all'. Charles realized that it was good politics to live up to this. In the Declaration of Breda, the manifesto that had helped win him the throne, Charles had made an unequivocal promise of 'liberty to tender consciences', or religious toleration, for all the disparate groups that had rebelled against the Stuart monarchy. All the other undertakings of Breda – about disputed title to land, war crimes and arrears of army pay – were swiftly passed into legislation by the Convention Parliament, often using the precise, carefully chosen words of the Declaration itself.

But not religious toleration. Before the Civil War, Parliament had split over the intertwined issues of royal power and religion. The king's Anglican supporters took as their biblical text Paul's letter to the Romans, in which he states that 'the powers that be are ordained of God'. Anglicans interpreted this to mean that their highest religious duty was to obey the monarch, no matter what he did.

Opposing them were the Presbyterians, and other more extreme Protestant dissenting sects, who countered with Peter's saying in the Acts of the Apostles: 'It is better to obey God than man.' These opponents of absolute royal power had won the Civil War, but with the Restoration they had lost the peace.

In the elections to Charles's first parliament those who had fought alongside his father to defend the established Church of England and the king's role as its supreme governor were returned in large numbers, hence its nickname, the 'Cavalier Parliament'. In the political ascendant at last, the Cavaliers insisted on the enforcement of rigid Anglican conformity by oaths to be administered on all clergymen, dons, teachers and members of town and city corporations.

The result was known as the Clarendon Code, after Charles's chief minister and Lord Chancellor, Edward Hyde, Earl of Clarendon. There is dispute as to whether Hyde had planned to subvert Charles's offer of toleration all along or whether he simply took advantage of circumstances. But there is no doubt that the Code reflected Clarendon's view that the Church of England was the only true Church and that only the Church of England taught the proper obedience of subjects to the king.

Charles had little sympathy with the Church's Protestant opponents, whom he blamed for the Civil War and his father's execution. But with Roman Catholics it was a very different story. The queen mother, Henrietta Maria, was a proselytizing Catholic, and there were persistent rumours that Charles himself had converted to Catholicism, or at least was dangerously partial to it. In fact he had few firm beliefs, and deplored the intolerant zeal of every group. As he said, he 'should be glad that those distinctions between his subjects might be removed; and that whilst they were all equally good subjects, they might equally enjoy his protection'. Charles sought to address these problems – and to salve his conscience over the broken promise of toleration in the Declaration of Breda – by issuing a second declaration in December 1662. It referred to the king's discretionary power to 'dispense' with the Clarendon Code for both Protestants and Catholics who 'modestly and without scandal performed their devotions in their own way', and called on Parliament to pass an Act to make such a suspension of the Code general and permanent.

But the ultra-royalist Cavalier House of Commons, with its hard-line Anglican majority and absolute loyalty to the monarchy, refused their monarch point blank. They had not fought the Civil War and suffered under Cromwell to see the monarchy adopt their enemies' principles. And Charles, aware above all that Anglicans were the strongest supporters of the restored monarchy, had to acquiesce.

II

After these domestic frustrations, foreign policy seemed to offer an opportunity for the decisive action – and the glory – of war.

The seventeenth century had been the Golden Age of the Dutch Republic. After surviving – with English help that was neither consistently given nor very effective when it was – the Spanish attempt at reconquest in the late sixteenth century, the Dutch had gone on to become an economic superpower that threatened to take over English trade. The English had already tried to cut them down to size in the first Anglo-Dutch War in the 1650s. Now Charles was persuaded that he should seek to outdo Cromwell by launching a second conflict.

The war began well with the great victory of Lowestoft in 1665, when the fleet, commanded in person by Charles's brother James, Duke of York, as Lord Admiral, defeated the enemy and blew up the Dutch flagship, together with the Dutch commander, Admiral Opdam. But then the attempted seizure of the Dutch East Indies fleet in a neutral port misfired; the domestic disasters of the Great Plague in 1665 and the Great Fire of London the following year hampered the war effort and things hit rock bottom when the Dutch admiral De Ruyter sailed up the Medway, where the English fleet was anchored, captured the flagship the *Royal Charles*, on which the king had returned to England in 1660, burnt others and forced the rest to scatter and beach themselves. As was said in London, 'The bishops get all, the courtiers spend all, the citizens pay for all, the King neglects all, and the Dutch take all.'

It was a national disaster, which led to a profound bout of introspection. 'In all things,' reflected the diarist Samuel Pepys, who was in the thick of events as a naval administrator, 'in wisdom, courage, force, knowledge of our own streams, and success, the Dutch have the best of us, and do end the war with victory on their side.' Why was England apparently so feeble in defending even its own shores? A spate of books on the Dutch rushed to offer the explanation. The most interesting is Sir Josiah Child's *Brief Observations Concerning Trade and the Interest of Money*. Written even before the war was over, it argued that the Dutch Republic was so strong because it had developed secure financial institutions that gave it long-term security and the ability to wage war and expand its commerce, in spite of its geographical disadvantages. Most European monarchs had made a habit, when financially squeezed by the demands of war, of repudiating their creditors, which meant they could only borrow at a high rate of interest. But through the Bank of Amsterdam, with its enviable reputation for honouring its debts, the Dutch could borrow cheaply: a financial advantage that translated into military strength. And Child is to be taken seriously, since he was an expert on finance, having built up one of the greatest City fortunes of his day. Other authors pointed to Dutch religious toleration, which gave the republic domestic peace, as opposed to the civil wars produced by persecution in England. And others again to the superiority of Dutch hygiene, education, poor relief and technical expertise.

Why not, in short, imitate the Dutch instead of fighting

them? Why not even ally with them? Especially since a new potent threat to England's security was arising in Louis XIV's aggressive, Catholicizing France.

III

France offered an alternative model for a modernizing monarchy. If the Dutch owed their success to innovative republican institutions and consensual government that had made a small and disunited country a world power, then France had become strong by following the opposite path.

France, like England, had been torn apart by civil war in the middle decades of the seventeenth century. But the wars, known as the *Fronde*, were very different. Instead of pitting the king against his subjects, they were a quarrel *within* the highest ranks of the nobility and the royal family itself. They came to an end at roughly the same time, however, when in 1661 the twenty-three-year-old Louis XIV, who had been king since the age of five, began his personal rule.

Louis was Charles's first cousin and the two were similar in appearance, with their powerful physique, swarthy complexion, full lips and hooked nose. They also shared the same insatiable sexual appetite. But there the resemblance ended.

For Louis – despite his lustfulness – was a man of rigid dignity, inflexible will and unbending self-discipline. His iron self-control meant, for instance, that he was able to give a public audience immediately after an operation, without anaesthetic of course, to treat an anal fistula. And what he expected of himself, he demanded of others.

Louis's motto, seen to this day on the ceiling of the Hall of Mirrors at the heart of his great palace of Versailles, was *Le Roy gouverne par lui-même*: 'the King rules by himself'. This meant that there would be no great minister or corrupt court faction – or even parliament – to come between the king and his people. Instead, he, Louis, would personally direct a close-knit group of departmental officials. They came from modest backgrounds and shared Louis's appetite for hard work and belief in discipline. Above all, they were at one with his commitment to the glory of France and her king.

Colbert, the minister of finance, directed an ambitious programme of state-sponsored industrial growth and overseas imperial expansion; Vauban, a military architect of genius, protected France's borders with vast fortifications; Louvois, the minister of war, reorganized the army and oversaw a series of aggressive campaigns that expanded French territory towards her 'natural frontier' on the Rhine and beyond; even the arts – painting, music, architecture, the theatre and science – were subjected to central direction and made to hymn the glories of *le Roy soleil,* 'the Sun King'.

And the medicine seemed to work as, in little more than a decade, France turned from the sick man of Europe into the European superpower. It also became the very model of a modern monarchy.

The rise of France posed for the English the same dilemma as the earlier rise of the Dutch. How would the English see the new France? As a threat? Or as a model?

For most of Charles's subjects, Louis's aggressive Catholicism meant that the issue was not in doubt: France not only threatened to become a universal monarchy but – what was even worse – a universal *Catholic* monarchy.

The result was that when, less than a year after the debacle of the Battle of the Medway, England not only made peace with the Dutch but joined them in an alliance against France, the news was greeted with widespread rejoicing.

But not by Charles. The king harboured a grudge against the Dutch for the stain on his honour of defeat by a mere republic. He also took a very different view of both Louis and Catholicism from most of his subjects. Partly it was a matter of family connection. Charles himself was half French through his mother, Henrietta Maria. And the ties were strengthened when his youngest sister, also named Henrietta Maria, married Louis's brother, Philippe, Duke of Orleans. Henrietta, who was as intelligent as she was pretty, promptly became a firm favourite of Louis (indeed, his interest was rumoured to be more than brotherly) and a powerful conduit between the two courts.

And there was a similar family inclination to Catholicism. So when in 1668 Charles's brother James informed him that he had converted to Rome, Charles, far from expressing horror, confided in him his intention to do the same. It remained only to work out the means.

A secret meeting was summoned on 25 January 1669 in James's private closet or study, at which only the king, his brother and three confidential advisers were present. Tearfully Charles explained his determination to adopt the true faith. But how? The fear of a Catholicized monarchy was, as everyone knew, enough to rouse Englishmen to arms. In the face of this threat the rest unanimously advised him to inform Louis and seek his powerful advice and assistance.

Charles and Louis had already opened secret negotiations, with Henrietta Maria, Duchess of Orleans, as go-between, for a *renversement d'alliances* that would see England and France joining together to make war on the Dutch. Now Charles's professed resolution to convert to Catholicism drove the stakes still higher.

It took over a year to reach agreement. Finally, in May 1670, under cover of a flying visit by the Duchess of Orleans to see her brother, the secret Treaty of Dover was signed. (It was so called because it was so closely guarded that most of Charles's ministers were not informed of its existence.) In it, Charles reaffirmed his 'plan to reconcile himself with the Roman Church', while Louis, for his part, promised Charles a subsidy of 2 million livres to help him suppress any armed resistance to his conversion, together, if need be, with 6000 French troops. The two monarchs were then to coordinate an attack on the Netherlands, with Louis bearing the brunt of the land war and Charles the naval.

Was Charles's undertaking to convert real? Or a diplomatic ploy that proved too clever by half? In any case, though the actual text of the Treaty of Dover remained a closely guarded secret, the rumours surrounding it led to a dangerous polarization in English politics. The worst fears of Charles's opponents were confirmed by the final steps that led to the outbreak of war. On 5 January 1672 Charles unilaterally suspended all payments from the Exchequer for a year; on 15 March he published the Declaration of Indulgence, which, on the model of the abortive declaration of a decade earlier, used the royal prerogative to suspend the Clarendon Code for Catholics as well as Protestant dissenters. Then, two days later, he joined Louis in declaring war on the Dutch.

The effect was to reconfirm the fatal association in the public mind of arbitrary government with Catholicism and an unpopular – and, as it turned out, unsuccessful – foreign policy. For the Dutch, despite the French occupying five out of their seven provinces, refused to roll over. Instead, they broke the dykes and used the flood waters to stop the French advance into the heartland of Holland. Still worse, from Charles's point of view, the man who led the heroic Dutch resistance was his own nephew, William, Prince of Orange.

For the system of hereditary monarchy meant that the rivalries of the great European powers were also family quarrels. France was ruled by King Charles's cousin, Louis XIV, while France's Continental rival Holland was ruled by his nephew William, the son of Charles's eldest sister, Mary, Princess Royal of England, and William II, Prince of Orange.

But William III was a very different ruler from Louis, the Sun King, the absolute monarch of all he surveyed. For the head of the House of Orange was not sovereign in the Dutch Republic, but first among equals. Sovereignty instead resided in the Estates of the seven provinces. But ever since William the Silent's leadership of the Dutch Revolt against Spain in the late sixteenth century, his descendants as Princes of Orange had traditionally been made *stadholder* or governor of each of the provinces and captain general and admiral of the armed forces of the republic.

It was an important position. But to exploit its potential required talent and tact on the part of the reigning prince. He also had to cope with strong republican elements among the Dutch urban elites, who were jealous of the quasi-regal pretensions of the House of Orange and were determined to cut it down to size. William would prove more than equal to the task.

His beginnings were inauspicious enough, however. In 1649 his English grandfather, Charles I, was executed, and the following year his own father died of smallpox at the age of only twenty-four. Eight days later, on 14 November 1650, William was born as a posthumous child in a black-hung bedchamber.

Quarrels between his widowed mother, Princess Mary, and his grandmother, Princess Dowager Amalia, for his guardianship played into the hands of the anti-Orange faction in the republic, led by the Grand Pensionary or chief administrator of Holland, De Witt, who not only managed to withhold the family's traditional offices from the young prince but even went so far as to abolish them.

None of this had much impact on the young prince, who was brought up in his birthplace, the Binnenhof Palace in The Hague – first in his mother's apartment and then in his own. At the age of six he was given his first tutor, a local clergyman, and at the age of nine a governor, who came from the cadet Nassau branch of the princely house.

From his tutor he absorbed a firm Calvinistic Protestantism and from his governor a sense of the historic destiny of the House of Orange – and a passionate love of hunting. He also emerged as a man's man, with little time for women but a lot for attractive young men.

And all of these things – his religiosity, his family pride, even his homoeroticism – came together in the crisis of 1672 when he discovered his lifelong vocation as leader of the military resistance to French hegemony and the champion of Protestantism – first in the Netherlands and then throughout Europe.

William was not the only Protestant in Charles's family. Only a few months after the Restoration, Charles's brother James, Duke of York, had married Anne Hyde, daughter of Lord Chancellor Clarendon, the author of the notorious Code that defended the Church of England against Catholics and dissenters. Many, including the queen mother, Henrietta Maria, were scandalized at the *mésalliance* between a prince and a commoner. But Anne proved a dignified duchess and a loyal wife. She also brought up her two daughters, Mary and Anne, as committed Anglican Protestants despite their father's zealous devotion to the Roman Catholic Church.

And this Protestant grouping within the royal family became even stronger in 1677, when, as a result of the perpetual switchback of politics at Charles's court between Protestantism and Catholicism and France and the Netherlands, it was decided that William of Orange should marry his cousin, James and Anne's eldest daughter Mary. Charles's alliance with Louis and James's Catholicism had outraged the nation. It seemed as if the suspiciously Catholic royal court was subverting the national religion by joining Louis's campaigns against the Netherlands. The sudden U-turn to a marriage alliance with the Protestant Dutch Republic was intended to reassure the public and Parliament.

The wedding took place at Whitehall on 4 November 1677, the prince's birthday. Despite the auspicious anniversary, however, the marriage was hardly a meeting of minds – or bodies. The fifteen-year-old Mary, beautiful and vivacious, towered over the dour bridegroom, who, despite his reputation as a warrior prince, was weak in body, hunched and asthmatic. She is said to have wept for a day and a half when she was told she was going to marry the Dutchman; while William, for his part, had made prudential enquiries via the wife of the English ambassador in The Hague as to Mary's suitability for a man like himself, who 'might not perhaps be very easy for a wife to live with'.

The answers seem to have satisfied him. And, after a shaky start, the forecast proved to be correct. Rumours of pregnancies soon dried up and Mary was jealous of William's quick and, as it turned out, lifelong attachment to her lady-in-waiting, Elizabeth Villiers. But this was an affair of the head rather than the heart, and William and Mary soon became mutually devoted. Indeed, Mary would put her loyalty to her husband above that to her own father. English history would have been very different otherwise.

IV

The marriage of William and Mary took on a further significance. Mary would inherit the English throne after her father James died, and would then, of course, bring her kingdom's might into alliance with William's Holland. For Mary and her younger sister Anne were the only legitimate children of the royal house of the younger generation. William himself was fourth in line, after his wife and sister-in-law.

For King Charles, so philoprogenitive with other women, had no children with his wife, Catherine of Braganza. When Charles had first seen the princess, with her hair dressed in long projecting ringlets in the Portuguese fashion, he is supposed to have exclaimed, 'they have brought me a bat!' But, despite her repeated miscarriages and at least one serious exploration of the possibility of divorce on grounds of her barrenness, Charles – perhaps out of guilt, perhaps out of affection – stuck with her.

The result was a replay of the twin crises of religion, in the form of the Royal Supremacy over the Church, and the succession, which had plagued English politics since the reign of Henry VIII. Known as the Exclusion Crisis, because it focused on the attempt to exclude Charles's brother James from the succession, it threatened to set the Stuarts on their travels once more. And his handling of it showed Charles at his best – and worst.

James was made of very different stuff from his sinuous elder brother Charles. Every bit as highly sexed (indeed, he slept with a stream of common whores so ugly that wits claimed they had been prescribed as penance by his confessor!), James was otherwise formal, unimaginative and good at receiving orders and delegating them to subordinates. In short, there was something in him of the centurion in the Bible who told Jesus: 'I am a man under authority, having soldiers under me: and when I say to this man, Go, and he goeth, and to another, Come and he cometh.'

So it was with James. Unlike Charles, who regarded his secret and half-hearted attachment to Catholicism as a matter of mere diplomatic and political expediency, James, after he had embraced the true faith as he saw it, never once deviated from it in word or deed: 'it was like a rod of steel running through thirty years.'

It was also to prove an absolute line of divide in English history.

The first test of James's resolve came quickly. In February 1673 the strongly Anglican Parliament was recalled and immediately set itself to force the king to overturn the Declaration of Indulgence. Lured by a generous promise of taxation, Charles agreed. Parliament then pressed home its advantage by passing the Test Act. This banned from all public office, civil or military, anyone who would not swear to the Acts of Uniformity and Supremacy; take communion according to the rite of the Church of England; and – just to make sure – sign a declaration against the key Catholic belief of transubstantiation, by which the bread and wine in the mass were held to become the actual body and blood of Christ.

James, as Lord Admiral, held such a public office; but, as a now convinced Catholic, he could take neither the required oaths nor the Anglican sacrament. The deadline for swearing the oaths was 14 June; that day James surrendered the Admiralty to the king. His resignation resolved the immediate issue; it raised, however, a much bigger one: if, as a Roman Catholic, James could not be Lord Admiral, how could he be entrusted with the infinitely greater responsibility of kingship? And, if not, could Parliament break the sacred line of succession and the integrity of its monarchy for the sake of its religion? It seemed like another version of resistance theory, this time in the name of the Church of England.

But down that route most respectable Englishmen, traumatized by the execution of Charles I, were not prepared to go – unless something very extraordinary occurred.

In the late summer of 1678, the extraordinary duly happened in the shape of the Popish Plot. It is one of the strangest episodes of mass delusion and hysteria in English history; it starred one of the most remarkable hoaxers, Titus Oates, while its setting was the teeming metropolis of London, where Parliament, court and city all lived cheek by jowl with what was now the largest urban population in Europe. It was where men went to make their careers – and to disappear.

One of those – perhaps with more to escape from than most – was Titus Oates. Lame, stunted, homosexual and extraordinarily ugly (his mouth was described as being in the middle of his face), he had failed at everything. He had been expelled from school; passed through two Cambridge colleges without getting a degree; been ordained on false pretences and driven out of his parish for making a false accusation of sodomy; been cashiered as a naval chaplain for committing buggery himself; and finally, after a probably false conversion to Catholicism, he had been frogmarched out of no less than three Jesuit seminaries.

By July 1678, the twenty-nine-year-old Oates was back in London and desperate for survival – and for revenge on the world in general and on Catholics in particular. His scheme was to invent a gigantic Catholic conspiracy, masterminded by his erstwhile teachers, the Jesuits, to murder Charles and forcibly reconvert England. He found a willing listener in a fanatically anti-Catholic clergyman and, at his suggestion, wrote the whole thing up in the form of a deposition of forty-three articles.

On 13 August, a copy was handed to Charles while he was taking his usual brisk morning walk in St James's Park; on 6 September Oates also swore to the truth of his deposition before Sir Edmund Berry Godfrey, a fashionable, rather publicity-seeking magistrate; and on 28/29 September Oates appeared before the Privy Council itself.

Charles shredded his evidence from his own knowledge. But his advisers, from a mixture of motives, were inclined to take Oates more seriously and gave him a free hand to arrest the alleged plotters. And here Oates, for the first time in his life, struck lucky. Anne, Duchess of York, had died in 1671, and two years later James had remarried the Catholic Mary of Modena. One of those Oates accused was Edward Coleman, Mary of Modena's secretary.

Coleman was almost as great a fantasist as Oates himself. Unfortunately, he had tried to put his schemes into action by soliciting money from Père la Chaise, Louis XIV's highly influential confessor. Copies of the correspondence were discovered when his papers were searched and they contained a damning paragraph: 'Success for his schemes', Coleman wrote, 'would give the greatest blow to the Protestant religion that it had received since its birth . . . They had a mighty work on their hands, no less than the conversion of three kingdoms, and by that perhaps the utter subduing of a pestilent heresy, which had so long domineered over great part of the northern world.' Here at last, it seemed, was proof positive of Oates's allegations, with a conspiracy extending to the heart of the royal family itself.

Oates's winning streak continued, even more sensationally, when Justice Godfrey, before whom he had sworn his deposition, disappeared in mysterious circumstances on 12 October. Already that evening rumours were sweeping through the city that he had been murdered by the Papists. Five days later the rumours seemed to be confirmed when his body was found face down in a ditch on Primrose Hill. There was heavy bruising round his neck and his own sword had been driven through his heart so hard that the point protruded several inches from his back. Despite the violence, however, none of his valuables had been taken.

Even at the time, some suspected that the death was a suicide disguised as a murder. But such doubts were brushed aside and the coroner's jury returned the verdict of 'murder'. And there was no doubt in the popular mind that it was murder by Oates's Papist conspirators. Godfrey was now reinvented as a Protestant martyr. His body was laid in state in his house and, on 31 October, given an impressive funeral at St Martin-in-the-Fields, at which the preacher preached a fiery sermon on the text 'As a man falleth before the wicked, so fallest thou'. Medals were struck in his honour and pamphlets written.

Fears of a massacre of Protestants now swept the capital; the preacher at Godrey's funeral stood between two heavies dressed as clergymen and ladies carried daggers inscribed 'Remember Justice Godfrey' for their own protection from Catholic assassins.

In the midst of all this, on 21 October 1678, Parliament

assembled. As the hysteria of the plot gathered force, no fewer than thirty-five people, mostly Catholic priests, were condemned to the hideous death of a traitor on the mere say-so of Oates and his steadily increasing band of associate informers.

But the parliamentary opposition, led by the Earl of Shaftesbury, aimed at the biggest Catholic target of all: James, Duke of York, the king's brother and the heir presumptive of the imperial crown of Britain.

V

Anthony Ashley Cooper, first Earl of Shaftesbury, was one of the most complex and controversial figures of a complex and controversial age. He was very short, had strongly marked features and was known as 'Tapski', from the tube and tap which, in a dangerous and innovatory operation, had been inserted by his physician, John Locke, into his abdomen to drain an abscess on his liver.

His career was pretty fraught too, as he shifted, not always in the same direction, from being one of Cromwell's ministers to Charles's Lord Chancellor. From that exalted position he moved into opposition once again, to become one of the king's greatest and most dangerous opponents. For he was bold, unscrupulous, demagogic and a master of propaganda. As such, he chose the most modern and emotive icon as the symbol of his political strategy. The Monument, built to commemorate the Great Fire of London, and finished in 1677, just a year before the outbreak of the Popish Plot, was a modern marvel – at 202 feet, the highest vantage point in the city and rivalled only by the spires of one or two of Wren's equally new, rebuilt churches, which had likewise risen phoenix-like from the ashes of the fire.

And the Monument was the sensational setting of the most effective piece of propaganda to emerge from Shaftesbury's circle. Entitled *An Appeal from the Country to the City*, it enjoined Londoners to climb the 311 steps to the top of 'your newest pyramid' and admire the rebuilt city. Then they should imagine it on fire once more; the guns of the Tower turned on the city; the streets running with blood and the fires of Smithfield burning their Protestant victims at the stake again, as they had done in the reign of the last Roman Catholic monarch, Bloody Mary.

All this would happen, the *Appeal* insisted, if a Catholic king were allowed to succeed.

The *Appeal* didn't name James directly. Instead, keeping up the topicality, it alluded to the bas-relief on the base of the Monument, which shows James assisting his brother Charles to extinguish the Great Fire. All this was a sham, it announced. Instead 'one eminent Papist' – James – had connived at the disaster, 'pretend[ing] to secure many of the incendiaries' – thought to be Catholic, of course – 'but secretly suffer[ing]them all to escape . . . for a Popish successor cannot but rejoice in the flames of such a too powerful city'.

Fired by such propaganda, between 1679 and 1681 the electorate returned three parliaments in which there was a clear Commons majority for James's exclusion. Each was quickly dissolved by Charles, who was prepared to concede limitations on

James's powers as king but would not yield on his brother's indefeasible hereditary right to succeed.

Charles also had more cards than it at first seemed. The first was the division among his opponents about who should succeed if James were excluded. The more moderate Exclusionists favoured the Dutch line and wanted the succession to leapfrog a generation so that James's daughter Mary would become queen on Charles's death. Her marriage to the champion of Protestant Europe, William of Orange, satisfied everyone that the monarchy's association with French Catholicism would then be over for good. But Shaftesbury and the radicals backed instead Charles's eldest illegitimate son, James, Duke of Monmouth.

Born in 1649 of Charles's affair with Lucy Walter, his first serious liaison, and made Duke of Monmouth in 1662, James was handsome, charming, charismatic and amorous. He was also spoiled, badly educated, sensitive about his illegitimacy and, having been personally involved in both a mutilation and a murder, had an ugly streak of violence. The army was a natural career for such a man, and by 1678 he had succeeded to Oliver Cromwell's old office of Captain General or Commander-in-Chief and won what military glory was available under Charles. More importantly than all that, Monmouth was unequivocally, ostentatiously Protestant.

The Popish Plot and the ensuing Exclusion Crisis made Monmouth – popular, Protestant and princely – an obvious alternative to the dour and Catholic James and a natural ally for Shaftesbury.

The only problem was his illegitimacy. But *was* he illegitimate? Rumours, carefully fanned by Monmouth himself, circulated to the effect that his parents had been secretly married. There were supposed to be witnesses and a black box containing irrefutable written evidence.

But Charles, fond though he was of the strapping first fruit of his loins, was not prepared to allow Monmouth to shunt his legitimate brother James aside. Indefeasible hereditary right could not be undermined, however high the stakes. For this was the deepest principle of the Stuart dynasty. The result was one of the stranger scenes in English history when, in early January 1679, Charles, having summoned the Privy Council, solemnly declared 'in the presence of Almighty God that he had never given or made any contract of marriage, nor was ever married to any woman whatsoever but his wife Queen Catherine'. The declaration was then signed by the king, witnessed by those present and enrolled in the records in Chancery.

In a further, vain attempt to lower the temperature, both rivals for the throne, first James and then Monmouth, were packed off into honourable exile. James, unwisely, went to Catholic Brussels before being made Governor of Scotland, while Monmouth went to Holland, where he was correctly but coolly received by Mary and William of Orange, his Protestant rivals for the succession.

The inability of the Exclusionists to agree on a single candidate was one thing strengthening the hand of Charles and James; the other was the perceived extremism of the Exclusionists of whatever stripe. For everything – their language, their demagogy, their violent anti-popery, their allies among the Protestant sects – revived uncomfortable memories of the Civil War.

The result was a pamphlet war and a clash of ideas out of

which was born our modern two-party system. The Exclusionists were known as Whigs, or Scottish Covenanting rebels; the anti-Exclusionists as Tories, or Irish outlaws and cattle thieves.

The Whigs believed in religious toleration, limited government and a kingship that finally answered to the people; the Tories in divine right monarchy, indefeasible hereditary succession, passive obedience and a monopolistic Church of England that was equally hostile to Catholics on the right and to Protestant dissenters on the left. The Whigs were pro-Dutch; the Tories generally pro-French. The Whigs had made the running in the Exclusion Crisis; now it was the Tories' turn.

For they made the forceful point that there was no precedent for preventing the next in line from taking his or her rightful inheritance. Mary Queen of Scots was an example of a Catholic heir. She had been executed before she could succeed Elizabeth, but that was because of her treason, not her religion. The Tories also pointed out that if James were excluded from the throne, the monarchy would be ruined for ever. In effect, England would become a republic. The nominal ruler would come to the throne only if he or she met the conditions laid down in advance by Parliament. However much Anglicans detested Catholicism, the alternative prospect of an elected, circumscribed monarchy was many times worse. In this Tory scenario, the Exclusionists were portrayed as modern Cromwellians, who were refighting the Civil War and attempting to destroy the monarchy and the Church of England. It was an emotional – and effective – appeal to English loyalties.

Charles met his fourth parliament in the Convocation Hall at Oxford. The Commons and Shaftesbury's group in the Lords were, as usual, hot for Exclusion. But Charles, sensing the turning of the political tide, stood firm. 'I have law and reason and all right-thinking men on my side; I have the Church' – and here the king pointed to the bishops – 'and nothing will ever separate us.'

After sitting for a bare week, the parliament was dissolved. Nor, thanks to a new subsidy from Louis XIV and booming revenues from trade, did Charles ever have to summon another one. Instead, he could turn to the congenial task of taking his revenge on Shaftesbury and Whigs for the Popish Plot and the Exclusion Crisis. Charles began by attacking the stronghold of the Whigs in the City and the other towns' corporations. Their charters were revoked and their governing bodies purged of dissenters and Whigs and packed with Tories.

In despair at the sudden turn of events, the Whig leaders now made the mistake of dabbling, very half-heartedly, in treason. A faction plotted to assassinate Charles and James, and put Monmouth on the throne. It was badly planned and attracted few followers. But the king struck them down ruthlessly. And, although the plot was the work of a small group, the Exclusionists as a whole were tainted by their treason. One Whig lord committed suicide in the Tower, two were publicly beheaded and most of the rest, including Shaftesbury and Monmouth, fled into exile in the Netherlands. There Shaftesbury died. But his secretary and intellectual factotum, John Locke, who had devised the operation for the insertion of the tube and tap into his master, continued writing and working in the congenial atmosphere of Dutch tolerance and freedom, completing his great work, *An Essay Concerning Human Understanding.*

Meanwhile, England witnessed a Tory triumph, which, like the French absolutism it so much resembled, expressed itself in soaring stone and brick. The statue of Charles I – the Tories' martyred hero – was re-erected in London; at Winchester, a huge new palace, destined to be the English Versailles, was being rushed to completion; and, above all, the huge bulk of St Paul's was rising over the City of London as the noblest, most eloquent and most crushing symbol of an Anglican absolutism.

If St Paul's was the symbol of the Tory triumph, its intellectual centre was Oxford. And it was there that, in Convocation on 21 July 1683, the University of Oxford issued a solemn declaration 'against certain pernicious books and their damnable doctrines'. It is an Anglican syllabus of errors, in which all the doctrines of Whiggism and their authors are condemned as 'false, seditious and impious, and most of them . . . also heretical and blasphemous'. Instead, the university proclaimed that Toryism was an eternal verity and the duty of 'submission and obedience [to kings] to be absolute, and without exception'.

In other words, Anglicanism and royalism were one, as they had been from the beginning under Henry VIII and right through the Civil War.

But what would happen if the King ceased to be Anglican?

England would soon find out. For on 6 February 1685 Charles II died, having converted at last to Catholicism in his very final moments, and was succeeded without a struggle by the proudly Catholic James. The result would test the relationship of Church and state to destruction and send a Stuart on his travels once more.

ROYAL REPUBLIC

JAMES II, WILLIAM III, MARY II

WE ALL KNOW that England was conquered by William the Conqueror in 1066. But we have forgotten, or do not care to remember, that, 600 years later, England was also conquered by another William. William of Orange was Dutch, rather than Norman, and, while there's no doubt that the Norman Conquest changed England radically, the consequences of the Dutch conquest of 1688 were similarly profound, and not just for this country but, arguably, for the whole world.

It began to heal the breaches of Civil War, which the Restoration of 1660 had tried but failed to do. It turned England from a feeble imitator of the French absolute monarchy into the most powerful and most aggressively modernizing state in Europe.

In short, it invented a modern England, a modern monarchy, perhaps even modernity itself.

I

All this would have seemed like the dream of a madman only a few years previously in 1685, when James II had succeeded to the throne. Then, England was a country still shaped by Henry VIII's religious settlement and the vast dynastic mural of Henry, which showed him as head both of his family and the Church, was still one of the wonders: Whitehall Palace for the new king to admire – and to imitate. For successive monarchs had tried to exploit the vast powers of the Supremacy to build up power and wealth and rule unfettered by influence from Parliament.

And towards the end of his reign, it looked as if Charles II had finally succeeded. Bolstered by the support of the High Anglican Tories (as well as secret subsidies from his cousin Louis XIV) Charles managed to rule without Parliament for the last four years of his reign, although the cost was a passive foreign policy that gave France a free hand in Europe. And when Charles unexpectedly died in February 1685, aged fifty-five, the strength of the Stuart monarchy he had restored was underlined by the unchallenged accession of his brother James to the throne.

Just a few years earlier James's position as his brother's rightful heir had been in grave jeopardy following his open conversion to Catholicism. Yet together they had ridden out the storm, even if Charles, acutely aware of the power of anti-Catholic sentiment, had been heard to prophesy that James would be king for no more than three years.

But no one paid much attention, least of all James himself.

Now, as he was proclaimed king on 6 February, crowds of Londoners toasted him in free wine and cheered. The fellows and undergraduates at Oxford 'promised to obey the King *without limitations or restrictions*'. There were similar oaths throughout the country and no sign of resistance to the first openly Catholic monarch since Bloody Mary. It seemed a miracle. And such James devoutly believed it to be.

That a convert to the Church of Rome could nonetheless become head of the Church of England was testimony to the power of the idea that underlay the Royal Supremacy: that the highest religious duty of an Anglican was to obey the king, who was God's anointed Vice-regent on Earth.

The smoothness of James's accession was underscored by the magnificence of his coronation. It took place on St George's Day and it was the king's command to do 'All that Art, Ornament and Expense could do to the making of the Spectacle Dazzling and Stupendous'. Henry Purcell, Master of the King's Music, composed and directed the music, which culminated in his great anthem 'My heart is inditing'. Samuel Pepys, as one of the Barons of the Cinque Ports, helped support the canopy over James in the initial procession from Westminster Hall to the Abbey. The final grand firework display centred on a blazing sun, the emblem of the absolute monarchy of Louis XIV of France, while the great crowned figure of *Monarchia* ('Monarchy') strongly suggested that England was going the same way.

Not everyone was happy, of course, in particular a group of Whig exiles in the Dutch Republic. They had been the architects of the parliamentary attempts to keep James from the throne, and they had been forced to flee when they had lost the political battle to Charles's Anglican Tory supporters. Now James's accession and the election of a complaisant Tory parliament that seemed ready to do James's bidding were the fulfilment of their worst fears. Only an armed invasion, they thought, could save England from Catholic absolutism. Its natural leader was Charles II's bastard son, James, Duke of Monmouth, who, unsatisfactory as he was, had been the Whig candidate for the throne during the Exclusion Crisis.

Monmouth, who had come to enjoy the ease of a comfortable exile, took some persuading, however. But eventually he felt honour bound and, on 24 May, he set sail from Amsterdam with a pathetically small force of three ships and eighty-three men. They made for Lyme Regis in Dorset because this was an area where the Good Old Cause of English republicanism lived on. It was also a stronghold of dissenting Protestantism. And Monmouth's manifesto, which even seemed to leave the issue of the monarchy open, was designed to appeal to such men. He promised to free the English from the 'Absolute Tyranny' instituted by his uncle. He accused James of responsibility for the Papal Plot against Charles, the murder of Sir Edmund Godfrey and even of Charles II. Given the success that Titus Oates had enjoyed in working up the country to a pitch of anti-Catholic hysteria, and the popularity of the Exclusion parliaments, Monmouth believed that the country would be eager to rebel against the new Catholic king. But just three thousand at most joined his ranks. And they included no gentlemen.

Desperate to win over such leading figures in society – the so-called 'better-sort' – Monmouth had himself proclaimed king.

It was intended to give his cause the veneer of legitimacy and demonstrate that a successful outcome of his rebellion would be nothing more radical than a restored Protestant monarchy. The result was to alienate his existing supporters without gaining any new ones. It also meant that, as a rival king, he could expect no reconciliation with his uncle. James II, for his part, worried about his hold on both Scotland and London, was able to spare only two or three thousand troops against Monmouth. They were badly led but at least they were professional soldiers. And that proved decisive.

The showdown came at Sedgmoor in Somerset on 6 July 1685. Boxed in by the royal army, Monmouth decided that his only chance was to launch a surprise night attack. The tactic made sense but his scratch forces were incapable of carrying it out and, once day broke, were routed by the king's troops: 500 were killed and 1500 taken prisoner.

By then Monmouth had already fled, disguised as a shepherd. But it was only two days before King James II of England, as he called himself, was found hiding in a ditch in his disguise, captured and taken to London. There was no need for a trial, since he had already been condemned as a traitor by an Act of Attainder rushed through by the Tory Parliament. Nevertheless, Monmouth humbled himself by begging for his life on his knees before James. At once his boastful claims to majesty disappeared as he pleaded that he had been forced against his will to declare himself king. His uncle, appalled at such cowardice, was implacable. Monmouth was brought to Tower Hill for execution on 15 July.

Monmouth's death, like his life, was a mixture of tragedy

and farce. The two Anglican bishops who accompanied him to the scaffold tried to force a public acknowledgement of guilt out of him. He reluctantly said 'Amen' to a prayer for the king but refused absolutely to swear to the Anglican shibboleth of non-resistance to royal power.

Finally, the wrangling, widely felt to be indecent in the face of death, stopped, and Monmouth prepared himself for execution. He begged the executioner not to mangle him and bribed him heavily. Then he knelt down. But the first blow merely gashed him, and he turned his head as if to complain. Now thoroughly unnerved, the headsman took four further strokes but still failed to kill him. At last, he severed the duke's head with a knife. Many of Monmouth's supporters followed him to a bloody end at the hands of the public executioner.

The Whigs had another martyr and James, so he thought, another miracle. But the challenge to James's monarchy was to come not from the divided and dispirited Whigs but from the apparently all-powerful and all-loyal Tories. The Tories had given James rock-solid support throughout the Exclusion Crisis; now in return they naturally expected that he – Catholic though he was – would be equally unwavering in his support for the Church of England. And, at first, it looked as though he would be.

Things got off to a good start with James's speech to the first Privy Council meeting of his reign. He spoke off the cuff. But an official version was worked up and published with royal approval:

> I have been reported a man for arbitrary power; but that
> is not the only story which has been made of me. I shall

make it my endeavour to preserve this government, both
in church and state, as it is by law established. I know
the principles of the Church of England are for monarchy,
and the members of it have shown themselves good and
lawful subjects: therefore I shall always take care to
defend and support it.

His audience applauded and James basked in their approval.
Parliament voted him a vast income. Few kings had come to the
throne with such wealth, loyalty and goodwill.

In fact, there was misunderstanding on both sides: the Tories
thought that James had promised to rule as though he were an
Anglican; James assumed that the Tories and the Church would
continue to support him whatever he did. Both were quickly
disillusioned.

For James was a man with a mission. The last Catholic
monarch to rule in England was Mary Tudor. The piety, the
sacrifices and the vicissitudes of his ancestor gave James hope.
Like James, Mary had succeeded to the throne against overwhelming odds, which she took to mean that God had given her
a mission to reconvert England to the true faith. The new king
had overcome the full force of Parliament and the country's
inbred hostility to Catholics. Divine purpose must lie behind
these miracles. What clearer sign could God give that he supported the Catholic cause? The king also believed that he was
on a personal journey of salvation. He had sinned by sleeping
with innumerable women of easy virtue. He had to atone for
those sins, and the one sure way of doing so was to fulfil his
mission. James, we know from his own private devotional writ-
ings, was driven by this burning sense of divine purpose: "'T'was

the Divine Providence that drove me early out of my native country and 't'was the same Providence ordered it so that I passed most of [the time] in Catholic kingdoms, by which means I came to know what their religion was . . .' 'The hand of God' was demonstrated in the failure of the attempt to exclude him from the throne: 'God Almighty be praised by whose blessing that rebellion [of Monmouth] was suppressed . . .'

Such was James's mission. But what of the *method* of Catholic conversion? Was Britain to become Catholic within his lifetime, or was this the beginning of a long process of counter-reformation? Would it be by coercion? Or persuasion?

Here memories mattered. Bloody Mary had used the rack and the stake and, thanks to Foxe's *Book of Martyrs*, the memory was still fresh in England. So too were the stabbings, drownings and defenestrations of Protestants in the Massacre of St Bartholomew's Eve, the pogrom of Protestants which had occurred in Paris during the French Wars of Religion in 1572. Now these memories, which had scarcely faded, were reanimated in the most dramatic possible fashion by Louis XIV of France, the outstanding contemporary Catholic king and James's model and mentor.

For on 22 October 1685 Louis revoked the Edict of Nantes, which, by granting toleration to French Protestants, had brought the Wars of Religion to an end. News reached England quickly and the effect was dramatic. John Evelyn recorded in his diary:

> The French persecution of the Protestants raging with the utmost barbarity . . . The French tyrant abolishing the Edict of Nantes . . . and without any cause on the

sudden, demolishing all their churches, banishing, imprisoning, sending to the galleys all the ministers, plundering the common people and exposing them to all sorts of barbarous usage by soldiers sent to ruin and prey upon them.

In fact James, who was no lover of persecution, protested, albeit discreetly, to Louis. But in vain. From now on, every move James made to ease the burdens on English Catholics and bring them back into political life would be read against the background of the events in France. Only six months after his accession, James's honeymoon was over.

II

Could something like the Revocation of the Edict of Nantes happen in England? A Catholic army harass English Protestants and compel them to convert or to emigrate? Circumstances in England made it infinitely improbable. But James, by his single-minded determination to allow Catholicism a level playing field in England with the established, Protestant Church, did his best to make the improbable seem a real possibility.

In response to Monmouth's Revolt, James had recruited a professional army 20,000 strong. And included in the officer corps were a hundred Roman Catholics. This was acceptable in an emergency; it was a red rag to a bull once the revolt was suppressed, since the employment of Catholics in the army, as in all public posts, was forbidden by the Test Act, which had been passed under Charles II in response to James's own conversion to Catholicism.

This was the background to the recall of Parliament, which James opened on 9 November 1685, just as the first wave of French Protestant refugees, numbering several thousand, reached London.

Like his father, Charles I, the king came to Parliament 'with marks of haughtiness and anger upon his face, which made his sentiments sufficiently known'. Then, with characteristic bluntness, James tackled the issue of Catholic officers head-on in his speech from the throne, when he vowed that nothing would ever make him give them up: 'to deal plainly with you, after having had the benefit of their services in the time of danger, I will neither expose them to disgrace, nor myself to the want of their assistance, should a second rebellion make it necessary.'

This was to fling down a challenge to both Houses of Parliament. In the Commons, a backbencher invoked the spirit of the Long Parliament in 1641, on the eve of the Civil War: 'I hope we are Englishmen and not to be frightened from our duty by a few high words.' He was arrested and sent to the Tower for his disrespectful words. There were other, more influential voices being heard. In the Lords, the Bishop of London declared that the Test Act was the chief security of the Church of England.

Furious and frustrated, James dismissed Parliament. He would have to get round the Test Act some other way. The only other body whose authority remotely compared with that of Parliament was the judiciary. During the period of his personal rule, James's father, Charles I, had used the judges to authorize the collection of taxes that Parliament refused to grant; now James turned to the judges to get round the Test Act that Parliament refused to repeal.

First the bench of judges was purged of waverers; then a test case was brought on behalf of a Catholic army officer to whom James had granted a royal 'dispensation' or waiver from the requirements of the Test Act.

The Lord Chief Justice read the verdict on behalf of his almost unanimous colleagues. It could hardly have been clearer. Or more subversive:

> We think we may very well declare the opinion of the court to be that the King may dispense in this case . . . upon these grounds:
>
> 1. That the Kings of England are sovereign princes.
> 2. That the laws of England are the King's laws.
> 3. That therefore 'tis an inseparable prerogative of the Kings of England to dispense with penal laws in particular cases, and upon particular necessary reasons.
> 4. That of those reasons and those necessities the King himself is sole judge.
> 5. That this is not a trust invested in . . . the King by the people, but the ancient remains of the sovereign power and prerogative of the Kings of England.

This ruling transformed Parliament into a mere sleeping partner in the constitution: it might pass what laws it liked; whether and on whom they were enforced was purely up to the king.

But, most of all, the judges' ruling was exquisitely uncomfortable for the Tories since it turned one of their fundamental beliefs, in the unconditional nature of royal power, against their other, in the sanctity of the Church of England. And James's subsequent exploitation of the judges' ruling only impaled them on the horns of the dilemma more cruelly.

James made the most of the intellectual quagmire in which the Tories found themselves. Their loyalty to the monarchy, they said, was unlimited, and they preached against any form of resistance. How far could this be pushed? James was convinced that Protestantism flourished in England only because it had banished religious truth by monopolizing education. If Catholic thinkers were only given equality with Protestants, the country, he believed, would learn that they had been lied to, and that the truth resided in Roman Catholicism. Then his mission of conversion would be possible. He therefore ordered the fellows of Magdalen College, Oxford, to elect a Catholic master. The fellows had vowed to obey their king in everything. Now they were being ordered to break the law of the land and their own college's statutes and acquiesce in the destruction of the Anglican monopoly on education. They refused James's order, arguing that it was illegal. The king, outraged that his loyal churchmen should defy him, went in person to Oxford. 'Is this your Church of England loyalty?' he demanded of them. '. . . Get you gone, know I am your King. I will be obeyed and I command you to be gone.'

James did not understand – or affected not to understand – the distinction that Anglicans were beginning to make between resistance and obedience. Although they had sworn oaths not to rebel against the king, many were coming to believe that this did not necessarily mean that they were obliged to aid James's policies. Moreover, this was especially true when they felt that he was breaking the law. They believed that this was not just a matter of letting a handful of Catholics serve as army officers or academics, but rather that it presaged a full-scale assault on the Church, the laws and the nation itself.

For James saw the *dispensing* power, which enabled him to exempt individual Catholics from the Test Act on a case-by-case basis, simply as a first step. Instead, his Holy Grail was to secure a recognition of the *suspending* power, which would enable him to abrogate the laws against Catholics (and Protestant dissenters too) in their entirety. This would have the effect of the king's repealing, unilaterally, legislation that had been agreed by all three elements of the Crown-in-Parliament – king, Lords and Commons.

French kings could do this, as Louis XIV had shown with the Revocation of the Edict of Nantes. English kings could not. They were supposed to seek the consent of their subjects and respect the permanence of the law. But if any English king had the potential to go down the path of French absolutism, it was James, with his ample tax revenues, his standing army, his iron will and his sense of divine mission. England was at a dividing of the ways.

James chose his ground with care. First he issued the Declaration of Indulgence, which tried to press all the right buttons. It invoked the 'more than ordinary providence' by which Almighty God had brought him to the throne; and it offered universal religious toleration as a guarantee of Dutch-style economic prosperity – as opposed to Louis XIV-style religious persecution, which 'spoiled trade, depopulated countries and discouraged strangers'.

It was powerful bait. But would the Church of England be prepared to sell its monopoly position for a mess of pottage?

On 27 April 1688 James ordered the clergy to read the Declaration of Indulgence from their pulpits. The Archbishop of Canterbury, William Sancroft, who, only three years before, had crowned James in the magnificent ceremony at Westminster Abbey, summoned his fellow bishops to a secret supper party at Lambeth, where seven of them signed a petition to the king against the Declaration.

In it, the bishops contrived both to have their Tory cake and to eat Whig principles. On the one hand, they invoked 'our Holy Mother the Church of England [which was] both in her principles and her practice unquestionably loyal [to the monarchy]', and, on the other, they argued like good Whigs that 'the Declaration was founded on a dispensing power as hath often been declared illegal in Parliament'.

It was a frontal and – as the petition was soon circulated in print – public challenge to royal authority.

James determined to slap the bishops down by prosecuting them for seditious libel. But the bishops showed unexpected courage and a surprising flair for public relations. First, they stressed their loyalty. When James accused them of rebellion they recoiled in horror. 'We rebel! We are ready to die at your Majesty's feet,' said one bishop. 'We put down the last rebellion, we shall not raise another.' Then, by refusing to raise securities for bail, they got themselves imprisoned (rather briefly) in the Tower. It was a terrific coup: crowds of Londoners cheered them from the river banks as they were taken there by water; the soldiers of the garrison received them on their knees and the governor treated them as honoured guests.

Even more importantly, the bishops' trial, in the huge space of Westminster Hall, turned into a public argument about the legality of the dispensing power itself. Decorum broke down as the spectators cheered counsel for the bishops and booed and hissed the royal lawyers, and even the judicial worm turned against the king as one of the bench declared in his summing up that, if the dispensing power were allowed, 'there will need no Parliament; all the legislature will be in the king, which is a thing worth considering'.

'I leave the issue to God and your consciences,' he concluded to the jury. The jurors stayed out all night in continuous deliberation. Then, the following morning, they returned the verdict: 'Not guilty'.

Instead, it was James's government which had been condemned.

III

James II's zealous desire to legitimize Catholicism in England had brought him into open conflict with Parliament, the bishops and now the courts. But it was an unexpected event that took place at St James's Palace which finally brought matters to a head, an event that would under other circumstances have been an occasion for national rejoicing. Mary of Modena, James's second, Catholic wife, came from famously fertile stock. And she duly conceived frequently. But all the babies either miscarried or died in infancy, leaving James's Protestant daughters by his first marriage, Mary and Anne, as his heirs presumptive.

In the late summer of 1687, however, James went on pilgrimage to Holywell while Mary took the waters at Bath. Both medicine and magic seemed to work, and in December her pregnancy was officially confirmed. James was elated. The Jesuit monks who surrounded the pregnant queen promised that she would give birth to a boy. Now, with a Catholic heir on the way, the programme of converting the country could be continued long into the future.

The news was a disaster for English Protestants. There was sheer disbelief that the pregnancy could be genuine. Surely it must be another Catholic plot to subvert the laws and religion of the country? And the most important among these disbelievers were the members of James's own, Protestant first family: his daughters Mary and Anne and his son-in-law, William of Orange. William had expected that his wife Mary would eventually inherit the throne, thus bringing England on to his side in his struggle against Catholic France. They were now, by the pregnancy, to be dispossessed and disappointed.

Anne, who was still resident at her father's court despite her marriage to Prince George of Denmark, had also taken a hearty dislike to her stepmother's airs and graces when she became queen. Now she played a key role in endorsing and disseminating the malicious rumours about her pregnancy. It all looked suspiciously trouble free. Mary of Modena was too well. James, bearing in mind his wife's previous disastrous gynaecological

history, was too confident. And he was too confident in particular that he would have a son.

Anne wrote to her sister Mary to tell her that the queen was
only pretending to be pregnant. There was, she said, 'much
reason to believe it a false belly'. Even so, the supposedly fake
pregnancy ran its full course. The queen's pains began at
St James's on the morning of 10 June 1688, and, after a short
labour impeded only by the crowd of witnesses crammed into
her bedchamber, she gave birth at about 10 a.m.

The baby, christened James Francis after his father and
maternal uncle, was indeed the prophesied boy and – once his
doctors had stopped feeding him with a spoon on a gruel made
of water, flour and sugar, flavoured with a little sweet wine, and
allowed him human milk from a wet-nurse – he was healthy and
destined to live.

But was he the king and queen's child or a changeling?

Normally, the birth of a Prince of Wales would have crowned
James's attempt to reassert royal authority and re-Catholicize
England. When, for instance, such an attempt had been made a
century before, under Mary Tudor, it had been shipwrecked by
the queen's failure to produce a child and so guarantee the
permanence of her legacy. But the birth of James Francis had the
opposite effect. Faced with the prospect of a Catholic succession,
James's opponents decided that they could tolerate the course
of his government no longer. Before the birth of a healthy
prince, at least James's actions were reversible when his solidly
Protestant daughter, with her husband William at her side, came
to the throne. But now they must instead bring him to heel –
or even bring him down.

The first step was to develop the rumours about the queen's pregnancy into full-scale assault on the legitimacy of James Francis. The pregnancy, the story went, had been supposititious all along, as Anne had said, and therefore the child must be a changeling, smuggled into the queen's bed in a warming-pan by the cunning Jesuits after a carefully stage-managed performance of childbirth. It was all nonsense, of course. But Princess Anne believed it. She persuaded her sister Mary in the Netherlands to believe it. And her brother-in-law, William of Orange, found it convenient to believe it too.

By 1688, William, now in his late thirties, was a hardened general and politician. But his goal – to unite the Netherlands and England in a Protestant crusade against the overweening Catholic power of Louis XIV's France – remained unchanged. Bearing in mind his position as both James's nephew and son-in-law, he had every reason to suppose that Mary would inherit England naturally. But James's Catholicizing policies and, still worse, the birth of a Catholic son and heir threatened to rob him of the prize. William would not let it go without a struggle.

He needed a decent justification for action, however. He took the birth of Prince James to be an act of aggression against him on James's part: 'there hath appeared, both during the Queen's pretended bigness, and in the manner in which the Birth was managed so many just and visible grounds of suspicion.' In view of these, William was compelled to take action because 'our dearest and most entirely beloved Consort the Princess, and likewise ourselves, have so great an interest in this matter, and such a right, as all the world knows, to the Succession of the

Crown'. He was, in short, fighting not for his own selfish ends, but for his wife's rights and the rights of the English people.

William made his preparations on two fronts: in England and in the Netherlands. Learning from the mistake of Monmouth's puny expedition, he realized that he must invade in overwhelming force. During the course of the summer, he assembled a formidable armada on the Dutch coast, consisting of 60 warships, 700 transports, 15,000 troops, 4000 horses, 21 guns, a smithy, a portable bridge and, last but not least since it enabled the pen to assist the sword, a printing press.

William also benefited from Monmouth's experience in England. Monmouth had struck too soon, before the extent of James's intentions had become apparent. William, instead, reaped the fruits of the mounting disillusion with the king, which united Tories with Whigs in resistance to the Crown and reached its high water mark with the controversial birth of James Francis. The result was that on 30 June, three weeks after the birth of James Francis, four Whig peers and gentlemen and three Tories signed an invitation to William to invade Britain, since 'nineteen part of twenty of the people . . . are desirous of a change'. They exaggerated, of course. But their sense of the popular mood was right.

But none of this would have been possible but for a fateful decision taken by Louis XIV. There were two crisis points in Continental Europe in 1688: one in Cologne, where the pro-French Prince Archbishop had been replaced by one hostile to Louis, and the other much farther south, where the Habsburg Emperor Leopold was engaged in a life-or-death struggle with the Ottoman Turks, who had laid siege to Vienna. If Louis decided to strike against Cologne, which lay near the Dutch border, William could not risk denuding the republic of troops for his English expedition. Instead, in late summer, Louis resolved to pile the pressure on Leopold by invading southern Germany. The fate of James, Louis's English would-be pupil in absolutism, was sealed.

But at first the weather seemed to offer James the protection that Louis XIV had not. William had intended to sail on the first high tide in October. Instead he was first bottled up in port for several days by adverse winds and then driven back to shore by a storm. Meanwhile, James was still clinging to Divine Providence. 'I see God Almighty continues his Protection to me,' he had written on 20 October, after learning that the storm had driven William back to shore, 'by bringing the wind westerly again.'

But then the wind turned easterly and stayed that way. It blew hard due east, giving William a smooth voyage down the Channel and bottling James's fleet up in port. It was not lost on people that, a hundred years before, Protestantism had been saved by the destruction of the Spanish Armada. Now, for the hotter Protestants, England would be delivered from Catholicism by a very different sort of armada. But again, it was done by a wind. In 1588, the Armada medals were inscribed 'God's winds blew and they were scattered'; in 1688 the breeze that blew William towards England was called 'the Protestant Wind'.

William landed at Torbay in Devon on 5 November – another auspicious date for Protestants – and marched through cheering crowds to Exeter, where he set up camp and his print-

ing press to churn out carefully prepared propaganda. The 'Protestant wind' that blew William to England also blew away
James's confidence and with it his authority as the signs, which
for so long had been in his favour, turned against him. On
19 November, he arrived in Salisbury intending to stiffen his
army with the presence of their undoubted monarch. Instead, he
underwent a psychosomatic crisis and succumbed to repeated
heavy nosebleeds. Incapacitated and depressed, on 23 November
he decided to retreat to London, his army and his subjects'
loyalty untested.

That night, his up-and-coming general, John, Lord Churchill, fled to join William, whither he was followed twenty-four
hours later by James's other son-in-law, Prince George of
Denmark, husband of Princess Anne.

Behind every great man, it is said, is a strong woman. John
Churchill's strong woman was his wife, Sarah. But Sarah was
also, as Princess Anne's principal courtier and closest friend, a
power behind the throne. When Churchill and Prince George
deserted to the enemy, James immediately ordered the arrest of
their wives, Sarah and Anne. But Sarah was ahead of him and
she and Anne fled secretly from Whitehall late at night on
25 November. Their flight went undetected for seven hours and
when James re-entered his capital on the afternoon of the 26th
he was greeted with the news that his youngest daughter too
had joined the rebels. 'God help me,' he cried, 'my very children
have forsaken me!'

Abandoned by his God as well as his children, James's only
thought now was for flight. He believed wrongly that history
was repeating itself and he was in the position of his father,

Charles I. His enemies would execute him and murder his beloved baby son. It was clear that he was suffering a mental crisis and was incapable of judging the true nature of the situation. Outwardly, he conducted negotiations with William. But they were only to provide a cover for his real purpose. He contrived to bungle even this. The escape of the queen with the Prince of Wales had to be postponed several days and took place only on 10 December, when she left Whitehall disguised as a laundry woman. James himself quit the capital next day, first flinging the matrix of the Great Seal in the Thames. After his embarrassing capture by the fishermen on the Kent coast, he was taken as a prisoner to Faversham, whence he was rescued by a loyal detachment of his guards and escorted back to London.

There he received a rapturous welcome and, for a moment, thought of making a stand. Many believed that if William ever tried to use force to snatch the throne, the army would rally behind James. This was never put to the test. James's resolution crumbled when William sent a powerful detachment of his army to occupy London, seize Whitehall and order James to withdraw from the capital. The ultimatum was delivered to James in bed at midnight. Twelve hours later he was sent under guard to Rochester, whence, on 23 December, he was allowed to escape to France. This time, with his son-in-law's connivance, he succeeded.

As James left London for the second time, William entered it. In six weeks, and without a shot being fired, England was his. But on what terms?

IV

A late-seventeenth-century engraving shows William the Conqueror swearing to the laws of his sainted Anglo-Saxon predecessor, Edward the Confessor, and thus preserving the traditional rights of the English.

Faced with their own William the Conqueror, the men of 1689 determined to tie him down even more firmly; others were resolved not to have him as king at all. As part of the propaganda for his invasion, William had committed himself, irretrievably, to be everything that James apparently was not: a friend of English law and liberties, of England's religion, and, above all, a supporter of Parliament. He could do nothing, therefore, without a free parliament. The assembly – in the event called a Convention since only a King could legally call a parliament – met on 22 January 1689, a month after William's entry into London.

The Tories retained a small, but weighty, majority in the Lords. But the Commons was made up of the men of the last parliaments of Charles II's reign, who had voted to exclude James from the throne in the first place and had subsequently been marginalized during the Tory ascendancy.

For the first fortnight of the Convention, the two Houses fought over the implications of the extraordinary last few months, which had left James still very much alive, if not in full possession of his mental faculties or indeed present in the country itself. Faced with these facts, the Commons made up of

James's Whig enemies and under the chairmanship of Richard Hampden, son of Charles I's implacable enemy, made a bold resolution. It was also a daring constitutional innovation. James II, they declared, had broken the 'original contract' between king and subjects. He had also violated the 'fundamental laws' of the realm. And, most importantly, by removing himself from the country, he had abdicated the throne. The country had not been conquered by William; James had not been deposed. The king had deserted his people, not the other way round. It was a piece of fiction, but it was a very convenient one.

Nevertheless, the Tory-dominated lords hestitated long and hard before they accepted it. But swallow it they did. James II having been disposed of, the key issue was now the succession. What was to become of the monarchy, now that there was no one on the throne? The Tory peers were determined to preserve the principle of Stuart hereditary right by denying William the title of king – a title to which they believed he, as fourth in line, had no right. He must wait his turn, and let the next in line take the throne. But the next in line was the baby Prince James Francis, the so-called 'pretended Brat'. The implication of sticking to indefeasible hereditary succession was yet another Catholic monarch.

The Whigs were not so wedded to such unyielding principles of monarchy. The Commons neatly sidestepped the problem of James Francis by declaring that it had been found 'by experience' that it was impossible for England to have a Catholic monarch. Whether the baby was legitimate or a changeling did not now matter. It was his Catholicism which rendered him ineligible to inherit the throne. The next Protestant in line for the succession

James II saw his smooth accession as a miracle, which he celebrated by an unusually splendid and well-recorded Coronation. This engraving, taken from Francis Sandford's lavishly illustrated book on the event, shows the king's crowning by Archbishop William Sandcroft of Canterbury. But James misunderstood the warmth of his welcome. He thought that it meant that the English and the Church of England in particular would tolerate his moves to give Catholicism a level playing-field. Instead, he alienated every powerful interest group in the country and paved the way for his overthrow in the Glorious Revolution of 1688-89.

2

Royal rivals: Ever since (1) Louis XIV of France had almost conquered the Netherlands in 1672, (2) William of Orange had been determined to topple the power of autocratic Catholic France. His opportunity came in 1688, when, as the husband of James II's elder Protestant daughter (3) Mary, William launched a successful invasion of England, and with Britain's power added to the Netherlands, began a second Hundred Years War against France.

3

2

The Apotheosis of William and Mary. Sir James Thornhill's ceiling (1) in the Painted Hall of the Royal Naval Hospital at Greenwich employs the visual language of Louis XIV's Catholic absolutism to celebrate his defeat at the hands of the limited Protestant monarchy which was established in England after the Glorious Revolution of 1688. William, with Mary at his side, is borne aloft in the centre, as he uses a barbaric-looking Louis as his footstool. But the succession was a problem once more: (2) Anne, Mary's younger sister, succeeded the childless William and Mary but her only surviving child, shown with her, had already died.

2

The reign of Anne was the most triumphant so far in English history, thanks to a remarkable power couple, (1) John and Sarah Churchill, seen with their children. Sarah, as Anne's favourite, managed the home front while John won victory after victory over Louis XIV. His greatest triumph was the (2) Battle of Blenheim (1704), shown here in the commemorative tapestry he commissioned, when the French commander was captured and personally surrendered to Churchill. Churchill, who had already been created Duke of Marlborough, was rewarded with the vast palace, also called (3) Blenheim and grander by far than any royal residence, which was built at public expense on the site of the old royal palace of Woodstock near Oxford.

The triumph of George I and the House of Hanover, from the Upper Hall at Greenwich. In view of the childlessness of Anne, it was decided to pass over fifty Catholic claimants and give the throne to the Protestant George, Elector of Hanover, the grandson of James VI and I's daughter Elisabeth. George, who landed at Greenwich in 1714, enjoyed a trouble-free accession, while his son and grandson, who appear beside him, guaranteed the continuity of the new, thoroughly German dynasty. Thornhill, the painter, shows himself observing the scene on the right.

was, of course, Mary. But it was clear that William would not accept being second string to his wife. The only realistic solution was to have William – the saviour of the country – as king, whether it was constitutionally correct or not.

In the event, it took William himself to break the deadlock. The Tories hoped to string out the debates so that they could preserve the principle of monarchy. William threw cold water on their endless constitutional nit-picking. He would act neither as regent for his self-exiled father-in-law, James II, nor as consort for his wife Mary; instead, he would be king or he would return to the Netherlands and leave England to constitutional squabbles, anarchy and the possibility of a restored James II. Even Tories found that, even if they would rather do without King William, in practice England could not do without the Dutchman now that the country had no legitimate ruler.

Faced with his ultimatum, Lords and Commons agreed to a face-saving compromise. William and Mary would rule as joint king and queen to give the impression that the Stuart line of descent was still valid. But in practice, the exercise of sovereignty would be vested solely in William.

But having given William the crown he wanted, Whigs and Tories united to limit the powers that he or any future monarch could exercise by drawing up the Bill or Declaration of Rights. The rights in question are not so much those of the individual against the government; rather they are 'the ancient rights and liberties' of the nation as represented in Parliament against the Crown.

So, the Bill declared, the Crown could not dispense with or suspend laws made in Parliament; it could not raise taxation except through Parliament and it could not have a standing army without the consent of Parliament. On the other hand, the Crown should allow elections to Parliament to be free and parliaments frequent. Finally, and above all, the Bill declared it 'inconsistent with the safety and welfare of this Protestant kingdom' for the monarch to be Papist or to be married to a Papist.

The principle of the Royal Supremacy, that the English should have the religion of their king, had been stood on its head. It was a revolution indeed.

All was now ready for the formal offer of the crown to William and Mary in the Banqueting House at Whitehall. Mary, who had arrived in England only the day previously and, it was widely felt, had stepped into Mary of Modena's apartments, her possessions and her very habits with indecent glee, joined her husband under the Cloth of Estate. The Lords on the right and the Commons on the left, led by their Speakers, approached the steps of the throne; the clerk read out the Bill of Rights and a nobleman offered William and Mary the crown in the name of the Convention as the 'representative of the nation'.

William then accepted on their joint behalves, promising in turn to do all in his power 'to advance the welfare and glory of the nation', and they were proclaimed king and queen to the sound of trumpets. Two months later, William and Mary were crowned in Westminster Abbey, with the ceremony and the oath in particular having been transformed to reflect the new realities of power.

Each in turn swore to govern 'according to the statutes in parliament agreed on'; to maintain 'the Protestant reformed religion established by law' and to do 'justice in mercy' – with no damn nonsense about 'discretion' as previously. Just as inno-vatory was the coronation sermon. Ever since the coronation of Henry VIII's young son, Edward VI, when Archbishop Cranmer had proclaimed that oaths could not bind the boy king nor holy oils add anything to his inherent, God-given sanctity, preachers at the coronation had vied with each other to elevate the monarch-cum-Supreme Head of the Church to an almost God-like plane.

In 1689, however, all this changed. 'Happy we,' the preacher proclaimed prosaically, 'who are delivered from both extremes: who neither live under the Terror of Despotick power [as in Louis XIV's France], nor are cast loose to the wildness of govern'd multitudes [as England had been during the Civil War and Commonwealth].'

As the preacher finished, the congregation broke into 'infi-nite applause'. They were responding as though the ancient mysteries of the coronation had transmuted into the inaugur-ation ceremonies of a popular prince-president of a middle-of-the-road republic – as of course William was, in effect, in his native Holland. But not only was the monarchy brought down to a merely human level, so too was the Church, which, since the Royal Supremacy, had been its most stalwart supporter and mouthpiece.

William's propaganda had promised, and the Convention speedily enacted, freedom of conscience, of worship and security from persecution to all outside the Church of England – Roman Catholics as well as Protestant dissenters – who would live 'as good subjects', recognize William and Mary as king and queen and repudiate the temporal authority of the Pope.

The effect, and on the part of the Whigs the intended effect, was also to diminish the Church of England. The Church remained uniquely privileged and only its members could hold public office, from the throne down. Nevertheless, it had ceased to be a monopoly and become one church among many.

The Church split over the changes – between diehard Tories and Whigs, like Gilbert Burnet, the preacher at the coronation, who not only accepted the new dispensation but also understood that the Church would have to argue for Christianity, not in the old voice of absolute authority, but by reason and persuasion. Chance and taste played their part too. William (among his many other ailments) was asthmatic and detested the urban, riverside position of Whitehall Palace with its fogs and mists. So too did Mary, who felt able to see nothing but 'water or wall'. Within a few months, therefore, the royal couple bought Nottingham House, with its extensive gardens and pleasant suburban situation on the edge of Hyde Park, and rebuilt it at breakneck speed as Kensington Palace. The result, described by a contemporary as 'very noble, though not great', was exactly the kind of residence that William was used to as *stadholder* and prince in the Netherlands.

Meanwhile, Whitehall, called 'the largest and ugliest palace in the world' by the Duc de la Rochefoucauld, and seat of all English kings since the time of its builder, Henry VIII, was abandoned for all save ceremonial occasions. Neglected and forlorn, like so many underused buildings, it burnt down in 1698 and was never rebuilt.

Perishing in the flames and ruins was the great dynastic mural of Henry VIII and his family, which, more than any other single image, represented the awesome powers of the Royal Supremacy over Church and state. The painting had survived the destruction of the Supremacy and the royal absolutism it had entailed by less than a decade.

BRITANNIA RULES

WILLIAM III, MARY II AND ANNE

Two years before her death in 1714, a statue of Queen Anne was placed equidistant, as wags said, between her two favourite places, St Paul's Cathedral and a brandy shop. Whether the queen's preference was for the bottle or the building, certainly St Paul's was the setting for the high points of her reign.

The queen herself came to the cathedral in solemn procession in 1704 to lead the service of thanksgiving for Blenheim, the great victory won over Louis XIV of France by her general John Churchill, Duke of Marlborough, husband of Anne's favourite, Sarah, who rode in the queen's coach and accompanied her every move.

The last monarch to come to St Paul's for a victory service had been Elizabeth I, and the parallels between the two queens were invoked in the celebrations:

> As threatening Spain did to Eliza bow
> So France *and* Spain shall do to Anna now.

But whereas the dire state of Elizabeth's finances had never allowed the defeat of the Armada to be followed up with a crushing offensive campaign against England's enemies, each year of Anne's reign brought fresh victories and another state procession to St Paul's, until, by 1712, the year Anne's statue was erected, Britain could name her own terms for peace with France.

And by then it was no longer England, but Britain. She was the dominant power in Europe. Fifty years later, another victorious war was celebrated at St Paul's. The country's crushing defeat of France in Europe and the Americas marked Britain's emergence as the *world* power.

Few countries have risen to great-power status so quickly and so unexpectedly. Why had the England of Anne succeeded where the England of Elizabeth had failed? The answer can be found in the events that followed the revolution of 1688, which had settled most of the political and religious disputes that had torn England apart since the Reformation.

But much of the credit must also go to the man Anne abused in her private letters as 'Caliban' or 'the Dutch monster': her cousin, brother-in-law and predecessor, William III. It was William who created a new kind of English monarchy, with a new relationship between Crown and Parliament, and in doing so transformed Britain from a divided, unstable, rebellious and marginal country into the state that would become the most powerful on the planet.

I

Soon after their inauguration as joint monarchs in February 1689, William of Orange and his queen, Mary Stuart, escaped from London to enjoy the country air at Hampton Court. It was love at first sight, and the palace and gardens we know today are essentially their creation.

But though William and Mary could flee the capital, they could not escape so easily from the quasi-religious rituals that hedged the divinity of the Tudor and Stuart kings. The dour Calvinist king was not impressed. He had mocked 'the comedy of the coronation', which was full of 'foolish old Popish ceremonies'. But his obligation to enact the spiritual dimension of English monarchy did not stop there. Many of these rituals centred on the Chapel Royal and followed the ancient rhythms of the Church's calendar. A particularly important group of dates clustered round the great feast of Easter, which in 1689 fell on 31 March.

On the day before Good Friday, the monarch, re-enacting the role of Christ, would wash the feet of as many poor persons as he was years old in the ceremony of Maundy Thursday. Three days later, on Easter Sunday, he would take his place in the Royal Pew, then, at the climax of the service, descend the stairs, process to the altar and receive communion alone to symbolize his unique relationship with God. Acknowledged now by God and man, there was also a clamour for William and Mary to follow in the footsteps of their predecessors and heal the sick by Touching for the King's Evil.

William and Mary managed to go through the Easter Day ceremonies, though they thought the practice of receiving communion alone a 'foolish formality' and changed it as soon as possible. But William baulked at other, more outlandish ceremonies. On Maundy Thursday he refused to wash the feet of the poor, limiting himself instead to giving them the traditional alms. Even more extreme was his reaction to touching for scrofula. Since the Stuart Restoration in 1660, this ceremony had been the primary point of contact between monarch and subject and the symbol of the divine nature of kingship. Charles II had touched vast numbers of the people. James II had gone beyond Charles's enthusiasm for the practice and had reintroduced the old Latin Catholic ritual as well. For William, this was to add idolatrous superstition to old-fashioned absurdity and he suspended the practice entirely. 'God give you better health and more sense!' he mocked the hopeful afflicted.

Within days, William's refusal to continue the old royal rituals was hot news in Paris. It signalled to his French rival – and everybody else – that here was a different kind of king. For William's Tudor and Stuart predecessors, the monarchy and its powers, prerogatives and titles was a sacramental trust, committed by God to their ancestors, and, with God's will, to be transmitted to their descendants. But none of this, despite his own Stuart mother and wife, applied to William. He had come to the throne not through strict lineal succession, but because of the mess of purely human affairs. And since he was childless and with no prospect of offspring, he had no descendants to worry about. Finally as a strict Calvinist, he didn't – as his attitude to the Coronation, the Maundy and the Touching shows – believe in sacraments, royal or otherwise.

What William *did* believe in was predestination or divinely ordained destiny: in particular his own God-given mission to be the champion of Protestantism and the nemesis of Louis XIV's France. To become King of England, therefore, was only a step to this goal and not an end in itself. This meant that William's view of kingship was *instrumental*, in contrast to the jealous *sacramentalism* of his Tudor and Stuart predecessors. And this meant in turn that for William literally nothing was sacred (following the Dutch custom, he even kept his hat on during religious services). He was not sentimental about the trappings and symbols of monarchy. Nor was he in thrall to the sacred mystique of kingship. So William was willing, if not necessarily happy, to bargain away the powers of the monarchy for the hard cash that was needed to fight his great war against France.

This, it turned out, was a good thing, since the attitude of William's subjects to the monarchy had changed as well. The change was neatly summarized for the king by one of his ministers. During the last few decades, kings had known where they stood: the Tory half of the nation supported royal power while the Whig half opposed it. But the revolution that had brought William to power had muddied the waters. For the Whigs, though they were William's natural supporters, retained their habitual mistrust of monarchy. While the Tories, though remaining theoretically committed to royal power, did not, in their heart of hearts, think that William was the rightful king. They had made solemn and binding oaths to James II, which they were painfully conscious of having broken. And so the Tories mistrusted William at least as much as the Whigs did.

The result was that, divided in everything else, William's leading subjects were united in their determination to drive a hard bargain with their new King William. One MP spoke for all when he told the House: 'If you settle such a revenue as that the King should have no need of a Parliament, I think we do not do our duty to them that sent us hither.'

Parliament had made this error of rendering themselves useless by granting the king enough money to rule on his own in the Restoration Settlement of 1660 and, even more flagrantly, at the beginning of James II's reign in 1685. It was not to repeat the mistake again.

So in 1689 it refused to make any permanent settlement of the revenue at all, postponing it for another year. And even in 1690 it granted William only the Customs (or taxes on foreign trade) for life, while the Excise (or internal indirect taxes) was to be reviewed four years later. In personal conversations, William freely expressed his outrage at such ingratitude, as he saw it. 'The Commons used him like a dog,' he would say. 'Truly, a King of England ... is the worst figure in Christendom,' he moaned at another time. And, in exasperation at the carpings and criticisms of the English, he snapped: 'The nation entertained such distrust and jealousies of him that he intended to go abroad.'

But, having vented his frustrations in private, in public (as he had learned to do by bitter experience in the Netherlands) he calmly settled down to bargain. The result was a financial and constitutional revolution far greater in effect than the revolution itself. In 1689 he offered the Commons scrutiny of public accounts. He surrendered his prerogative of calling and dissolving parliaments at his own pleasure in 1694 by agreeing to the Triennial Act, which provided instead for the automatic summoning of a new Parliament every three years. And in 1697, by agreeing to a Civil List to cover the expenses of the royal household and peacetime domestic administration, he yielded to parliamentary control over the expenditure, as well as the raising, of all revenue for the army and the navy.

Thanks to this subtle give-and-take diplomacy, Parliament, which in 1690 had been barely willing to finance William's expedition to reconquer Ireland from a French-financed invasion personally led by a reluctant James II, by the middle of the decade was raising an unheard-of £4 million a year in taxation. And every penny was needed. For the war that William declared against France within days of his coronation was the largest, longest, most expensive conflict England had engaged in since the Middle Ages. John Churchill, Duke of Marlborough and after the king himself England's leading general, predicted that it would last 'forever'; in sober fact it was to be merely a new hundred years' war which was not finally settled till the Congress of Vienna in 1815.

The scale of the war and the taxation it entailed completed and made permanent the revolution of 1688–89. The result was – literally – built in stone. The Board Room of the Admiralty in Whitehall, which is still in use, was built to put the administration of England's hugely expanded navy on a proper footing. The Royal Hospital at Greenwich, founded by Queen Mary in 1692 after the great naval victory over the French of La Hogue, was built to care for invalided and aged sailors. Grander than any royal palace, it became a monument both to England's naval greatness and, with its lavishly painted interiors, to the Glorious Revolution and William's own triumphs over France.

If England was gaining secure and permanent civil and military institutions safely ensured by sturdy buildings, surely the most innovative and durable was the Bank of England, established in 1694 at Mercer's Hall in the City of London. Its origins had, like much else, less to do with root-and-branch reforms than with William's pressing need to manage the government debt incurred in fighting the war against France. Copied, once again, from the Dutch model of the Bank of Amsterdam, the bank's security was based, not on the king's credit (for kings, including Louis XIV, could and did go bankrupt), but on the guaranteed steady income stream of parliamentary taxation.

Security of payment meant that English interest rates plunged, while those in France, which stuck to the old system of royal credit and experienced the familiar crises of royal bankruptcy, soared. Thus, though pound for *livre* the English tax base was smaller than that of France (which is four times as big a country and then had three times as big a population), gearing meant that the English could match or even outspend the French.

In his own lifetime, William was only able to fight Louis to a standstill rather than inflict the crushing defeat for which he yearned. But he had created the financial, military and political machinery which, as events would show, swung the balance of power decisively in England's favour. It was an extraordinary achievement, which makes this Dutchman one of England's greatest monarchs.

II

William got little thanks from his subjects at the time, and posterity has been no kinder. For William, with so many great gifts, had few of the small ones that humanize greatness and make it popular, or at least bearable. He had no small talk. He suffered fools not at all. He hated company, preferring instead to unwind with a handful of intimates.

Secure in the privacy of the suburban or rural royal courts, William was free to carouse with his mainly Dutch male cronies in seclusion. English ministers who were used to a royal court where the king was accessible and business could be conducted face to face were annoyed by William's reclusive tendencies. Rather than sleep in the magnificence of the State Bedchamber, which was traditionally the buzzing hub of the royal court, William took his rest in a simple private chamber. And it was very private indeed. The king could not be troubled by overly attentive servants, demanding ministers or prying eyes. The locks wore on the inside and only one other man had the key, Arnold Joost van Keppel, whose extensive apartment was next door. And Keppel's good looks and easy and exclusive access to the king fuelled ugly rumours of homosexuality.

Worst of all, perhaps, William and his favourites remained obstinately Dutch, and that the xenophobic English found intolerable. His wife and joint monarch, Queen Mary, however, deflected much of the bitterness over the fact that England had been conquered by a warmongering Dutch obsessive. Mary represented the unbroken Stuart descent and continuity with the past. Above all she was English. If William had delivered England from a Catholic king and waged war on France, Mary represented English virtue and piety. As far as William was concerned this was a good arrangement. For Mary believed that ruling was a man's business, and she was no threat to William's sole exercise of power. At the same time, she was indispensable to him as a figurehead to quell his new subjects' xenophobia. As William stated: 'He was to conquer Enemies, and she was to gain Friends.'

But when Mary died of smallpox in 1694, the Stuart fig leaf was torn from William's throne. Mary was loved by the people, and her death provoked an outpouring of grief from the country. But William had always been a very unpopular king, nicknamed the 'Rotten Orange', 'Hook Nose' or 'The Little Spark'. King Louis and the exiled James II celebrated when they heard of the death of Queen Mary. They did not believe that William could survive long on his own. He was hated by the English, and if he wasn't deposed or assassinated, then at least he would never risk leaving the country to go and fight France.

But William was able to face down his enemies. The king's evidently sincere grief at his bereavement won him some temporary popularity, and his supporters urged the population to respect the memory of the late lamented queen by remaining loyal, as she had done, to her husband. The PR campaign worked. Despite Louis's and James's predictions, William was secure enough to leave the country to continue the war against France as usual during the campaigning season. If the English did not love William as they had loved Mary, or even respect him that much, they were at least prepared to tolerate him for all his faults.

But by the turn of the eighteenth century Parliament had begun to resent William's aggressive foreign policy – and to resent paying for it most of all. The Commons demanded that he disband most of the army and send home his Dutch guards. Once again, the stage appeared to be set for another round in the chronic conflict between king and Commons that had removed two monarchs within living memory. As he had done before, William petulantly threatened to return to Holland and wait until the English came to their senses and begged him to come back to save them from France and James II. He even drafted an abdication speech. For the sake of a few pounds, William said, the English were prepared to reduce the army and invite invasion. 'It is impossible to credit the serene indifference with which they consider events outside their own country,' William wrote of his truculent and insular subjects.

Things got worse as Parliament and king clashed over foreign policy and England's rights and responsibilities in Europe. But then the rule of the House of Orange came to an abrupt and unexpected end. On 21 February William was hunting in Hampton Court Park when his favourite horse Sorrel stumbled at a mole hill, throwing him and breaking his collar bone in the fall. The bone was set successfully but a chest infection set in and William died at his other favourite palace of Kensington on 8 March, aged fifty-one. Five weeks later, on

12 April, he was buried privately at midnight in Westminster Abbey. The Privy Council announced plans for a monument in the Abbey and another in a 'public place'. But no one could be bothered to build them – least of all his successor Anne.

Anne was thirty-seven. She had never been a beauty like her sister Mary. But she had a handsome, womanly figure, rather running to seed after repeated miscarriages and stillbirths. Her best feature, however, was her beautiful speaking voice, for which she had received professional coaching in her youth. Above all, she knew how to rise to a public occasion.

This meant that her first speech to Parliament, only three days after William's death, was a triumph. She wore a magnificent crimson robe, lined with ermine and bordered with gold. She blushed prettily. And she proclaimed in her thrilling voice that 'I know my heart to be entirely English'.

It was a deliberate distancing of herself from William, the foreigner who barely respected England and Englishmen. The English, pleased as they were to be rid of William, loved her for her bullish and patriotic sentiments and from that moment she became, and remained, as popular as William had been disliked. Her accession seemed like the best of all possible worlds. She was a Stuart, but she was fiercely committed to the Protestant Anglican Church. She was a supporter of the modernized monarchy, but she had an instinctive and inbred regard for the ceremonies and mystique of the ancient monarchy. Touching for the King's Evil was back in fashion.

But despite these changes of personal style and belief, the substance of government altered very little. She would, Anne confirmed in her first speech to Parliament, continue her predecessor's policies at home and abroad. And that meant, above all, that she would continue with the war against France. She told the Dutch Republic that she would do everything that 'will be necessary [for] preserving the common liberty of Europe, and reducing the power of France to its just limits'. But this was an English queen speaking, and Anne was determined to cast herself in the mould of historic warrior queens; this would be an English war, and the country would fight it for its own interests and glory, and not on behalf of others.

For the stalemate peace that Louis and William had been forced to sign in 1697 quickly collapsed. The issue was the succession to the childless King Carlos II, who ruled Spain and her still vast empire in Europe and South America. Among the intermarried royal families of Europe, the choice lay between two remote cousins: the Austrian Habsburg Emperor was one candidate, the other was Philip, the younger grandson of Louis XIV of France. In the event, it was Philip whom Carlos left as his heir on his death in 1700.

For William the prospect of such a gigantic addition to French power was intolerable and, just before his death, he had reassembled the Grand Alliance against France, consisting of Britain, the Netherlands, the Empire and the German princes. But the declaration of war, on 5 May 1702, was left to Anne. Louis is supposed to have replied mockingly that he must be old indeed if women waged war on him. But oddly it *was* the fact that Anne was a woman which proved his downfall. For William, as was still commonplace among kings, had acted as his own commander. This was a mixed blessing: he was brave to the point of foolhardiness and indomitable; but he was no general.

But the man Anne chose to act in her stead as commander was. Indeed, ranking with Caesar and Napoleon, he is the only world-class general that England has ever produced. John Churchill had defected to William during the revolution, but, like many leading Englishmen, he had been pushed aside by the new king's Dutch intimates. In 1692 he was dismissed from court and deprived of his commands for spreading dissatisfaction in the army against the Dutch generals. Forgiven at last, he was appointed captain of the forces by William near the end of his reign, in 1701. He was retained in this leading post by the new queen, not just for his qualities, but because his wife was the queen's best friend.

Losing her mother at the age of only eight and quickly separated from her father because of his conversion to Catholicism, Anne became shy, reserved and lonely. She had found consolation in a series of close friendships with women. Much the most important and long lasting was that with Sarah Churchill, and testimony to it are the countless letters they wrote each other under the levelling pseudonyms of Mrs Freeman (Sarah) and Mrs Morley (Anne). Back in 1692, when the Churchills had been disgraced, William had demanded that Anne dismiss Sarah and John from her household. But Anne won the lasting hatred of her brother-in-law the king when she refused. Anne had pledged herself to Sarah as follows: 'never believe your Mrs Morley will ever submit, she can wait for a Sunshine Day, and if she does not live to see it, yet she hopes England will flourish again.' Now, with William's death, the Sunshine Day had arrived – for England and, especially, for the Churchills.

Within a week of her accession, Anne had delivered her person and her kingdom to John and Sarah. Sarah was made Groom of the Stole and head of the royal bedchamber. The office was known, after its official symbol, as 'the key to the prince', and it controlled access to the queen's private apartments, her jewels and robes, and her personal cash. At the same time, John was appointed captain-general, master-general of the ordnance and ambassador extraordinary to the Dutch Republic, which in turn appointed him its own captain-general with the elegant Mauritshuis in The Hague as his residence.

His occupation of the Mauritshuis, which had belonged to the junior branch of the House of Orange, emphasized that John had now inherited William III's role as joint commander of the Anglo-Dutch alliance. Indeed, in military terms the Dutch were still the senior partner, as they had once been in trade and public finance. Their army was professionally drilled and equipped with the most modern weapons, like flintlock muskets with fixed bayonets, while the Dutch logistics and commissariat were the most efficient in Europe.

But the English, as in other areas, copied them, and, thanks to their superior resources, soon outdid them. In all this Marlborough was the beneficiary of William III's pioneering efforts. But he achieved what William had only dreamed of doing. In 1702–03 he freed the Dutch Republic from the French stranglehold. That won him the dukedom of Marlborough. In 1704 he shattered the French threat to the emperor, the other key member of the Grand Alliance, with the victory of Blenheim on the Danube. The French commander was captured, along with 13,000 of his men, and 20,000 were killed. It was a crushing defeat for France, and England's greatest victory since Henry V's at Agincourt.

Marlborough scribbled the news to Anne on the back of a tavern bill and was rewarded with the royal estate of Woodstock in Oxfordshire. Here a vast palace – grander by far than any of Anne's own – was built for him and his wife at public expense. Called Blenheim, it is a temple to Marlborough's series of victories in the 1700s. Its every feature memorializes his triumphs: Blenheim itself; the victory at Ramillies in 1706 which drove France out of modern Belgium; and Oudenarde, the victory in 1708 which opened up the door to France itself.

But, despite Marlborough's triumphs, there remained profound tensions in Britain. For the issue of the succession had reopened. Back in 1689, the full implications of dethroning James II, whose general Marlborough had once been, had been masked because the House of Stuart would, it seemed, continue in the persons of his daughters and their issue.

Indeed, that very July Anne, despite her unfortunate tendency to miscarriages, had had a son who lived. He was christened William, created Duke of Gloucester and became the apple of his uncle William III's eye. The succession would continue – and it would be through a male, a Protestant, a descendant of the direct Stuart line and an Englishman. The people could be reassured that the rule of a foreigner was only a temporary sacrifice. But in 1700 the boy died. Who should now replace him in the succession after Anne?

There was always the possibility of reverting to the male Stuart line, still temptingly near in their exile in France. The dethroned James II died in 1701 but was succeeded by the 'warming-pan baby', James Francis, whose birth in 1688 had started it all. Known to history as the Old Pretender, he was recognized by Louis XIV as King James VIII of Scotland and James III of England immediately on his father's death.

The Old Pretender was brave, moderately intelligent and charming – one to one at least. But he had his father's stiffness of public manner, his arrogance and his unyielding rigidity in his commitment to Catholicism. In short, the Old Pretender was the kind of man to arouse loyalty but, almost invariably, to disappoint it.

A few English and more Scots remained devoted to the cause of James III and were known, from the Latin form of his name, as 'Jacobites'. But, overwhelmingly, the English elite remained opposed to a Catholic king. Instead, Parliament – Tories as well as Whigs – passed the Act of Settlement in 1701. This reaffirmed the principle of the revolution that a Roman Catholic should never be king. The problem was that they had to look very far to find a Protestant in the line of descent from the Tudor and Stuart dynasties. Parliament passed over fifty other Popish claimants who stood legitimately in the line of succession, including the Old Pretender. At last, it gave the succession, after Anne, to the impeccably Protestant Sophia, granddaughter of James I and Electress Dowager of the insignificant north German principality of Hanover. It was a link with the royal line, but a very distant one.

Two months after the passing of the Act of Settlement an English embassy arrived in Hanover to honour the future dynasty. They presented the widowed Electress Sophia with a copy of the Act of Settlement and her son, Georg Ludwig, with the Garter. (Georg was ruling prince of Hanover, because there, unlike in England, women were prevented from reigning in their own right.) Five years later, Sophia's grandson, the electoral prince, Georg August, was also made a Knight of the Garter and created Duke of Cambridge as well.

But though Anne was happy to shower honours on her successors, she refused absolutely to allow any member of the electoral family to set foot in England. Successors were a magnet for opposition – as the queen knew, for she had been a difficult heir herself. Anne, wisely, was taking no risks. In England the choice of the House of Hanover was widely welcomed. But in Scotland, which shared a monarch with England but not a parliament, it precipitated an immediate rupture in relations with its southern neighbour. It was not automatic that the House of Hanover would succeed to the throne of Scotland. The spectre of renewed hostility between the two kingdoms raised its ugly head once again.

Would Marlborough have to break off the greater ambition of taking on Europe, in order, like that earlier captain-general Cromwell, to subdue the rebellious northern kingdom?

III

In March 1703 the Scottish Parliament was opened with the customary 'riding'. The mounted procession set out from Holyrood Palace, rode up the High Street, past St Giles Cathedral, and turned into the Scottish Parliament House. First came the nobles in their robes; then the barons representing the shires; and finally the town burgesses. The members were accompanied by their armed retainers and rode through a lane of citizens, also armed.

The carrying of arms was traditional. But, on this occasion, the atmosphere was feverish with barely suppressed real violence: 'our swords' were in our hands or at least our hands were at our swords', one leading member remembered. And the object of this impassioned feeling was England.

Before the revolution, the Scottish Parliament was a poor thing, managed for the absentee monarch by a committee called the Lords of the Articles. But the revolution liberated Parliament in Scotland as well as England. Freed from royal management, it could take an independent line against the Crown – and a Crown that was seen, above all, as the prisoner of its English ministers. Indeed, there was now talk of actual independence – or at least of selling freedom dearly.

The bargaining counter was the Hanoverian succession. The English Act of Settlement, which gave the Crown to the House of Hanover, had been passed without consulting the Scots. Now the Scots would play the English at their own game and settle *their* succession independently too. The Scottish Parliament of 1703 did so in the Act of Security. This provided that, after Anne's death, the next monarch of Scotland should be a Protestant and of the royal line, but need *not* be the same person as the successor to the English Crown. The English Parliament had actually named who the successor would be. This was to ensure that none of the fifty or so Catholics who stood in the line converted to Protestantism in order to fulfil the obligations of the Act of Succession and claim their right. As the Scots framed their Act of Security, there was nothing to stop the Old Pretender, the so-called James VIII of Scotland, from converting to Protestantism to claim the throne, and then switching back to Catholicism when circumstances suited. The British Isles would once again have two monarchs facing each other with mutual enmity.

Anne refused to give her consent to the Act of Security for almost a year, until overwhelming pressure forced her to yield. A few days later, news of Marlborough's great victory at Blenheim reached London. Freed from the immediate threat of a French-sponsored Jacobite invasion of Scotland, the English Parliament could now respond in kind to the Scottish.

The result was the Aliens Act, passed in spring 1705. All Scots, except those resident in England, were to be treated as aliens, and the major Scottish export trades to England banned *unless*, by Christmas 1705, significant progress had been made to agreeing a union of the two kingdoms.

The Aliens Act aroused predictable outrage in Scotland. But the deadline did concentrate minds. Two sets of commissioners, thirty or so on each side, were appointed to thrash out an agreement. The commissioners began work in April 1706 in government offices in what had been Henry VIII's cockpit at Whitehall. To soothe Scottish sensibilities, the two sets of commissioners met in separate rooms, communicated by written minutes only and strictly avoided socializing with each other.

On 22 April, the English room sent the following proposal to the Scottish:

> That the two kingdoms of England and Scotland be for
> ever United into one kingdom by the name of Great
> Britain. That the United Kingdom of Great Britain be
> represented by one and the same parliament, and that the
> succession to the monarchy of Great Britain [be vested
> in the House of Hanover].

On the 25th, the Scottish commissioners came back with a counter-proposal. They would accept union and the Hanoverian succession *but* on condition of freedom of trade, not only within the United Kingdom but also within 'the Plantations'. The English replied promptly that they regarded such mutual freedom of trade as a 'necessary consequence of an entire Union'.

It had taken only three days to work out the bones of an agreement. For both sides had got what they wanted. The English wanted Scotland unshakeably onside during their newly embarked-upon geopolitical struggle with France; while the Scots, having tried but failed catastrophically to establish a colonial empire of their own, wanted free access to the English 'Plantations' as a way out of their own desperate national poverty.

The 'Plantations', or colonies, largely in North America, were the great English success story of the previous hundred years, as, in spite of civil strife at home, the English had built an empire abroad. By Anne's reign, indeed, America seemed a separate realm and appears symbolically as such on the base of Anne's statue outside St Paul's, alongside figures representing her three other kingdoms of England, Ireland and Scotland. Henceforward, this American realm was to be as much Scottish as English. Or rather, like the empire itself, it was to be British.

And it was to St Paul's that Anne, wearing the combined orders of the English Garter and the Scottish Thistle and accompanied by 400 coaches, came to celebrate Union on 1 May 1707, the day that it came into effect. It was, she said, even among so many victories, the day that would prove the true happiness of her reign.

The Union was a nice mixture of the conservative and the radical. Most that was distinctively Scottish (or indeed English) was preserved, and along with 'the most ancient and most noble order of the Thistle', Scotland kept its own law and law courts (complete, at the outset, with the torture that was an intrinsic part of its criminal law), its universities and educational system and, above all, the intolerant, monopolistic Presbyterian Kirk that had been restored in the religious upheaval that was Scotland's peculiar contribution to the Glorious Revolution.

But equally, the institutions of the United Kingdom were new and were framed with the innovative, rational methods of Anglo-Dutch political economy. Most pressing, however, was the issue of Scottish representation in the Union Parliament at Westminster. It could be determined either by population or (since the principal business of Parliament was to vote taxation) by taxable wealth. Using the former basis would have given Scotland eighty-five MPs; using the latter (since Scotland's wealth was only a fortieth of England's) only thirteen. Eventually the commissioners compromised at forty-five, and honour was more or less satisfied.

Nevertheless, there were no celebrations for Union in Scotland. But, as the intellectual and economic transformation of eighteenth-century Scotland would show, the Scots probably got the better deal.

On 19 August 1708 Anne processed once more to the spiritual home of her reign, St Paul's, to give thanks for Marlborough's victory of Oudenarde. Accompanying her in her coach, as etiquette demanded, was Marlborough's duchess, Sarah. There had been much resentment at the Duke and Duchess of Marlborough's influence over the queen. Sarah was a committed Whig, contemptuous of princes and princesses, proudly atheist and opposed to the Anglican monopoly. She believed that it was her job to keep Anne from the Tories, whom the queen instinctively supported. Many detested Sarah as the malign power behind the throne.

All this came to a head on the way to St Paul's. En route, the two women had a terrible quarrel because Anne, who hated cumbrous clothing, had refused to wear the rich, heavy jewels that Sarah, as Groom of the Stole, had put out for her. As they stepped out of the coach, Sarah was heard to hiss 'Be quiet' to the queen, lest (she claimed) others overheard their quarrel. It seemed to confirm Sarah's unnatural power over the monarch. But more importantly, Anne never forgave the insult to majesty and the long and fraught friendship was over.

The quarrel was in fact only the straw that broke the camel's back. For Sarah had fought her own war at home – against the Tory leaders whom she accused, not altogether wrongly as it turned out, of being secret Jacobites. Aware of James III's insidious charms, Sarah campaigned, with all her husband's relentlessness but none of his panache, for the Tories to be removed from government and for her Whig friends to retain power. But

Anne, desperate to preserve her freedom of action between the competing political parties, refused. The result was that Sarah's company became increasingly disagreeable to the queen, who resented the political lectures and nagging. Lonely, unwell and in need of friendship, she transferred her affections to another courtier, Abigail Masham, who, unlike the domineering and high-handed Sarah, was demure and undemanding. Abigail was also close to the Tories, and her favour with the queen threatened to break the Whigs' monopoly on power. Sarah, outraged in turn, then accused the queen, in barely concealed terms, of lesbianism.

Sarah's loss of favour dangerously exposed Marlborough on the home front. For in any case, Anne, and much of the nation, was getting sick of the war, the deaths and the spiralling taxation. The turning point was Marlborough's last great set-piece battle of Malplaquet. It was an English victory of sorts. But the casualties were enormous and the French, faced with the invasion of their own soil, dug their heels in to fight a patriotic war. Marlborough's reaction was to demand the captain-generalship for life, like Oliver Cromwell. Anne's was to exclaim, 'when will this bloodshed ever cease?' and to decide that Marlborough must go.

Marlborough was dismissed in December 1711 and his Whig allies were replaced with a Tory ministry determined to make a unilateral peace with France. Secret negotiations were opened and agreement quickly reached. Louis XIV's grandson Philip would retain Spain and her American Empire, but renounce any future right to France. England would be granted huge exclusive commercial concessions in the Spanish Empire, including a

thirty-year monopoly on the slave trade. The Tories also had a
secret plot. They had provoked outrage in Europe by abandoning their allies. One very important loser in this matter was
Georg Ludwig, the Elector of Hanover and heir to Sophia, who
stood to inherit the English Crown. Once on the throne, Georg
would be unlikely to forget or forgive this gross betrayal. The
outcome of the Act of Succession would be to place the Tories
in danger. The leaders would therefore dump Hanover and
offer the Crown to the Old Pretender, *provided* he renounced
Catholicism.

The separate peace was formally agreed at Utrecht in 1713
and celebrated with yet another grand thanksgiving service in
St Paul's. And there was much to celebrate, since the peace,
despite its consciously moderate terms, marked England's
eclipse of the two powers that, only half a century before, had
overshadowed her: England was now more powerful militarily
than France and more commercially successful than the
Netherlands.

And she had found her own unique way to modernity. At
the root of this success was a new relationship between monarch
and Parliament, in which the sovereign reigned, but for the
most part the ministers ruled. Forged in the revolution of 1688,
developed under William and consolidated under Anne, this new
constitutional monarchy had proved more than a match for
the absolutist political model represented by France. Over the
coming centuries it would do so time and again.

But Anne, despite her passionate personal support for the
peace, was too frail to attend the ceremonies. On Christmas Eve
she fell suddenly and dangerously ill. She made a recovery of

sorts. But it was soon clear that she had only months, if not weeks, to live. The Tory ministers now made a secret offer of the Crown to the Old Pretender, subject only to his conversion. But James III had inherited his father's arrogance as well as his unyielding commitment to Catholicism. He now calculated that the Tories had so alienated Hanover that they would have to bring him back, conversion or no conversion, and refused point blank to change his religion.

That was the end of the Pretender's chances – and, it turned out, of the Tories' as well.

IV

On 30 July Anne suffered two violent strokes, which left her able to say only yes or no. Two days later, at the age of only forty-nine, she was dead, and Marlborough and his duchess, who had gone into ostentatious voluntary exile in disgust at the peace, returned in triumph to London.

Anne's reign was a paradox, between public power and popularity and personal physical weakness. The latter was unsparingly described by one of the Scottish Union commissioners in his account of an audience with the Queen:

> Her Majesty was labouring under a fit of the gout, and in extreme pain and agony . . . Her face, which was red and spotted, was rendered something frightful by her negligent dress, and the foot affected was tied up with a poultice and some nasty bandages . . . Nature seems to be

inverted when a poor infirm woman becomes one of the rulers of the world.

This was possible, of course, only because of the machinery of England's new constitutional monarchy, in which the queen was a powerful figurehead, but the actual government was left to ministers.

Nevertheless, a woman who could resist and finally face down Marlborough and his formidable duchess was nobody's tool. Likewise the peace with France was hers, as much as the Tories'. But her most important contribution was to remain steadfastly loyal – after her own fashion – to the Hanoverian succession. And so, England and Scotland were likely to get another female ruler, Sophia of Hanover. But Sophia died before she could inherit, and the heir to the British Crown was her son, Georg Ludwig.

When Anne died shortly after, the two principal claimants were both several hundred miles from London: Georg Ludwig in Hanover and the Old Pretender in Lorraine, where he had been forced to withdraw after the peace with France. If he had made a dash for it, the Old Pretender could have given the Hanoverian a run for his money. But James III did not do dashing.

Instead, correctly confident in the machinery of the Act of Settlement, George, as he now signed himself in English, took a leisurely six weeks to arrive in England. He landed at Greenwich on 18 September at 6 p.m. Accompanied by his son, Georg August, and a great crowd of nobles, gentry and common folk, he walked through the grand colonnades and courtyards of the Royal Naval Hospital to the Queen's House in the park, where he spent his first night in England.

The following morning, in the Queen's House, George held his first English court. He made plain his high regard for the leaders of the Whig party and he administered a very public snub to the Tory leader: he allowed him to kiss his hands but said nothing to him in return. If George had anything to do with it, the sun, it was clear, would shine on the Whigs, while the Tories were destined for the wilderness.

And George *did* have a lot to do with it, despite the constitutional nature of the monarchy. And royal influence, combined with distaste at the Tories' slitheriness about the Hanoverian succession, helped win the Whigs a comfortable majority in the Commons. They now turned the Tory defeat into a rout by impeaching the former Tory ministers for the treachery in the peace negotiations at Utrecht. One was sent to the Tower; the other fled to the Old Pretender to encourage his bid for the throne.

But at this moment, Louis XIV of France, the inveterate enemy of the new English monarchy and the principal casualty of its success, died and was succeeded by a regency that was committed to good relations with England. Deprived of French active support, a Jacobite rising conducted by northern English Catholics was easily defeated at Preston. But in Scotland, though the rebels were held back from the Lowlands by the drawn battle of Sherrifmuir, they took the Highlands and occupied Perth.

After lengthy delays and disguised as a French bishop, the Old Pretender finally set sail for Scotland, where he landed just before Christmas 1715. At first, it was a triumphal progress: the magistrates of Aberdeen paid him homage; he made a state entry into Dundee; and proclaimed his forthcoming coronation as King James VIII and III at Scone. He then took up residence at Scone Palace and kept his court with the royal state of his ancestors.

But, after this good start, things began to crumble. With his shy, cold public manner, James couldn't even keep the loyalty of his existing followers, let alone recruit new ones. 'If he found himself disappointed with us', one of his soldiers wrote, 'we were tenfold more so in him.' It was no basis on which to stand and fight the government forces that were marching on them through the snow of winter.

After retreating to Montrose the Old Pretender took ship secretly to France on 3 February 1716, abandoning his army to their fate. He never saw Britain again. The House of Hanover had seen off the Stuart dynasty.

The arrival of George I and ensuing triumph of the House of Hanover were also commemorated in the Painted Hall at Greenwich, a few paces from where George actually landed.

But that was the only realistic thing about the painting. Done in *grisaille* (or shades of grey) to imitate a Roman stone relief, it shows George arriving in a Roman triumphal chariot, while personifications of Tyrannic Power and Rebellious Despair quail before his harbinger, Liberty, with her cap.

The reality had been very different as the painter, James Thornhill, who had been an eye-witness and shows himself as such at the edge of the composition, well knew. It was night, he noted. George's clothes were unworthy of the event. And most of the receiving peers were Tories, which was the wrong political party. Hence, he explained, his decision to go for high-flown allegory.

But the sober reality had been right. George *was* a modest man and would preside over a modest monarchy. No British king would ever again inhabit a palace as large as Greenwich or hold court in a space as splendid as the Painted Hall. And if more and more of the globe would indeed be British, it was not the king but his ministers who made it so.

Nevertheless, Thornhill's vast swirling allegories were not wholly disproportionate to the events they represent. For the Revolution and its aftermath in the Hanoverian Succession *were* glorious. By good luck, as well as good management, Britain had freed herself from political and religious absolutism and in so doing freed herself for the rapid and most significant expansion of any European power since Rome. No wonder Thornhill, like most subsequent commentators on the British monarchy, was uncertain of what language he should use to describe the limitation the Crown and the triumph of the Nation.

EMPIRE

GEORGE I, GEORGE II, GEORGE III

IN 1782, FACED WITH a Commons motion to make peace with Britain's rebellious American colonies and recognize their independence, George III resolved to abdicate and return to his other kingdom of Hanover in Germany. He even got so far as drafting his abdication address:

> His Majesty ... with much sorrow finds he can be of no further utility to his native country, which drives him to the painful step of quitting it forever.
>
> In consequence ... his Majesty resigns the Crown of Great Britain ... to his ... son and lawful successor George, Prince of Wales, whose endeavours for the prosperity of the British Empire he hopes may prove more successful.

Was the House of Hanover about to go the way of its unlucky predecessors the Stuarts? And the British to lose the empire they had only recently won? If it had been left to the Hanoverians themselves, who were the least able and attractive house to sit on the British throne, it is unlikely there would have been much to lose in the first place.

But in fact Britain in the eighteenth century witnessed an extraordinary and unprecedented political development: the rise of a second, parallel monarchy in Britain – the premiership. It was monarchs of this new kind who created the first British Empire, and the old monarchy which eventually destroyed it.

The seeds of the premiership lay in the Glorious Revolution of 1688–89. But it was the accession of the House of Hanover in 1714, and the awkward, unattractive personalities of the first two Hanoverian kings, which accelerated its development and made it irreversible.

I

For most of the eighteenth century, the monarchy veered between deep unpopularity and a national joke. When George I became king in 1714 the English had, for the second time in thirty years, a foreign monarch. Indeed, George of Hanover was much *more* foreign than William of Orange. For William had an English mother, spoke fluent English and was married to an English princess. George, on the other hand, was resolutely, unremittingly German: he arrived with German ministers, German-speaking Turkish body-servants, and German mistresses. (Indeed, the mistresses had been a necessary part of his life since he condemned his wife to life imprisonment in a German castle following the discovery of her sensational affair with a Swedish count.) Even subsequently, he never learnt more than a few words of broken English and his interests remained essentially German too, centring on the welfare of his beloved north German principality, where he went whenever he could and stayed as long as possible.

It was all neatly symbolized by his heraldry, which showed the white horse of Hanover superimposed on the British royal coat of arms. Moreover, the German takeover of 1714 had consequences almost as momentous as those of the Dutch conquest of 1688. The conquest and the ensuing Glorious Revolution had been the work of Tories as well as Whigs and, for the following thirty years, the two parties had continued to alternate in power.

But George saw things very differently. Passionately interested in the military glory of Hanover, he blamed the Tories for the Peace of Utrecht, which halted the Grand Alliance's chances of a crushing victory over France and, more importantly for George, the aggrandizement of his beloved Hanover. He blamed them even more for their flirtation with his rival, the Old Pretender. The Tories, for their part, believed that the new monarch was really the puppet of the Whigs. Under the control of their opponents, they feared, the monarchy would become the powerless figurehead of a republic and the Church of England would lose its privileged status. For them, 1714 was the victory of the old parliamentary cause of the Civil Wars and the triumph of the Protestant dissenters.

Nor was George popular with the country. On the day of his coronation banners mocking the new king were displayed throughout the country. There were riots and talk of plots to restore the Stuarts. The general election of 1715 was violent, with more banners proclaiming 'No Hanover' and 'Down with the Roundheads'. And if the country seemed turbulent and dangerously polarized at the beginning of the reign, the king blamed it on the troublemaking Tories. Thus their prophesy that the new dynasty would exclude them in favour of the Whigs became self-fulfilling. Tories were deprived of office at every level, down to the gardener at Dublin Castle. George was certainly no natural supporter of the Whigs, but circumstances dictated that if he had anything to do with it, the sun would shine on them and not the Tories.

And George *did* have a lot to do with it, and royal influence, combined with distaste at the Tories' slitheriness about the Hanoverian succession, helped win the Whigs a comfortable majority in the Commons. The Whigs now turned the Tory defeat into a rout by impeaching the former Tory ministers for the treachery in the peace negotiations at Utrecht. One was sent to the Tower; the other fled to the Old Pretender to encourage his bid for the throne.

It was a century before the Tories would win a general election again, and sixty years before a Tory held high political office. The resulting long Whig domination has been hailed as the Restoration of Political Stability. It could equally be characterized as six decades of one-party rule, with all the problems of one-party rule that our own times have familiarized us with once more. For the Whig consensus was dogged by bitter internal division and competing factions. And this struggle became linked with another poisonous dispute – within the new German royal family itself.

'The Hanoverians', it has been cruelly said, 'like pigs, trample their young.' The dictim was exemplified by the very public mutual loathing of fathers and eldest sons. There was good reason for this in 1714. At first sight, George's eldest son, George Augustus, Prince of Wales, was a much more attractive character than his father. He was married to a vivacious, intelligent wife, Caroline. He was as fond of public pomp and circumstance as his reclusive father detested it. He had displayed conspicuous bravery at the Battle of Oudenarde, where he fought on the English side under Marlborough and had his horse killed under him in the thick of the fighting. He spoke voluble, if heavily accented, English and had thoroughly acquainted himself with English affairs. Indeed, he played the English card shamelessly and proclaimed, rather unconvincingly, 'I have not one drop of blood in my veins dat is not English.'

Matters between father and son came to a head in 1716, when the king, who had been pining for Germany, returned to Hanover for a six-month visit. Custom dictated that the prince should have been left as regent; instead, an obscure precedent was dug out from the Middle Ages and he was created 'guardian and lieutenant of the realm' with severely restricted powers. All important decisions would be referred to the king in Hanover, as if his son were simply incapable of any kind of responsibility. The prince was left feeling humiliated and sidelined.

But still the prince *was* the figurehead of government and he and Caroline determined to exploit the fact for all that it was worth. On 25 July the prince and princess and their daughters moved to Hampton Court, where, with a short interval, they remained for four months. Many people were angry that the new king had so little respect for his new people that he had left the kingdom as soon as he could. As was said, George 'is already become the Jest, the Contempt and Aversion of the Nation'. He had been cuckolded by his wife, whom he had been forced to lock up; he had two ugly mistresses nicknamed 'the elephant and the maypole' for their mismatched appearance; and he was stiff and humourless. All this was ripe for jokes and innuendo. But George's ill-disguised dislike for England was offensive. His son and daughter-in-law, on the other hand, made great effort to show that they at least were pleased to be in England. And the young couple won popularity and loyalty for it.

Hampton Court Palace had lain unfinished and largely neglected since William III's death. But now it burst into life as George and Caroline moved into the state apartments, which had been specially refurbished for them, and kept the kind of splendid open court that had not been seen in England since the days of Charles II. It attracted the aristocracy and politicians, poets such as Alexander Pope, the writer Joseph Addison and scientists including Isaac Newton and Edward Halley. Once again, there was a flourishing court culture and a popular prince. The royal couple dined in public, held balls, fêtes and picnics; they also went on a successful tour of the South-East.

George I reacted to his son's public favour with jealous rage and, when he returned to England, entered – against all his instincts and preferences – into a public-relations war with the prince. So in the following summer of 1717, the king himself took up residence at Hampton Court, alongside the prince and princess. In uncomfortable proximity in the same building, the two adjacent but rival courts continued to maintain different styles: the king's studiously informal, the Waleses' preserving something of the traditional formality of the English court, with the consequent need for grand state apartments, like the Guard Chamber and, beyond it, the Presence Chamber, which were designed for them by Sir John Vanbrugh. It was a war of style and culture, and the prince and princess seemed to be winning it.

But King George had his own genius with whom to strike back: George Frideric Handel. On 17 July, just before his departure for Hampton Court, the king bade farewell to the capital in fine style with a grand water party to Chelsea and back. Accompanying the royal party was a barge with a large band of fifty musicians, who played the music that Handel had composed for the occasion. The king liked it so much that he had it 'played over three times in going and returning'. And no wonder, for it was Handel's *Water Music*. Let the Prince of Wales try to beat that!

In November the royal family returned from Hampton Court to London for the winter season. Within a few weeks the quarrel between father and son became an open breach, and the king ordered the Waleses in writing to leave St James's Palace. In the new year they took up residence at Leicester House, in what is now Leicester Square. There were now two rival courts in London; Tories and dissident Whigs flocked to Leicester House in the expectation that when Prince George came to the throne they would be the favoured few. And the Jacobites rejoiced at the family feud, which, they hoped and prayed, presaged the fall of the House of Hanover.

II

One of the leading members of the Leicester House Set, as the followers of the Prince of Wales were known, was the up-and-coming Whig politician Sir Robert Walpole. Walpole, the son of a middling Norfolk squire, was a mountain of a man, with a gigantic appetite: for food and drink, sex, money, power – and work. He was shrewd, affable (when it suited him) and knew the price of everything and everyone. But, despite his coarseness and corpulence, he was attractive to women and understood them thoroughly.

What he understood most of all, however, was the House of Commons, of which he was the long-time undisputed master. For such a man, opposition, even when sanctioned by the Prince of Wales, was of limited appeal. For one thing, George I showed no signs of dying any time soon and no man could gain power without access to the patronage that was the gift of the monarch, even if he had Parliament on his side. So in 1720 Walpole brokered a general reconciliation of sorts: between the king and the prince and within the fractured Whig Party. But what propelled him to undisputed power was his handling of the financial crisis known as the South Sea Bubble.

For the Glorious Revolution not only brought in modern public finance, with the Bank of England and the national debt, it also introduced other, less obviously desirable features of capitalist modernity such as the stock market, speculation and boom and bust. And the South Sea Bubble was the mother of all busts.

The centre of this feverish activity was the Royal Exchange, where shares in ventures like the South Sea Company were traded. The company had been established in 1711 as a Tory riposte to the Whig-dominated Bank of England. Its original purpose was to reduce the burden of the national debt by converting loans to the government into shares in the company. The company did have real assets, in particular the *assiento* or forty-year monopoly on the slave trade to Spanish America, which the Tories had won at the Peace of Utrecht. But its value was talked up beyond all reason. In March 1720 South Sea Company shares stood at 170, before peaking at 1050 on 24 June. Then they crashed, bottoming out at 290.

Everybody got their fingers burnt; still worse, everybody seemed to have their fingers in the pie: from the king, who had been made governor of the company, to his mistresses and his ministers, who had all received significant gifts of shares. Everybody, that is, apart from Walpole. With his usual good luck, he had been out of favour when the final scam was launched and so, for once in his life, appeared as whiter than white. He also used his financial skill to wind the crisis down, without provoking either a financial or a political meltdown.

On the other hand, his Whig rivals fell victim to the cry for vengeance: one died of a heart attack after angry scenes in Parliament; another committed suicide; and a third was sent to the Tower. With rivals eliminated and his own reputation riding high, Walpole emerged as unchallenged first or 'prime' minister.

And he made sure to advertise the fact to the world. Houghton Hall, which Walpole built on the site of his modest ancestral home in north Norfolk, symbolized his immense power. He moved with his usual purposeful expedition. Designs were commissioned in 1721, the year his premiership began; the foundation stone was laid the next year and the building was finished in 1735. And for 'the Great Man', as he soon became known, nothing but the best would do. Walpole built with the best materials; he used the finest architects and designers, such as William Kent, who was responsible for the opulently gilded interiors and furniture; and he embellished the house with the biggest and best collection of pictures in England.

The result was perfection: according to one contemporary connoisseur, it was 'the greatest house in the world for its size' and 'a pattern for all great houses that may hereafter be built'. But at first it seemed as though Walpole might have counted his chickens before they were hatched. For in the summer of 1727 George I died, fittingly en route to Hanover. At first, his son refused to believe the news, thinking that it was another trick played by his father to entrap him into incautious expressions of joy. But once George II was persuaded of its truth, he made clear that the monarchy would be transformed from the dour, reclusive and Germanized version that Britain had suffered for thirteen years.

He indulged his love of splendour by having a magnificent coronation with music by Handel, whose great anthem, *Zadoc the Priest and Nathan the Prophet crownèd Solomon King*, has been played at every subsequent coronation. He vowed that unlike his father he would rule as a *British* king, not a reluctant German. Queen Caroline said that she would 'as soon live on a dunghill as return to Hanover'. There would be other radical changes with the new reign. Above all, George told Walpole, whom he had never forgiven for going over to his father, to take his marching orders.

But Walpole kept his head. He still had a large following in the House of Commons and showed his usefulness by getting it to vote George a bigger Civil List (or personal income) than his father. But for all his abilities and backing in Parliament, Walpole could remain in office only as long as he retained his favour with the king. He tried to make sure of this by appointing his followers to court positions so that no faction could be built against him. Such Walpole courtiers controlled access to the royal family, and they could exclude the Prime Minister's enemies from gaining the king's ear.

But most importantly, he had a powerful ally. Other politicians had paid court to George's insipid mistress. But Walpole knew better. Instead, he rebuilt his close friendship with Queen Caroline, whom he had betrayed in 1720: 'I have the right sow by the ear,' he boasted ungallantly. He was right and Caroline played a vital role in managing her husband – who quickly turned out to be even more curmudgeonly and more in love with Hanover than his father and much less intelligent – on Walpole's behalf. Together they subtly governed the king, directing him towards Walpole's policies. The minister and the queen would meet in secret, so that she could discuss matters with the king before Walpole had his private interview. Thus primed when the Prime Minister met George, the king would already have been manipulated into agreement. Walpole had nothing but praise for the queen's arts in moulding the king's mind: she 'can make him propose the very thing as his own opinion which a week before he had rejected as mine'. And

Walpole was skilful at keeping Caroline herself onside, flattering her with carefully chosen compliments. 'Your Majesty knows that this country is entirely in your hands,' he would lie, to the queen's delight.

In fact, the country was in Walpole's hands, as his premiership sailed on over the blip of George II's accession. But it trembled once more ten years later. George and Caroline had an odd marital relationship: he had numerous affairs and snubbed her all the time in public, but she always bounced back and was able to control him. Nevertheless, when Caroline fell fatally ill in 1737, George was heartbroken and tearfully refused her deathbed injunction to marry again by exclaiming: 'No! I'll have mistresses!' Walpole's premiership survived, even though he was terrified that the easily led George would fall under the spell of someone hostile to him now that Caroline was dead. He remained as Prime Minister, however, despite being deprived of his greatest ally. But now his enemies were gathering strength. Most important was the group known as 'Cobham's Cubs', who gathered round Richard Temple, Viscount Cobham. Cobham was a soldier, a statesman – and a landscape gardener.

His greatest creation was the garden at Stowe, his Buckinghamshire estate. Vistas, trees and water were punctuated with artfully sited temples to create the sort of idyllic classical landscape imagined by painters like Nicolas Poussin and Claude Lorrain. It was intended to delight the eye – but also to exercise the mind. One of the classical monuments was the Temple of British Worthies. It is a Whig pantheon, with, on the left, the proponents of political liberty, such as the poet John Milton and the philosopher John Locke, and, on the right, the heroes of the struggle against Catholic Spain and France, such as Elizabeth I and William of Orange. But there was another, very different monument. It looked like a ruin containing a damaged, headless statue. Actually it was built like this. The ruin was satirically entitled the Temple of Modern Virtue, while the ugly, headless torso was 'the Great Man', Walpole himself.

For Walpole, Cobham and his Cubs believed, had comprehensively betrayed Whig principles by stealing the Tories' clothes. The Whigs had been the great anti-court party, determined to keep the powers of the king within bounds. But Walpole discovered that the way to keep office was to cultivate the king's favour and then use the royal patronage – of titles, jobs and straightforward bribes – to control Parliament. Whig heroes, or *Worthies*, should not be court toadies, as the oleaginous Walpole had become. The Whigs had also been the war party. But both the king and Walpole wanted peace with France: George to protect Hanover and Walpole to restore the public finances from the effects of the vast expense of Marlborough's wars.

Faced with mounting opposition, in 1742 Walpole won what amounted to a vote of confidence by only 253 votes to 250. The margin of victory was too small for effective government and three weeks later Walpole resigned. Within three years, deprived of the energizing effects of power, he was dead. And at first it seemed as though he might, like Samson, bring down the pillars of the Hanoverian temple with him.

For 1745 showed every sign of being a catastrophic year for Britain. In April, the French, against whom Walpole had reluctantly resumed hostilities, defeated the British under

William, Duke of Cumberland, the king's second and favourite son, at the great Battle of Fontenoy in Belgium. Still worse, the French victory opened the way to another Stuart invasion of Britain. It was led by the Old Pretender's eldest son, Charles Edward. Aged only twenty-four, and tall, handsome and dashing, 'Bonny Prince Charlie' had all the Stuart charisma and charm that his father and grandfather had so conspicuously lacked.

He landed in the Outer Hebrides in June. At first the Highlands were slow to respond. But over the summer the rebellion gathered force. By September, Charles had taken Edinburgh, routed the tiny Hanoverian army in Scotland and announced the dissolution of the Union. In November, he invaded England and got as far as Derby before the failure of the English to rally to his cause forced him to retreat back to Scotland.

The final battle took place at Culloden in April 1746, when Charles's Highland army was confronted by a much larger, better-disciplined professional force under Cumberland. This personal struggle between two royal princes for the Crown was like an episode of the Wars of the Roses, and both the battle and the repression of the Highlands after Charles's inevitable defeat were medieval in their savagery.

Charles, after many hardships and adventures, escaped, to die an early death of alcoholism and disillusionment; while Jacobitism itself died too – or rather, perhaps, was killed by Cumberland's scorched-earth policy after Culloden.

The Forty-Five was a turning point. Scotland threw itself more heartily into the Union, which was now yielding visible economic benefits; while in England the Tories, freed at last from the incubus of Jacobitism, were able to re-enter ordinary political life. But the greatest beneficiary of the year of crisis was Cobham's nephew by marriage, William Pitt the Elder, who was to emerge, despite George II's profound personal loathing, as the most remarkable politician of the age.

III

Of all the shades we can imagine wandering through the Elysian Fields of Stowe amid the follies and temples, William Pitt's is the greatest – and the strangest. The favourite grandson of Thomas 'Diamond' Pitt, a tough, irascible East India merchant who had made a fortune and founded a gentry family, Pitt had first been introduced to Cobham in his thirties when his dazzling parliamentary oratory against Walpole had immediately made him one of the leading Cubs. The connection became much closer when, years later, Pitt married the childless Cobham's niece, Hester. The couple were middle-aged – he was forty-six and she was thirty-four – but it was a passionate courtship that led to a devoted marriage.

Hester often acted as her husband's secretary; even more importantly, she was his nurse. For Pitt was plagued with illness, physical and mental, and subject to swings of emotion, from elation to prostration, that were so extreme as to sometimes amount to madness. At their worst, his mood changes laid him low for months on end; at their best they drove him to heights of oratory that convinced his hearers that he was the voice of destiny: Britain's destiny.

And that national destiny too was prefigured in the Temple of British Worthies at Stowe with its roll-call of naval heroes: King Alfred, who was honoured as founder of the English navy; Sir Francis Drake, who became the first Englishman to sail round the globe in an expedition of magnificent, insolent plundering of the riches of the Spanish Empire; Queen Elizabeth I, who had knighted Drake and gave her name to the first great age of English sea power and Sir Walter Raleigh, Drake's younger contemporary, who first projected an English colonial empire in America. Completing the pantheon of greats is the Elizabethan merchant-prince, Sir Thomas Gresham, who stabilized the coinage and founded the Royal Exchange. Britain, in this version of history, was founded on the marriage of buccaneering sailors and solid mercantile wealth.

And Pitt, himself the grandson of a merchant-robber-baron-cum-empire-builder, took these ideas and made them his own. The result can be boiled down to three axioms. First, the proper field of British endeavour was overseas and worldwide, not Continental and European; second, the navy, not the army, was the right instrument to advance British power; and third, overseas trade was the means to the wealth, and hence the power, of the nation.

All this was guaranteed to set Pitt on a collision course with George II that was both personal and political. For the king, who had led his army to victory against the French at Dettingen in 1743 at the ripe age of sixty, regarded the army as his own peculiar pride and joy. He was also as devoted to Hanover as his father and, like him, regarded foreign policy as the flower of his prerogative.

As such, he was overjoyed at the victory at Dettingen. And he expected that his subjects would share the celebrations of their victorious king when he returned home with Handel's *Dettingen te deum* ringing in his ears. He was the last British monarch to personally lead an army in battle, and he had done so bravely. But there were those who would downplay his success, in particular William Pitt, who sneeringly disparaged it in Parliament: 'His Majesty was exposed to few or no dangers abroad, such as the overturning of a coach or the stumbling of his horse.' But there was more pointed criticism than the merely personal. A sizeable group in Parliament did not think that Britain should be fighting in Europe for the sake of Hanover at all. Indeed, victory or no victory, it was a betrayal of Britain. Pitt spoke for them too: 'It is now too apparent that this great, this powerful, this formidable kingdom is considered only a province to a despicable electorate,' he declared. 'We need only look at the instances of particularity that have been shown; the yearly visits that have been made to that delightful country.'

Such language was unforgivable. And George was a good hater with an excellent memory for slights. The result was that Pitt spent the next decade in a sort of political limbo. He was admitted to government and in office because he was both too useful and too dangerous in Parliament not to be. But he was not in power because the royal veto prevented it. This was frustrating for someone as aware of his own abilities as Pitt. But it did give him the opportunity to reconsider his instinctive opposition to Continental alliances; indeed, he became something of a convert – as he proclaimed with his accustomed breathtaking effrontery. 'I have,' he confided to the House of

Commons, 'upon some former occasions, by the heat of youth and the warmth of a debate, been hurried into expressions, which upon cool reflexion, I have heartily regretted.' Being Pitt, he got away with it.

Being Pitt also, his moment came. War with France broke out again in 1756 and it began disastrously with the loss of Minorca and the control of the Mediterranean. Popular clamour arose for the punishment of the commanding officer, Admiral Byng, who was shot on his own quarterdeck – to encourage, as Voltaire acidly observed, the rest. The cry also went up for Pitt: 'I know', he said, 'I can save this country and no one else can.' In the circumstances, George had to yield to his appointment as secretary of state with the direction of the war, albeit with a bad grace.

Almost immediately, the tide of war began to turn. For Pitt was a new sort of minister, who demanded – and got – a new sort of control over both policy and its detailed execution. There was a uniform, overarching strategy, which combined Continental and overseas war. Britain's principal Continental ally, Frederick the Great of Prussia, was given money but no men, while both money and men were flung to the far corners of the globe against the key points of France's colonial empire. For this too was to be a new sort of war in which no quarter was given: 'his administration [would] decide which alone should exist as a nation, Britain or France.'

The result caught France in a vice. On the Continent, the military genius of Frederick the Great kept up the pressure, against formidable odds. But what was decisive in the wider struggle was the quality of the British navy. For Britain had moved fast to equip itself with the infrastructure to meet the requirements of worldwide war. The great dockyard at Chatham was the jewel in the crown of the new policy. The naval dockyards were then by far the largest industrial establishments in Britain, and only a hundred years later, in the nineteenth century, did private enterprise begin to catch up – in size, managerial efficiency and technical sophistication. Britain had four or five dry docks, like the ones that still exist in Chatham, to France's one. And they were bigger and better too. The pulleys and tackle for manoeuvring sails were much superior. British naval stores of food and drink were also better, longer lasting – and half the price.

This transformed the scope of British naval and combined operations. At the beginning of the eighteenth century a ship was lucky to be able to remain at sea for more than a fortnight; fifty years later cruises of three months and more were common. With voyages of this length, and the technical expertise to run them, all the world was now a stage for Pitt's great imperial drama.

It was fought in four principal theatres: Canada, the West Indies, Africa and India. In each, Pitt was victorious: General Wolfe defeated the French general Montcalm on the Heights of Abraham before Quebec in 1759 and all Canada fell the following year; at the same time, Martinique and Guadeloupe were captured in the West Indies and Dakar in Africa; Clive carried all before him in India, while both the northern and southern French fleets were smashed in European waters, giving Britain what she often asserted but rarely held: an absolute mastery of the sea. 'Our bells', wrote Horace Walpole, the witty, waspish son of the great Sir Robert, 'are quite worn threadbare with ringing for victories. Indeed, one is forced to ask every morning, "what victory is there?" for fear of missing one.'

It was a triumph too for Stowe and its new master, Pitt's brother-in-law, Earl Temple. The landscape was once more transformed with fresh shrines to British prowess and her new generation of heroes, more than equal to Alfred, Drake, Elizabeth, William III and all the other Worthies of history. An obelisk was erected in memory of General Wolfe, who had been killed at the moment of victory at Quebec. The Temple of Concord and Victory depicted an enthroned Britannia receiving tribute from the rest of the world. A selection of heraldic icons also mark a victory, one that was just as hard fought and won over a foe nearer home. They represent the august Order of the Garter, an honour on which Pitt's brother-in-law had set his heart.

But George loathed Temple even more than he did Pitt. Nevertheless, Pitt insisted and the king had to back down and confer the coveted honour. But he made his feelings plain at the investiture. Instead of decorously placing the ribbon over Temple's shoulder, as etiquette demanded, he threw it at him and immediately turned his back. Faced with the power of Pitt, the King of Great Britain was reduced to making an impotent protest, like a naughty child. Pitt was able thus to humiliate the king, not only because he was uniquely successful, but also because he had a new sort of power. He had been called to office, he asserted, 'by his sovereign' – which was conventional – and 'by the voice of the people' – which was a radical and bold claim.

Not even Walpole could boast that. Now, as George II

moaned, 'Ministers are Kings in this Country'. Frustration built up over the years; when he was in Hanover in 1755 he almost did not go back to England: 'There are Kings enough in England. I am nothing there. I am old and want rest, and should only go to be plagued and teased there about the damned House of Commons.' In 1727, when he had come to the throne, a minister as formidable as Robert Walpole had to win and retain royal favour, as his assiduous and unctuous flattery of Queen Caroline showed. Since then, the king had been forced to accept men he hated as ministers, above all William Pitt, who never ceased to denigrate his beloved Hanover and oppose Continental wars. Power was no longer gained by a minister's standing at court and personal relationship with the king, but by his ability to break down the doors and impose himself on the sovereign. How had George found himself in this situation at the end of his long reign?

Partly, it was simply a matter of Pitt's translation of his war aims into bold and vivid language that had a resonance far beyond Parliament. But there were also more concrete alliances, like the one commemorated in the Guildhall, the centre of the government of the City of London. Pitt's own statue dominates the hall. But standing up on high to equal the great Prime Minister is the statue of Alderman William Beckford, million-aire, City politician and radical press lord, who marshalled City opinion behind Pitt with his weekly paper, *The Monitor*. Imperial might, parliamentary legitimacy and prime ministerial power stood four-square with City finance, mercantile wealth and the press.

Winston Churchill, who resembled Pitt in so many ways,

called the Seven Years War 'the first world war'. But unlike the world wars of the twentieth century, it did not exhaust the country. When it began, Britain was one of two or three leading European powers. When it ended, she was all powerful and mistress of the first empire to stretch across four continents. But George was not there to see it and Pitt was not in office either.

IV

The morning of 25 October 1760 began like any other for George II. He rose early, drank his chocolate and retired to relieve himself on his close-stool. But there, without a day's illness or a moment's warning, he died, at about 7.30 a.m.

The gruff, choleric seventy-seven-year-old was succeeded by his grandson, the fresh-faced, twenty-two-year-old George III. George had been a late developer. Sulky, idle and apparently rather dim at first, he had been transformed in his late teens by a sympathetic mentor into a paragon of hard work and self-discipline. He was intensely musical, fluent in French and German, a competent draughtsman and an omnivorous bibliophile with a particular interest in history.

He had been a late developer sexually too. But following his marriage, eleven months after his accession, to Charlotte of Mecklenburg-Strelitz, he made up for lost time by fathering no fewer than fifteen children.

Above all, he was aware, unlike his two predecessors, that

he was English through and through – by birth and by inclination. He was also determined to fulfil his duties, as he saw them, as a patriotic British king. Perhaps, indeed, he was too determined, too demanding – both of others and, critically, of himself.

The clash with the great war minister, William Pitt, who saw himself as having something of a monopoly on patriotism, came within hours. In his accession speech, given at 6 p.m. on the day of his grandfather's death, George referred to the 'bloody war' in which Britain was engaged. At Pitt's outraged insistence, this was toned down to 'expensive but just and necessary war' in the published version. Within the year, however, Pitt had resigned and in 1763 the Treaty of Paris was signed, bringing the war to a triumphant conclusion.

Triumphant or not, the war still had to be paid for. So, too, did the new British Empire. The war had doubled the national debt, from £70,000,000 to £140,000,000. This meant that interest payments alone totalled £4,000,000 a year, or half the tax revenue. Ongoing costs had multiplied as well. Before the war, the annual cost of the American establishment was £75,000. Now it had increased more than fourfold to £350,000. All this fell on a British population of only eight million. Why shouldn't, ministers asked, British America bear a part? After all, the war, as Pitt had repeatedly stated, had been fought on their behalf, and they had been its principal beneficiaries with the removal of the threat from the French in Canada and the French allies among the Indian tribes. As Pitt had said in 1755, 'The present war was undertaken for the long-injured, long-neglected, long-forgotten people of America.' France had been expelled from much of North America while Britain and her allies tied up the French in Europe. 'America had been conquered in Germany,' Pitt bluntly asserted.

And there is no doubt that British America had deep pockets. Philadelphia, New York and Boston were large and rich; Charleston was catching up fast. And these were only the urban centres of an overwhelmingly rural economy in which about two million people were unevenly divided between thirteen colonies. The colonies were wildly different in size, religious complexion, economic interest and geographical focus, and were almost as suspicious of each other as of the British government. Nevertheless, there *was* a sense of British America – and of the fact that it was already four or five times the size of Old England.

February 12 1765 was a quiet day in the House of Commons, with only a Bill to tap American wealth by imposing stamp duty on American property and legal transactions to be debated. As colonial business rarely aroused much interest (unless Pitt was displaying his pyrotechnics), the Bill was nodded through an almost empty chamber with minimal opposition.

But the Stamp Act set America alight. For the British Parliament was not the only one in the British Empire. Indeed, in America there were thirteen such assemblies – one for each colony – which, in their own worlds, thought themselves the equal of the Westminster Parliament.

The eighteenth-century Capitol in Williamsburg, was the seat of the General Assembly of the Colony of Virginia. The Assembly was the oldest colonial legislative, first meeting on 20 July 1619. It was the closest in structure to Westminster, consisting of an elected Lower House, presided over by a

Speaker, a nominated Upper House and the Royal Governor, who opened the sessions with a speech and wielded the veto on all Bills. Above all, perhaps, the personnel of the Virginian Assembly was nearest to that of the Westminster Parliament, since it was dominated by wealthy gentleman-planters, like the Lee family of Stratford Hall.

Stratford Hall, built in the 1730s, is a not-so-miniature version of an English country house. And the Lees, with their wealth derived from the surrounding tobacco plantation cultivated by dozens of black slaves, lived a provincial version of the life of the English country gentlemen who made up the great bulk of Westminster MPs, and they displayed a similar self-confidence and sense of their own importance. Thus it was that, on 30 May 1765, with Lees in the lead, the Virginian Assembly passed the first resolution against the Stamp Act. This solemnly declared that 'the taxation of the people by themselves, or by persons chosen to represent them ... is the distinguishing characteristic of British freedom, without which the ancient constitution cannot exist'.

This was Whig language turned against the British Parliament that had first invented it. Less decorously, as the date for the coming into operation of the Stamp Act approached, Richard Henry Lee organized a protest procession, featuring his own slaves in costume and the mock-hanging of the collector of stamp duties. Similar resolutions and protests, many of them violent, spread like wildfire across the colonies, and British America became ungovernable. Wholly unprepared for the reaction, the Westminster Parliament repealed the Stamp Act. But it tried to preserve the principle of British parliamentary sovereignty by declaring that Westminster was competent to pass laws for the British colonies 'in all cases whatsoever'.

There remained only the little matter of translating the principle into practice. This every succeeding British government tried to do and failed. American resistance continued and the net yield of American taxation, at a few hundred pounds a year, was derisory. A final attempt was made in 1773. The usual British duty of 12 pence a pound on tea was lifted and a low American duty of 3 pence imposed. The effect was to make tea cheaper in America than in Britain, and the 'Sons of Liberty', as the American radical opposition called themselves, were afraid that Americans, who loved their tea, might sell their liberty for a nice, cheap cuppa.

To forestall them, in December 1763 they perpetrated 'the Boston Tea Party', in which forty or fifty 'patriots', disguised as Mohawk Indians, boarded three ships in the harbour and forcibly threw 343 chests of tea overboard. Goaded beyond endurance, the British government took a hard line at last. The port of Boston was closed, the Massachusetts Assembly remodelled and British troops exempted from trial by American juries.

But instead of being cowed, the Americans summoned a Continental Congress of representatives from all thirteen colonies to coordinate their response to the coercive British measures. Once again, the Virginian Assembly, meeting as usual in Williamsburg and steered by Richard Henry Lee, had taken the lead. But the most interesting Virginian initiative had its origins in the College of William and Mary, which lies at the other end of Duke of Gloucester Street from the Capitol.

The college was the Virginian University and the second

oldest of the seven university colleges in colonial America. And
it was here that Thomas Jefferson, who came from the same
wealthy, slave-owning background as Lee, became a student and
began to form the ideas expressed in the paper he wrote for
the forthcoming Continental Congress. Entitled 'The Summary
View of the Rights of British Americans', it takes the Whig idea
that all government ultimately depends on a social contract,
entered into by the people in a state of nature, and applies it
brilliantly to America.

In Old England the state of nature was a mere abstraction
– albeit a very useful one. But in America it was real – in
the endless, rolling acres of Jefferson's native Virginia. Here,
Jefferson points out, his ancestors had come, voluntarily, to a
New World, occupied and cultivated it by their own efforts,
formed their own societies and chosen and established their own
forms of government. Therefore, for the British Parliament,
which represented only the British people, to presume to legislate for the people of America, who already had their own representatives in their own assemblies, was a gross usurpation.
Instead, only George himself, as king and ultimate sovereign of
America, had a right to intervene.

This idea of a monarch who, as sovereign of free and independent peoples, holds an empire together was both ingenious and far
sighted. Indeed, it became the foundation of Britain's twentieth-
century imperial policy as the Empire evolved into the Commonwealth of self-governing dominions, united only by allegiance
to a common crown. But in the circumstances of the eighteenth
century it was impossible.

Parliament and premier had only just got some sort of

control of the monarchy. To allow George to become King of America would be to give the Crown a new and expanding power base that might once again allow the old monarchy to challenge the new. Nor did George want the power of an American monarch independent of Parliament, for he was far too loyal to the settlement that had brought the Hanoverians to the throne. Instead, he threw his weight behind the British Parliament's determination to impose its will on the rebellious colonies. 'I will never make my inclinations alone nor even my own opinions the sole rule of my conduct in public measures,' he said, confirming the power of the premiership. 'I will at all times consult my ministers and place in them as entire a confidence as the nature of this government can be supposed to require of me.' If the minister had been Pitt, there is little doubt he would have succeeded. But faced by a weak Prime Minister, the king himself increasingly emerged as the figurehead of the struggle. The result was indecision and disarray.

Troops, including German regiments personally raised by the king, were dispatched, and in April 1775 the first armed clash, in which the colonials acquitted themselves surprisingly well against seasoned professional troops, took place near Boston, at Lexington. The Americans took this as a declaration of war and a month later in May the Second Continental Congress convened in the State House in Philadelphia, the seat of the Pennsylvania Assembly, to organize military resistance. On 15 June Congress appointed George Washington as commander-in-chief of the American army.

It could not have chosen better. For Washington, though not a great general, *was* a great man. He was another product

of the planter gentry of Virginia, where his family were neigh-
bours of the Lees of Stratford Hall. As a younger son, he became
an officer in the Virginian militia; played an honourable part in
the Seven Years War against the French; and tried but failed to
get a commission in the British army. Marriage to a rich widow
and deaths in his own family now enabled him to acquire his
own plantation at Mount Vernon, where the mansion house,
modest at first, was steadily enlarged and beautified over the
years.

But despite his new-found wealth and status, Washington
never lost his interest in military affairs, and he turned up to
the congress in Philadelphia in uniform and using his rank of
colonel in the militia. As commander-in-chief, Washington
found himself in charge of a motley crew: badly armed, badly
fed and clothed and badly paid when they were paid at all. To
keep them in the field required tact, occasional firmness and
infinite dogged patience. Washington had them all. He also had
the natural leadership of a born-and-bred American gentleman.

The Continental Congress reconvened the following year at
Philadelphia. The fighting had hardened positions and in June
Richard Henry Lee of Virginia moved the resolution for indepen-
dence, while his fellow Virginian, Thomas Jefferson, drafted the
Declaration itself, which was adopted on 4 July 1776 and became
the Ark of the Covenant of the new republic.

Subsequent generations have focused on the grand principles
of the preamble, with its ringing assertion (written by a slave-
owner, of course) that all men, being born free and equal, have
the right to determine how and by whom they are governed.
Contemporaries were more interested in its violent and highly

NCORDIÆ ET VICTORIÆ

3

Contrasting ministers: (2) Sir Robert Walpole and (3) William Pitt the Elder.
The accession of the Hanoverians, with their German culture and interests, led to the
emergence of a second, elective monarchy in the office of Prime Minister, first held by
Walpole. Pitt, in contrast to the pacific Walpole, was the great war minister, who guided
Britain to the triumphs of the Seven Years War (1756-63). The war, celebrated in the
pediment of the (1) Temple of Peace and Victory, built by Pitt's brother-in-law at
Stowe, made Britain the first world power.

1

Two revolutions. In 1775, the thirteen British American colonies, ably led by (1) George
Washington, rose in rebellion; the following year, (2) Thomas Jefferson, a member of the same
Virginian gentry as Washington, drafted the Declaration of Independence. The Declaration turned
the Whig arguments, to which Jefferson had been introduced at the (3) College of William and
Mary in Williamsburg, against the British Parliament which had first formulated them.

George III in Coronation robes (4). The failure of the war against American Independence to which George had been deeply opposed, made the king very unpopular. Conversely, the war against revolutionary France highlighted his modestly straightforward virtues and made him, even in his long years of senility, Father of the Nation. The French absolute monarchy, which had aided the Americans, paid the price in 1789 with the French Revolution. (5) Louis XVI was guillotined in 1793 and the Terror began. Long before, (6) Edmund Burke, MP had prophesied the direction the Revolution would take and denounced its doctrine of change for change's sake as dangerous and destructive.

4

5

6

1

2   3

The French revolutionary wars, in which Britain led a European coalition against France, led to the emergence of the great general, (1) Napoleon Bonaparte, seen here dividing the globe with the British Prime Minister, William Pitt the Younger, as self-proclaimed Emperor of the French. Napoleon's flamboyant imperial style set the fashion for the older European monarchies, including Britain. Here, the Prince of Wales, acting as Prince Regent for his father, King George III who had lapsed into a demented senility, laid out (3) Regent Street in direct competition with Napoleon's rebuilding of Paris and, when he succeeded as (2) George IV, presided, in full Highland Dress, over a grand historical pageant in Edinburgh which succeeded in attaching Scottish nationalism to the Hanoverians.

1

2

3

Britain escaped revolution but, by the time the bluff ex-sailor (1) William IV succeeded in 1830, the pressure for Parliamentary Reform was overwhelming. But resistance from the Tories was equally strong and it was William, aided by his able private secretary, (2) Sir Herbert Taylor, who brokered the agreement which led to the (3) Reformed House of Commons, painted here in 1833.

Parliamentary Reform produced a new middle-class electorate with new, moralistic values. The monarchy adapted successfully to these, thanks above all to Prince Albert who married Queen Victoria in 1840. Albert created the royal domesticity shown in (1) the *Family Portrait of Victoria and Albert and their Children*; he also involved himself knowledgeably in the new industrial technologies by master-minding the (2) Great Exhibition, which he and Victoria are shown opening in 1851.

personal repudiation of allegiance to George III as a tyrant and 'unfit to be the ruler of a free people'. But the immediate importance of the Declaration lay elsewhere, in the claim that, as Free and Independent States, the United Colonies were entitled to contract what alliances they pleased.

And there was no doubt where their best hope of allies lay: the old enemy, France. For France was burning for revenge for its comprehensive humiliation by Britain in the Seven Years War. And how better to take vengeance than by separating Britain from the fruits of that victory – the better part of its newly acquired empire? Hence the bizarre marriage of convenience between the new republic and the oldest, proudest and most absolute monarchy in Europe. 'Do they read?' a French radical asked, as the French translation of the fiercely anti-monarchical Declaration of Independence was devoured at the Court of Versailles. He might well have asked, 'Do they think?', as the sweetly air-headed and super-fashionable queen, Marie Antoinette, demanded news of her 'dear republicans'.

And French help was desperately needed since, despite all Washington's efforts, the Americans barely hung on. New York and Charleston remained in British hands and the most likely outcome seemed a stalemate. The deadlock was broken at Yorktown, a few miles to the south-east of Williamsburg, where Lord Cornwallis, the British commander in America, set up his headquarters in 1781. Yorktown lies on the narrow peninsula between the estuaries of the York and James rivers as they debouch into the mighty Chesapeake Bay.

So long as the British navy controlled the sea, Cornwallis was impregnable. But the French threw money – all borrowed and at outrageous rates of interest – at their fleet while the British navy was overstretched and divided. The result was that Cornwallis found himself caught between a strong French fleet which blockaded the York river and Washington's army, which the French had also buoyed up with loans and gifts. Trapped and outnumbered by more than two to one, Cornwallis surrendered to Washington on 19 October with his whole army.

'Oh God, it is all over,' the British Prime Minister wailed when the news arrived. It was, though it took George III some time to realize it. In 1783 the Americans, in their first betrayal of their French allies, signed a separate preliminary peace with Britain that recognized American independence. George drafted and redrafted his abdication address. And the Holy Roman Emperor predicted that, with the loss of America, Britain would swiftly become a second-class power, like Sweden or Denmark. His words were echoed in Britain. 'America is lost,' said George. 'Must we fall beneath the blow?'

V

Thereafter, Britain and America went their separate ways. But only one remained loyal to its eighteenth-century roots.

These show clearly in Washington, the new American capital that was named after George Washington, who, after he had resigned his military command, became the first President of the new American Republic.

Laid out in the 1790s, its monuments, lawns and grand,

sweeping vistas are the lineal descendants of the landscape gardens of Stowe. Similarly, it is America today which best embodies the ideas of freedom, power and Empire which inspired that great denizen of Stowe, William Pitt, in the reign of George II.

And it does so for better or for worse.

THE KING IS DEAD,
LONG LIVE THE BRITISH
MONARCHY!

GEORGE IV, WILLIAM IV, VICTORIA

King Louis XVI of France was executed on 21 January 1793 on the guillotine, the revolutionary killing machine which had just been introduced to humanize – and industrialize – the process of execution.

The night before, Louis read David Hume's account of the execution of Charles I. But the French king was prevented from recreating any of the poignancy of the death of that English king. Instead, in his execution, everything was done to rob Louis of his dignity, both as a king and a human being. He was condemned as a mere errant citizen, Louis Capet; his hair was roughly cropped on the scaffold and he was ignominiously strapped to the movable plank before having his head and neck thrust into the guides for the twelve-inch, heavily weighted blade. Once severed, the bleeding head was held up to the mob before being thrown between the legs of the body, which was then buried ten feet deep in quicklime.

Not since the St Bartholomew Day Massacre had a foreign event provoked such horror in England. Audiences demanded that the curtain be brought down in theatres and performances abandoned; the whole House of Commons wore mourning dress; and crowds surrounded George III's coach, crying 'War with France!' In the event, the French Republic took the initiative by declaring war on Britain on 1 February.

Nothing would be the same again. The war, with only brief respites of short-lived peace, was to last eighteen years; it cost more in men and money than any before; and it rewrote the rules of politics. Henceforward, monarchies would be measured by their ability to respond to the new, post-revolutionary world. Those that could adapt survived; those that could not died, usually bloodily. Which the British would do was by no means a foregone conclusion.

I

Only four years earlier, in 1789, when the French Revolution broke out, nothing seemed less likely than this cataclysmic struggle. Much of the English elite welcomed the Revolution, which they saw in terms of France belatedly catching up with England's own benign and Glorious Revolution of exactly a century before in 1688–89. And, in any case, they took for granted that the revolutionary turmoil would cripple France as a great power for a generation.

Most confident of all was the Prime Minister, William Pitt. Son of the great mid-century Prime Minister of the same name, and known as Pitt the Younger, he had a meteoric career. Barely out of Cambridge, where he had excelled at mathematics, he became Prime Minister and Chancellor of the Exchequer at the age of only twenty-four in the aftermath of the American War of Independence, and quickly proved as great a peace minister as his father was a war leader.

This was because his qualities were almost the mirror-image of his manic-depressive father's. He was an optimist, a long and deep sleeper, and excelled as a financier, a fiscal reformer and a manager of his party and cabinet. He inherited few of the volatile passions of his father – he was somewhat rigid in demeanour and dry in speech – but was a relentless workhorse. Thus, under his sober guidance, Britain shrugged off the effects of the American War of Independence and even enjoyed a trade boom with her former enemies, France and America.

Pitt's best qualities were on display in the Budget speech he made in the Commons in February 1792. 'Unquestionably', he told the House, 'there never was a time in the history of this country when from the situation of Europe we might more reasonably expect fifteen years of peace, than we may at the present moment.'

Not even he could predict that the outbreak of the greatest war in which England had ever been involved was a year away.

One man who did not join in the cheers was Edmund Burke MP. Of a modest, half-Catholic Irish background, Burke had forged a remarkable career for himself in London as a writer, wit and politician. His maiden speech – a furious assault on the Stamp Act – brought him instant fame and he became a leader of the extreme Whigs, attacking, in classic Whig style, royal power and the king's influence in government. Indeed, his continued passionate defence of the American revolutionaries cost him his seat in populous Bristol, forcing him to seek re-election from a handful of compliant voters in the 'rotten borough' of Malton.

But – despite the famous mock epitaph, which accused Burke of giving to party the talents that were intended for mankind – he never lost his original love for literature or the imaginative powers that went with it. These were now powerfully excited by the tremendous spectacle of revolutionary France.

Crucial was Burke's interest in the 'Sublime'. This he had defined as a young man, in a notable, pioneering essay, which is the turning point in the whole history of the taste of eighteenth-century Europe, as 'a sort of delightful horror, . . . a tranquillity tinged with terror', which we get from the contemplation of darkness, danger and death. It was this insight which enabled him to perceive, long before anyone else, the enormity of the passions unleashed by the French Revolution. In doing so, it turned him from a mere politician into a prophet whose words echo down the generations.

Burke published his *Reflections on the Revolution in France* in 1790. The Revolution, though he already called it 'the most astonishing [thing] that has . . . happened in the world', was then barely a year old. Absolutism and feudalism had been abolished; Church property confiscated; the Bastille had fallen; the new Constitution and the Declaration of the Rights of Man had been promulgated; and the king and queen marched from Versailles to Paris.

But the Terror, the abolition of the monarchy and the execution of the king, the revolutionary wars that convulsed Europe for more than a decade and a half and led to the deaths of millions, still lay in the future. Burke, however, prophesied them all.

Burke did so because he correctly identified – from the beginning – that the operating principle of the Revolution was inhuman, abstract Reason, which thought that it could and should remodel politics, society and humanity itself from scratch. This levelling Reason saw history, habit and tradition as mere obstacles to progress that like any human opposition were to be destroyed in the joyous, all-consuming bonfire of the vanities: 'The Year One' of human history.

For Burke, on the other hand, history and tradition were the foundation of civilization and habit the thing that made us human. From time to time, they might need reform. But reform should preserve, not destroy, their essence. Monarchy, as the supreme embodiment of history and tradition, thus became a test case. Was it the key obstacle to the new world, as the French quickly came to see? Or was it the guarantor of stability and freedom, as the British had decided (on Burke's reading) in 1689, and would again, Burke predicted, once more?

Yet again, Burke was to be proved right. When he wrote the *Reflections* in 1790, his was a voice crying in the wilderness. But, over the next few years, public opinion swung, increasingly strongly, in his direction.

As in everything else, George, Prince of Wales, the king's

eldest son, was the barometer of fashion. Handsome (before he ran to fat), intelligent, charming, sensual and a brilliant mimic, his relations with his father followed the normal Hanoverian pattern of mutual loathing and contempt. He thought his father mean and puritanical; his father thought his son a wanton and a wastrel. The Prince of Wales also followed the traditions of his dynasty by putting himself at the head of the opposition party of radical Whigs, of which the pre-Revolutionary Burke had been the leading ideologue.

The prince's first reaction to the *Reflections* was thus, to Burke's immense hurt, to dismiss it as 'a farrago of nonsense' and the work of a turncoat. But, with the Terror, he changed his mind. The execution of Louis XVI, he wrote to his mother, Queen Charlotte, had filled him with 'a species of sentiment towards my father which surpasses all description'. He made his peace with the king (though it didn't last long); broke with the opposition and declared his enthusiastic support for Prime Minister Pitt. He even toyed with the idea of serving as a volunteer in the war against France.

And where the prince led, much of the Whig Party followed, joining Pitt in a coalition to wage war 'under the standard of an hereditary monarchy' against Republican France and all that she stood for. This increasingly ideological war irretrievably split the Whigs, and condemned them to the wilderness for a generation. The more conservative members, who believed that opposition to the war and calls for constitutional reform would culminate in the destruction of the constitution and the monarchy, as they had in France, soon followed the logic of their position and joined the government. This left only a rump of radicals in opposition, who were not only easily outvoted but were also tainted with republicanism and treason.

Once it was Jacobitism which had done for the Tories and left them in the cold; now it was Jacobinism (as the creed of the French ultra-Republicans was known) which dished the Whigs.

The great beneficiary was the monarchy. For much of his reign, as radicalism flourished in the cities and his American subjects rejected his authority, George III could do no right. Now he could do no wrong. Indeed, the *less* he did the better, as he turned (in the popular imagination at least) from a meddlesome would-be absolutist into the benign father of his people: uxorious, modest, moral, frugal and the very embodiment of a modern, eighteenth-century king. He liked to live simply, far removed from the formal ceremonies of monarchy, as an ordinary country squire. Those subjects who encountered him on his frequent walks found a man who conversed with them as equals. He enjoyed pleasant holidays in English seaside resorts, and when he was in Weymouth a year before Louis XVI was put to death, a lady of that town remarked on how wonderful it was to have George in their town, 'not so much because he was a King, but because they said he was such a worthy gentleman, and that the like of him was never known in this realm before'.

Thus, during the tumult of revolution and the recurring threats of French invasion, George III stood out as a reassuring symbol of stability who represented British virtues of simplicity, sincerity and good old-fashioned common sense. Indeed, he was the exact opposite of hot-headed Continental rulers or luxurious despots surrounded by the flummery of ceremony. He had the common touch without doubt. 'The English people were pleased to see in him a crowning specimen of themselves – a royal John Bull', in the words of the poet and journalist Leigh Hunt. The result was the astonishing popular success of his Golden Jubilee on 25 October 1810. There were illuminations, fireworks, dancing in the streets and celebratory verse:

> A People, happy, great, and free;
> That People with one common voice,
> From Thames' to Ganges' common shores rejoice,
> In universal jubilee.

But that very day, George, who had already had two mysterious episodes of apparent mental illness, began his permanent and irreversible descent into a twilight world of madness, blindness and senility.

II

At the time of his father's collapse in 1810, the Prince of Wales (disrespectfully known as 'Prinny' to his cronies) was already forty-eight and, under the combined influences of drink, drugs (like many of his contemporaries he took an opium compound known as laudanum) and a gargantuan appetite, his youthful good looks were fading fast and his skin had turned a deep coppery hue.

He spent gigantically too, and his own treasurer declared that his debts were 'beyond all kind of calculation whatever'. The contrast with his prudent and down-to-earth father could not have been greater and his profligacy and debauched antics had made him as deeply unpopular as the King was loved and respected. But worst of all was his disastrous marriage.

The marriage began hopefully as part of the closing of ranks within the royal family in the wake of the French Revolution. In return for the payment of his debts, the prince agreed to his father's urgent wish that he should marry and father an heir. German custom, however, dictated that his bride should be royal too. Best of a bad bunch of available Protestant princesses seemed to be his cousin, Caroline of Brunswick.

But when she arrived in England it was loathing at first sight. She was coarse, ill educated and none too clean. After his marriage in the Chapel Royal in St James's, George knocked himself out with brandy and spent his wedding night passed out on the bedroom floor with his head in the hearth. The following morning he recovered sufficiently to get Caroline pregnant, but only after he had steeled himself with more alcohol 'to conquer my person and overcome the disgust of her person'. A daughter, christened Charlotte, was born in January 1796. It was the first and last time the couple slept together, and they soon separated.

Such was the man who became Prince Regent of the United Kingdom. He got a bad press at the time, particularly from the great cartoonists like Gillray and Cruikshank, who had a field day with his shape and his private life. And posterity, on the whole, hasn't been much kinder.

But there's another side to the story. The Prince Regent wasn't much good at the business side of monarchy, which he found altogether too much like hard work. 'Playing at king', as he sighed shortly after becoming regent, 'is no sinecure.' On the other hand, few more imaginative men have sat on the British throne, and none has left more tangible results: in London, the royal palaces and the strange, hybrid concept of British identity itself.

Once again, it all goes back to the French Revolution. Burke's final prophecy and warning to the French had been that 'some popular general' would arise and become 'the master of your whole Republic'. This prediction too was fulfilled by the meteoric rise of Napoleon Bonaparte, the young, impoverished Corsican nobleman who became in quick succession France's most successful general, First Consul and finally, in 1804, self-proclaimed Emperor of the French.

Napoleon was self-crowned too in an extraordinary ceremony held in the hastily patched-up cathedral of Notre-Dame. Drawing on a range of royal and imperial symbolism, Napoleon and his stage designers came up with new rituals and regalia, a new imperial court, thickly populated with 'Grand'-this and 'Arch'-that, each in his own lavish new uniform, and a new imperial family, quarrelling as bitterly as any ancient dynasty.

Above all, the event, carefully recorded on canvas and in print, set new standards both for pomp and precision which the established monarchies rushed to copy. Not only, it seemed, could Napoleon beat kings and tsars on the battlefield, he could beat them at 'playing at king' as well.

The Republic had been bad enough for the Prince of Wales. But this upstart emperor was worse, and doing him down and outdoing him became – insofar as his easy-going personality allowed – an obsession. The Prince Regent had over a decade to wait. But at last the day arrived and on 18 June 1815, at

Waterloo, to the south of Brussels, Napoleon engaged with a British army commanded by Arthur Wellesley, Duke of Wellington. Each side played to their strengths: the French attacked with brio; the British doggedly resisted in defensive formations. 'Let's see who can pound longest,' said Wellington. In the event, the British did and held out until the arrival of the Prussian allied army gave them an overwhelming advantage.

The French retreat turned into a rout. On 3 July an armistice was agreed; on the 6th the allies entered Paris and on the 13th Napoleon wrote the most remarkable letter of his life. It was addressed to the Prince Regent. '*Altesse Royale* [Royal Highness],' it began, 'I have terminated my political career . . . I put myself under the protection of British laws, which I entreat of Your Royal Highness as from the most powerful, the most constant, and the most generous of my foes.' In this contest of the imperial eagle against the royal popinjay, the popinjay, it seemed, had won.

But even in defeat and exiled to the British possession of St Helena – a tiny, remote Atlantic island – Napoleon continued to fascinate his enemies. And none more so than the Prince Regent. It began with the contest of capitals: London versus Paris.

Napoleon, like many despots, was a megalomaniac builder, who started to refashion the then largely medieval warren of Paris into the worthy capital of an empire which, at its height, stretched from the Bay of Biscay to the gates of Moscow. This was to throw down the gauntlet to Britain, since London, fattened by overseas empire and trade, already dwarfed Paris in size and wealth. But it was a rather dingy world capital, shrouded in fog and coal smoke and traversable only by rutted and narrow streets and lanes. St James's Palace, it was said by sophisticated European visitors, looked like a workhouse and Parliament like a coffee house.

Now, 'Prinny' decided, the city must look like the capital of a victorious empire. The man charged with realizing his dreams was John Nash. Nash's brief was simple: he must outdo Napoleonic Paris. And, thanks to his unusual combination of qualities – as both visionary architect and shrewd property developer – he largely succeeded.

His scheme, which involved both landscaping and town plan-ning on a heroic scale, created a grand processional route from the newly laid-out Regent's Park in the north, through Regent Street, to Pall Mall and the gates of the prince's then London residence in the south. Nash worked in sweeping curves and artful vistas; while his buildings, which were really terraces of middle-class brick houses, were covered in stucco plaster and painted to look like a succession of noble palaces. This was archi-tecture as urban stage-set: as theatrical as Napoleon's coronation and as successful.

Then, in 1820 there arrived a day for which the prince had waited almost as eagerly as he had Napoleon's downfall. For almost a decade after he became regent, his father, George III, had lived the life of a recluse in a little three-room apartment at Windsor. Dead to the world, he spent hours thumping an old harpsichord. But his condition suddenly deteriorated and he died on 29 June.

The regent was king at last. And he was determined that everybody should know it. But there was unfinished business with an enemy who stood equal in his eyes with Napoleon. One of his first decisions as king was to order his government to pass a Bill in Parliament dissolving his marriage to his hated wife, who now exulted in her position as Queen Caroline. She had been in voluntary exile in southern Europe, where she had enjoyed herself to the utmost with a succession of male admirers. It was the government's duty to present evidence of the queen's outrageous behaviour to the House of Lords, and secure a divorce for the new king. The ministry, on the other hand, saw that depriving a queen of her rights was politically impossible and attempted to make George see reason. But the king would not be deterred.

In the end, the cabinet was proved right. The country rallied behind Caroline, whom it saw as a wronged woman and the embodiment of female purity. (If she was, it was only in comparison with her estranged husband.) The monarchy slipped to the depths of unpopularity, and even the Lords found it hard to stomach George's hypocrisy. The government dropped the Bill.

George's coronation finally took place on 19 July 1821. He had delayed it for over a year in the hope that the longed-for divorce would mean that he would not have to share the greatest day of his life with Caroline. Thwarted by the half-hearted efforts of his government and the truculence of his people, George got what he wanted by stationing prizefighters dressed as pages outside the doors of Westminster Abbey to exclude uninvited guests, with the queen top of the list.

Partly in compensation for the horrors of the past year it was, George resolved, to be the best-organized and most magnificent coronation in British history. It was certainly the most expensive, costing almost a quarter of a million pounds, while his father's had been staged for less than ten thousand.

For George IV was not measuring himself against a king but the Emperor Napoleon. Indeed, he was measuring himself literally, since his tailor was sent to Paris to copy Napoleon's coronation robe. The result imitates the form of Napoleon's robe and, being even more thickly embroidered and befurred, it took eight pages to carry it, and it was said that, had they let go, the king would have toppled on to his back.

George also copied Napoleon in demanding a precise and exhaustive record of the event in a series of coloured lithographs that preserved every detail of every costume for posterity. And, once again, the emulation was conscious and explicit. Sir George Nayler's *The Coronation of His Most Sacred Majesty King George the Fourth* was 'Undertaken by His Majesty's Especial Command', and Nayler received a £3,000 royal subsidy. For it had to be the best – or at any rate, better than Napoleon's: 'This work will excel any of the kind in the known world; and the folio History of Bonaparte's Coronation, the most important and perfect yet published, will sink into nothing by contrast,' the Preface boasts.

Eventually, but only a decade after George's death, the ambition was fulfilled with the appearance of a set of splendid volumes, with their hand-coloured plates, lavishly heightened in gold, which captured more than a little of the magnificence of the day.

One of the spectators at the coronation was the Scottish historian, poet and novelist Sir Walter Scott, who was bowled over by the combination of 'gay, gorgeous and antique dress which floated before the eye'. If the coronation was supposed to bewitch, the magic certainly worked on Scott. And he tried to transmit the wonder of the day in a newspaper article, which asked his readers to imagine the Abbey lit by the

> sun, which brightened and saddened as if on purpose, now beaming in full lustre on the rich and varied assemblage, and now darting a solitary ray, which catched, as it passed, the glittering folds of a banner . . . and then rested full on some fair form . . . whose circlet of diamonds glistened under it influence.

Conjure up, he enjoined them, the 'sights of splendour and sounds of harmony'.

Scott, born in 1771, belonged to the generation that had grown up with the French Revolution and had reacted strongly against it. Profoundly influenced by Burke and by Burke's German disciples, he lived history and tradition and gave them life in his poetry and novels.

One of the most famous was *Kenilworth*, which focused on the great revels presented at Kenilworth Castle for Good Queen Bess by her favourite, the Earl of Leicester. Published in 1821, the novel plugged into the same fashion for all things Elizabethan and Shakespearean that was tapped by costumes George devised for his coronation. Now Scott, who had first met George in 1815, was given the opportunity to devise his own grand historical pageant when he was put in charge of organizing the king's visit to Edinburgh in 1822.

The visit – the first to Scotland by a reigning monarch since Charles II's coronation in 1651 – began on 14 August with the king's ceremonial landing at Leith and continued for a fortnight with balls, receptions and a grand procession from Holyrood

Palace to Edinburgh Castle. There the king inspected the Scottish royal regalia, which had recently been unearthed by Scott himself.

Throughout, at Scott's insistence, all the gentlemen wore Highland dress, including the king, whose ample figure was compressed into something like the necessary shape by corsets and flesh-coloured tights. The climax came in the great banquet held in the Parliament House, where, a century earlier, Scotland's separate political existence had been extinguished by the passage of the Act of Union. The king called for a toast to the 'Clans and Chieftains of Scotland', to which the chief of the Clan Macgregor replied with one to 'The Chief of Chiefs – the King!'

It was all, as the hard-headed have not ceased to point out from then till now, nonsense. But, as befits Scott's genius as impresario, it was inspired, romantic nonsense. Above all, it was *successful* nonsense. It gave Scotland a proud cultural identity that, for over a hundred years, dwelt in a sort of parallel universe alongside the political subordination required by the Union. And, as the ardently Tory Scott intended, it firmly anchored this renewed Scots national identity to the Hanoverian monarchy.

For nationalism had played a part in the downfall of Napoleon's empire second only to British arms. The British monarchy instead, thanks in the first place to George IV's taste for theatrical pageantry, was able to harness the wild horses of nationalism, geld and domesticate them and turn them into the gaily decked palfreys pulling the royal state coach. Or, in the case of the Highland regiments, its foot-soldiers, marching alongside and winning the empire's battles under the Union Flag.

For that, parading through the streets of Edinburgh in a kilt was a small price to pay.

III

But George IV was unable to keep up the flurry of activity that marked the beginning of his reign. His health and mobility declined and his self-indulgence grew, as he washed down vast amounts of food with even larger quantities of alcohol and dulled what little sense remained with ever more frequent doses of laudanum. He died, unlamented, at Windsor on 26 June 1830 and, having been predeceased by his daughter and only child, was succeeded by his eldest surviving brother, William, Duke of Clarence.

At first sight, William IV, who was already aged sixty-four, was not a promising prospect as king. He had been sent to sea at the age of thirteen as a midshipman in the Royal Navy, where he had spent a few happy years drinking and womanizing around the world; on his return he shocked his staid parents and polished brothers with his compulsive swearing. Deprived of the chance to further his career, he had then spent most of his life as a relatively impecunious younger son. It was an empty existence with no meaningful role, and he filled his time fathering a numerous progeny of grasping bastards. And he had been cashiered from the only senior post he had (briefly) held – that of Lord High Admiral – for refusing to submit to the Prime Minister's orders. He was also personally ridiculous, with a strange, pineapple-shaped head and a tendency to talk at length and at some distance from the point.

On the other hand, he was a moderate Whig in politics, in contrast to the rabid Toryism of other members of the royal family, while his naval service had given him both a common touch and robust common sense. He was described as 'A little old, red-nosed, weather-beaten, jolly looking person with an ungraceful air and carriage', rather like a retired sea captain. He was also – in striking contrast to his predecessor – completely indifferent to ceremony and pomp and circumstance.

Testimony to this is Clarence House, the elegant but comparatively modest London residence built for William while he was still heir to the throne. The king continued to live there after his accession and showed no wish at all to move into the neighbouring Buckingham Palace, George IV's last, grandest, most expensive and still embarrassingly incomplete building project. Instead, he asked whether the palace could be converted into barracks.

William was equally unexcited about his coronation. Indeed, he suggested doing away with it entirely as a mere occasion 'for useless and ill-timed expense'. Could he not simply take the oaths to the constitution and the Protestant religion prescribed by the Bill of Rights and have done with it? When he was in the robing room of the House of Lords preparing to dissolve Parliament, he snatched the crown from a startled courtier and, placing it askew on his head, said to Lord Grey, the Prime Minister, 'Now, my Lord, the Coronation is over.'

Horrified Tory protests forced him to go through with the real ceremony. But it was done on the cheap (costing less than a fifth of George IV's, it was nicknamed the 'Half-Crownation'), while the ancient ritual was ignorantly butchered and abbreviated. And ever the boisterous and laid-back sailor, William conspicuously mocked the gravity of the occasion during the service.

All this was of a piece with his usual behaviour. Early in his reign he would walk up St James's Street unattended, but had to give up when he was mobbed. On another occasion, society was shocked when William took the King of Württemberg for a drive round London and 'set down the King ("dropped him", as he calls it) at Grillon's Hotel. The King of England dropping another King at a tavern!' And again, impatient at the delays in getting the state coach ready for the dissolution of Parliament, he threatened to go in a hackney coach (the ancestor of the modern taxi) instead. Never, in short, has Britain come nearer to a bicycling – or at least a taxi-ing – monarchy than under William IV. But would these decent, unpretentious qualities be enough?

Barely a month after William's accession there was a brutal reminder of the fate of unsuccessful sovereigns. Paris once again rose in anger: the 'Days of July', when the King of France, whose monarchy had been restored after the fall of Napoleon, was ignominiously driven from the throne. Now, news came, he was on his way to seek refuge in Britain.

He was packed off to Edinburgh, where he spent a miserable winter in unheated and unfurnished rooms at Holyrood, protected from a hostile mob only by Sir Walter Scott.

Just how secure was the throne of his reluctant and ungracious English host? For, despite forty-odd years of almost uninterrupted Tory rule, from the 1780s to the 1820s, the ideas of the French Revolution *had* taken root in Britain. But was it to be full-blown revolution? Or reform?

In the hard days after victory in 1815, when the economy had taken a serious downward turn and aberrant climatic conditions caused the harvests to fail, radical agitation had reached a peak. In 1819, for instance, a great demonstration took place in St Peter's Fields, Manchester, as 60,000 men, women and children marched on the town. The town magistrates panicked and ordered the local yeomanry cavalry to disperse the peaceful throng. The charge killed eleven and wounded about four hundred in what, in a savage parody of Waterloo, became known within days as the Peterloo Massacre.

But the demonstrators had not threatened violence. The huge crowd was carefully marshalled, with the brass bands accompanying each division playing patriotic tunes, like 'God Save the King' and 'Rule Britannia'. And when it was the turn of the national anthem most members of the crowd respectfully took their hats off. In 1820 the pro-Caroline demonstrators focused their anger on political corruption, not anti-monarchism. And the radical leaders paid court to the scorned queen, like any ardent royalist basking in the light of majesty.

Back in the heady days of the early 1790s, a minority *had* hoped for revolution red in tooth and claw. But this revolutionary group was quickly eclipsed by another, who wanted reform, not revolution. They thought change could be brought about *within* England's existing institutions, and by peaceful means, not revolutionary violence. They also differed from the ardently pro-French revolutionaries and their undercover, quasi-treasonable followers in that they paraded their John Bull British patriotism, as the Manchester and Caroline demonstrators had done. Finally, the striking thing is that the target of the reform agitation was *not* the monarchy, as it was in contemporary France and had been in seventeenth-century England, but Parliament.

In the early nineteenth century Parliament met, as it had done for centuries, in the medieval royal palace of Westminster, which had been long abandoned by the monarchy and handed over instead to Parliament and the Law Courts. Over the centuries, the ancient structure had been repeatedly hacked around and refurbished, the Commons most recently by Sir Christopher Wren in the eighteenth century and the Lords by James Wyatt at the beginning of the nineteenth.

The result was a kind of physical embodiment of Burke's ancient constitution, in which the antique buildings had been slowly and almost imperceptibly altered and adapted over the ages. They were also ramshackle, jerry-built and prone to fire.

Much the same could be said, by its critics, of the House of Commons itself. Many important and fast-growing towns had no MP at all, while tiny, half-abandoned villages with a handful of inhabitants returned two MPs each at the command of the owner of the rotten borough, as such constituencies were known. A handful of rich and powerful noblemen owned a dozen or more rotten boroughs each and could make or break governments.

It was William's misfortune that the pressure for parliamentary reform suddenly intensified at the beginning of his reign. For, five months after his accession, the Tory government fell and a Whig administration took office for the first time in almost fifty years.

The new government also looked to a different geographical

constituency. For the capital was not the only town to undergo radical change in the first decades of the nineteenth century. The noble townscape of Newcastle-upon-Tyne, for instance, is the equal of anything created by the Prince Regent in London. But its grand terraced main street and monumental column are a memorial not to a king or prince, or a general or admiral, but to Charles, Earl Grey, the Prime Minister of the Whig government of 1830 and a local Northumbrian grandee.

Grey's father was a successful general who was raised to an earldom. He first became an MP at the age of only twenty-two and quickly established a reputation as a brilliant, if reckless, speaker and an accomplished adulterer, who numbered Georgiana, Duchess of Devonshire, among his conquests.

In the Whig split during the French revolutionary wars Grey remained with the rump in opposition. But he disagreed with the leadership over their pro-French defeatism. Instead, he argued, the Whig Party must renew itself by discovering its earlier radicalism and joining – or rather leading – the movement for parliamentary reform.

For Grey was, and remained, a natural aristocrat, who saw himself acting on behalf of the people, and not at their command. Now, as Prime Minister, with nine out of thirteen cabinet ministers drawn from the Lords, he had the opportunity to put his ideas into practice. Over the next three years, three Reform Bills were submitted to Parliament each to much the same effect: fifty-six rotten boroughs to be abolished; forty-four seats to be given to large towns, and then the most modest property holders to be enfranchised. The first was defeated in the Commons and provoked a general election that, even on the unreformed franchise, produced a Whig landslide. The second was defeated in the Lords. And it looked as though the intransigent Tory majority in the Lords would do the same to the third.

The only way – it seemed – to break the deadlock was for William to create enough peers to give the Whigs a majority in the Lords as well.

So far, William had given Grey unstinting support. He had done so on practical grounds, since he recognized that reform was the only alternative to revolution. He also acted on principle, since he saw it as his duty, whatever his personal wishes, 'to support the Prime Minister until Parliament by its vote determines that the Prime Minister no longer possesses the confidence of the nation'. But a creation of up to fifty peers, which would radically dilute the composition of the Lords, was a step too far. William refused; Grey resigned and, on 9 May 1832, the king invited the Tories to form a government.

England now had its 'Days of May', when it looked as though London, Newcastle and the rest would follow in the steps of revolutionary Paris. There were mass demonstrations and strikes; newspapers whipped up the frenzy with provocative headlines like 'The Eve of the Barricades', while in Birmingham a speaker at a rally of 100,000 people proclaimed Tory 'incompetency to govern' and invoked the people's 'Right to Arm' in the face of oppression from the Bill of Rights.

When the American rebels had used that language, George III had dug his heels in; William IV instead sought compromise.

The Tories, he suggested privately, should simply cut their losses, bury their pride and abstain. Reform was inevitable, and that way at least they would retain their inbuilt majority in the

Lords. It was a bitter pill to swallow and they resisted as long as possible. But finally they had to admit that they couldn't form a government. William now had no choice but to recall Grey and to agree – in writing – to his demand for the mass creation of peers.

It was the most humiliating document a king had signed since the Civil War. But William turned it to his advantage by informing the Tory leaders of what he had done. Certain now that they would be swamped even in the Lords, they abandoned their resistance and the Reform Bill went through.

The key figure in these behind-the-scenes negotiations was the king's private secretary and long-serving courtier, Sir Herbert Taylor. Taylor wrote all William's letters (up to thirty or forty a day) and the suspicion must be that he helped shape much of their contents as well. If so, it was a job well done. For, by their joint actions in the 'Days of May', William and Taylor had invented, more or less at a stroke, both the modern constitutional monarchy and the role of the private secretary as the principal cog in the royal machine.

On 7 June the Reform Act received the royal assent by commission. Grey had wanted William to give it in person. But, because he disapproved of the popular clamour, the king refused. It was perhaps his only false step in the whole affair. The new House of Commons, elected under the new franchise, was unencumbered by such fear of public opinion.

Two years later, on the night of 16 October 1834, the chambers of both Houses of Parliament and all the rest of the Palace of Westminster apart from the Great Hall were consumed by a raging fire. Reconstructing Parliament from scratch now ceased to be a disputed metaphor and became a practical necessity instead.

IV

William himself, now in his late sixties and beyond hope of legitimate children of his own, would not long survive the Reform Act. His health was declining and his tetchiness increasing. But he was determined to live long enough for his heir presumptive, Princess Victoria, to inherit the crown in her own right. For if he died before she reached her eighteenth birthday, a regent would have to rule in her name. And that person would be William's detested sister-in-law and Victoria's mother, Marie Louise Victoria, Duchess of Kent. Contemplating the prospect of power, the duchess had become overbearing and nakedly ambitious. Outraged in turn, nine months before the young princess's birthday, William made an extraordinary speech to the court. He did not mince his words, saying that he was determined to prolong his life for a few months longer, for 'I should then have the satisfaction of leaving the royal authority to the personal exercise of that young lady . . . and not in the hands of the person now near me, who is surrounded by evil designs and who is herself incompetent to act with propriety in the station in which she would be placed'.

William made it with days to spare. Victoria celebrated her eighteenth birthday (her royal coming of age) on 24 May 1837 and William, his goal achieved, died on 20 June.

Victoria was at Kensington Palace when her uncle died. And it was here that she had been brought up and educated. Her education was strong in foreign languages and traditional female accomplishments like drawing and music. But it had neglected the male curriculum of classics and mathematics.

On the other hand, her governess, Baroness Lehzen, whose ideal monarch was Queen Elizabeth I, had made sure that, despite the bias of her education, Victoria would be no meekly submissive woman. Lehzen brought her up to rule, and Victoria had the appetite and will to do so. She was also prepared for the necessary hard work. During the king's illness, her lessons had been cancelled. 'I regret rather my singing lesson,' she said, 'though it is only for a short period, but duty and *proper feeling go before all pleasures.*' Just eighteen, she was showing the qualities that would define her reign.

The news that she was queen was brought at six o'clock in the morning by the Lord Chamberlain and the Archbishop of Canterbury, who were received by Victoria in her dressing gown. And the contrast between the glowing young queen and the sombrely dressed, elderly male political establishment was only underscored by her Accession Council, which was held later in the day. The next day she presided over another council meeting 'as if she had been doing it all her life'. All who saw her were bowled over by her confidence.

Particularly susceptible was the Prime Minister, Lord Melbourne. And the attraction was mutual. Charming, worldly wise and with the faint whiff of the danger of an ex-roué, Melbourne was the perfect mentor for the inexperienced young queen. He was also of the right political colour, since Victoria had been brought up as an ardent Whig.

The result was that the Tories soon called foul. But worse was to come when, only two years after her accession, Victoria displayed blatant partisanship during a ministerial crisis and wrecked a Tory attempt to form a government. Melbourne had won a crucial vote in the House of Commons by just five votes and resigned the premiership. Victoria, still under the sway of the paternal old politician, grudgingly offered the premiership to first the Duke of Wellington and then Sir Robert Peel. Peel, not feeling it the right moment to take power, would accept only on the condition that the queen replaced the ladies of her household, who were all aristocratic Whigs. Victoria took great pleasure in refusing this disrespectful order, and Melbourne, against *his* better judgement, was reinstated as the queen's pet Prime Minister. Even Whigs now had to acknowledge that a young, unmarried girl on the throne was a loose cannon.

But who was to be the husband? The front-runner was Prince Albert, a younger son of the Duke of the little German principality of Saxe-Coburg. The connection between the houses of Hanover and Saxe-Coburg was already strong, as both Victoria's mother and her cousin by marriage were Coburgs. Moreover, when Victoria (who was highly susceptible to male beauty) had first met Albert some years previously she had been very taken by his excellent figure and rather ethereal good looks. But she noted his tendency to tire easily, in contrast to her own boundless energy.

Albert was exactly of an age with Victoria. But otherwise their early experiences had been very different. Albert's father was an inveterate womanizer and, in revenge, his wife had taken a lover of her own. The result was divorce and Albert's loss of his mother at the age of only five. His own upright morality was a reaction to this loss and to the loneliness of a motherless child.

The gap left by his mother had eventually been filled by Albert's tutor, who discharged his duties with a rare zeal and thoroughness. He had also benefited from formal instruction, both in Coburg and later at the university in Bonn, which was then at the height of its academic fame. All this added mineralogy and science, anthropology, philosophy, literary criticism and music to the basic curriculum he had learnt at home. And, despite his rather weak constitution, he was no milksop either: he was a competent fencer and an excellent shot. In short, he was the very model of an accomplished, modern prince for the nineteenth century. All that he lacked, as a penniless younger son, was a wife.

Victoria was in no hurry to oblige: she was enjoying the delicious freedom of being a young Queen Regnant far too much for that. Nevertheless, despite her conspicuous lack of encouragement, Albert was sent over to England to be inspected a second time. He arrived at Windsor on 10 October 1839. Victoria was watching from the top of the stairs and confided her feelings to her diary: 'It was with some emotion that I beheld Albert, who is *beautiful*,' she wrote with a characteristically heavy underlining. It was love at second sight, but none the less profound for that. And it lasted for both their lives.

In view of the disparity in their status it was Victoria who had to propose. They were married at the Chapel Royal at St James's on 10 February 1840 and departed for a two-day honeymoon at Windsor. 'We did not sleep much,' Victoria noted of their wedding night. They revelled in each other's sensuality. Albert helped Victoria pull on her stockings; she watched him shave. Unsurprisingly, then, Victoria conceived within days and gave birth to a daughter in November. A son, Edward, Prince of Wales, came just eleven months later, followed by seven more children, with never more than two years between them.

And it was this uxorious bliss which began to alter the relationship between them. From the beginning, they had had adjacent desks. But Victoria had made it clear that, as was constitutionally proper, the business of queening was hers alone. Albert was allowed to blot her dispatches, but only as a concession.

But her repeated pregnancies, regularly followed by intense post-natal depression, began to swing the balance of power. And the change was completed by Albert's increasingly psychological dominance. She was tempestuous; he coldly rational. And he soon turned her temperament against her by making her ashamed of her uninhibited behaviour. The result was that Victoria not only became a submissive wife in private; she even surrendered public business to her husband, who acted as her private secretary with more power than any private secretary ever had. Once he had meekly blotted dispatches; now he dictated them.

This gave Albert a free hand to shape his own vision of monarchy. He had arrived in an England transformed by the Reform Act, which had created a new, predominantly middle-class electorate. And he had quickly attached himself to the most intelligent politician of the mid-century: the Tory leader, Sir Robert Peel. Peel, himself the son of a cotton manufacturer, saw it as his mission to adapt the Tory Party to the new world of industry and railways, powerful manufacturing cities and bourgeois morality which we call the Industrial Revolution.

In pulling it into the modern world, Peel split the Tory

Party, sending it into the political wilderness for two decades. But Albert succeeded in adapting the monarchy to the same forces beyond anyone's wildest dreams. He began at home.

The young royal family would spend their summers at Osborne House, which Albert built on the Isle of Wight. Victoria's uncle, George IV, true to his decadent nature and the flamboyance of the time in which he ruled, had summered in *his* holiday home, the Brighton Pavilion. With its exotic minarets and domes, it appeared to be the home of a fairy-tale oriental despot. At Osborne the contrast could not have been greater. In place of the fantastic architecture – and fantastic expense – all was sobriety and efficiency. The site was bought at a bargain price and building works completed to time and to budget.

But most innovatory was the layout. For Osborne is really two buildings in one. There was the Family Pavilion and the Household Wing. Servants and the business of state were shunted off into the latter, while the former provided the setting for 'The Home Life of Our Own Dear Queen' – which was really Albert's creation – and was a model of modern, almost bourgeois, privacy and respectability.

'That damned morality would undo us all,' snorted Victoria's first, old-school Prime Minister. Albert, on the contrary, saw the 'moral monarchy' as the one means by which royalty could appeal to the middle classes, perhaps even lead them.

And central to this was the mid-nineteenth-century faith in progress and entrepreneurial zeal. In the previous century, the monarchy had been at the forefront of innovation, patronizing nascent industry and sponsoring scientific experiments. But many of the great advances of the Industrial Revolution in the nineteenth century had been spurred by private effort. The Royal Society for the Encouragement of Arts, Manufactures and Commerce had been established by George III, but had slumped into dozy inactivity before Albert took over as president. Under his active patronage, it was revived with a successful programme of annual exhibitions of British manufactures.

Then it was suggested that the exhibition should become *inter*national to reflect the fact that one quarter of the world's population was now ruled by Britain. Albert took up the idea enthusiastically. But it required all his drive and determination to overcome the obstacles and objections. The projected event was riddled with impracticalities and dangers. For it to work, suitable space in central London would have to be found and all the international exhibitors would have to be carefully managed. The pessimistic predicted that it would be a Great British farce. The unruly lower orders would riot; the fine elms trees on the Hyde Park site would be damaged; none of the 245 submitted designs for the exhibition building would work.

The day was saved by Joseph Paxton's scheme for a prefabricated 'Crystal Palace' of iron and glass, like a gigantic conservatory. Albert took only nine days to get 'the most advanced building of the nineteenth century' accepted; seven weeks later the concrete foundations were laid and four months later it was finished. The statistics are staggering. The palace was 1,848 feet long, 108 feet high (easily accommodating the threatened elms) and covered by 300,000 panes of glass. Inside, 1¾ miles of exhibition space displayed 100,000 exhibits from 14,000 exhibitors drawn from Europe and the world. Machines hummed and whirred; telegraphs and cameras showed what the future might be like; both finely crafted and mass-produced artefacts were proudly on display; and the produce of the world – the fruits of empire and free trade – were brought together under the glass. All this was seen by 6 million people, or a third of Britain's entire population.

And it was all Albert's work. In a speech at the Lord Mayor's Banquet, Albert said that the Exhibition pointed to the future of mankind – unity through communication and mutual under-standing. 'The Exhibition of 1851', he said, 'is to give us a true test and a living picture of the point of development at which the whole of mankind has arrived in this great task, and a new starting point from which all nations will be able to direct their further exertions.'

On 1 May 1851, Victoria, wearing silver and pink and with Albert at her side, opened the Great Exhibition. 'It was the greatest day in our history', she wrote, 'and the triumph of my beloved Albert.' The crowds came, but they were not disorderly; they were decent and respectable. The Exhibition, true to its commercial origin, turned a handy profit, which was put towards founding the Victoria and Albert, the Science and the Natural History museums.

Eight months later, on 3 February 1852, Victoria and Albert opened another, very different, building. Indeed, at first sight it looks as reactionary as the Crystal Palace was progressive. For when the rules were announced for a competition to rebuild the Palace of Westminster after the fire of 1834, it was specified that the design must be in 'the Gothic or Elizabethan style'. The winner, Charles Barry, and his assistant, Augustine Pugin, responded enthusiastically, combining the native English Gothic with the resonantly patriotic Elizabethan; every inch of the building, inside and out, is a riot of medieval and Tudor-inspired ornament.

It is especially rich and colourful – a sequence of magnificent spaces, designed as a stage-set for the state opening of Parliament and used for the first time by Victoria and Albert in 1852. Albert was heavily involved here also, as chairman of the committee that chose the artists and the subjects for the wall-paintings, which were likewise exclusively historical and allegorical. The enormous Norman Porch has a stained-glass window showing Edward the Confessor. King Arthur and the Knights of the Round Table are painted on the walls of the Robing Room, where the monarch assumes the royal parliamentary robes and imperial state crown prior to the state opening. Paintings of the victorious death of Nelson at Trafalgar and the triumph of Wellington at Waterloo line the Royal Gallery. From here the sovereign processes to the Lords' Chamber, which was intended not only as a debating chamber, but as the magnificent climax of the state opening of Parliament. Stained-glass windows depicting the kings and queens of England and frescos with allegorical representations of Chivalry, Religion and Justice overlook the gold canopy and throne, upon which the monarch sits to open Parliament. Everything is crimson and gold and solemn splendour.

The result has been described and denounced as backward looking and Tory. Albert would have been astonished. He considered himself to be liberal, progressive and constitutionalist. He saw no contradiction between history and progress, or between the Crystal Palace and the Palace of Westminster. And

he regarded the state opening of Parliament as the perfect reconciliation of medieval and modern, in which the institutions of
English government showed themselves at once durable and
flexible.

And the monarchy, as guided by his hand, was all of these
things.

THE CHALLENGES OF MODERNITY

ONLY A DECADE after the triumphant openings of the Great Exhibition and the rebuilt Palace of Westminster, Albert was dead.

In November 1861 he had caught an infection while staying at Madingley Hall near Cambridge. It was described as a chill at first but later admitted to be typhoid fever. Albert was visiting Cambridge partly in his capacity as chancellor of the university, in which role he was as activist and reforming as in all his positions, whether nominally honorary or not. But he had a more personal motive as well. His eldest son, Edward, Prince of Wales, had turned out to be a dreadful disappointment. Albert had plunged him into a stringent educational programme that was intended to turn his son into a new version of his own younger self. But Edward proved idle and practically unteachable. Still worse, he had recently discovered his métier as a womanizer and was keeping a girl in his rooms at Cambridge, where he was also making a mockery of his stint in the university.

Depressed at his son's flippant response, Albert returned to Windsor in the pouring rain. Worn out with overwork, and overweight and prematurely aged, he put up little resistance to the disease. It is also possible that he was in the final stages of a stomach cancer. At all events, his condition rapidly worsened. But Victoria was oblivious and his doctors powerless, doing little more than drugging him with ever more frequent doses of brandy. Soon he was delirious, and on the night of 14 December his breathing began to change. Victoria was summoned and, confronting the truth at last, exclaimed 'This is death' and fell on his body.

One of the world's great love stories had turned into its most notoriously protracted widowhood.

But Albert's death was much more than a personal trauma for Victoria. 'With Prince Albert', the Tory leader Benjamin Disraeli wrote shortly after the funeral, 'we have buried our sovereign. This German Prince has governed England for twenty-one years with a wisdom and energy such as none of our kings has ever shown.' It was he who had, more or less single-handedly, adapted the monarchy to the modern, middle-class world created by the Reform Act and had made it respected by Nonconformist preachers, prosperous industrialists and an increasingly vociferous press.

Who would replace him now that he was gone? Not the queen, who, freed from his guiding hand, became increasingly wayward and self-indulgent. And certainly not the Prince of Wales.

Moreover, the world to which Albert had responded so effectively barely outlived him. For in 1867 Disraeli, now Leader in the Commons, 'dished the Whigs' by outflanking them with the second, much more radical Reform Act. This gave the vote to a third of adult males, thus spreading the franchise far beyond the solidly middle-class electorate created by the 1832 Act, in which the Liberals, as the Whigs were increasingly known, had a natural majority.

For a Tory (or Conservative, for the Tories were also sailing under new colours) to flirt with radical electoral reform was a step in the dark; it might also have been a plunge into the abyss. But Disraeli was buoyed up by his youthful 'Young England' philosophy and his romantic attachment to an imagined Middle Ages, in which there was a natural affinity, even an alliance, between the aristocrat and the working man, who, with all their differences, shared a certain generosity of spirit as against the mean, bean-counting materialism of the mercantile middle class. Disraeli's most distinguished twentieth-century biographer dismissed all this as 'gothic rubbish'. Actually, it proved to be surprisingly shrewd as sociology; it was even accurate as psephology, and in 1874 the Tories were returned (with Disraeli as prime minister) with their first clear majority for a generation.

This was also a world, as Disraeli similarly foresaw, that was much more sympathetic to the mystery and magic of monarchy than the 'desiccated calculating machines' of Liberal opinion-formers. Once again, the insight was a kind of self-projection of Disraeli's, since he too was an incurably romantic monarchist.

All this might have seemed to mark out Disraeli as the

predestined inventor of a new, popular monarchy, just as he is credited (not wholly unjustly) with creating the new, popular Tory Party. But Victoria, despite the increasingly warm, even flirtatious, nature of their relationship, was unpromising material. She had little respect for popular opinion and was firm that 'she would never be Queen of a democracy'; and, without Albert at her side to support her, she had no interest at all in public appearances.

So change was postponed for years, unil after Disraeli was dead and the queen was entering the twilight of her long life. In it, the Prince of Wales proved an unlikely hero of the hour. For though he was no good at doing, he was excellent at maintaining appearances: unable, for instance, to command a company, much less a regiment, he looked terrific in uniform and sat superbly on a horse. He was thus a natural star of the royal show. And he found his perfect ringmaster in Reginald Brett, Viscount Esher. Esher has been described as 'enigmatic'; he was certainly ambiguous: culturally, as he was half French; sexually, as he was more than half homosexual; and politically, as he was a Liberal monarchist. In view of this, he was a natural creature of the shadows, preferring to pull strings backstage rather than entering the limelight himself. But, for all that, he was a consummate man of the theatre.

His first royal employment was to act as pageant-master for the celebrations for Victoria's Golden and Diamond Jubilees, in 1887 and 1897. And he performed the same function at Edward VII's coronation in 1902. But his most important contribution came from his chairmanship of the committee to erect a worthy monument to Victoria. He used this to comprehensively redesign the centre of London – from Trafalgar Square to the front of Buckingham Palace, which was itself refaced – as a stage set for royal ceremony. It was the most ambitious rebuilding scheme in London since the time of the Prince Regent. But whereas Prinny was seeking to outdo the Emperor Napoleon, Esher was trying to placate and entertain King People.

For Esher realized that the old royal ceremony, which was performed, usually rather badly and more or less in private, for an inner circle of bored aristocrats, had had its day. Instead, the new franchise, which was broadened again in 1884, meant that the people were the political masters now. And they wanted – and got – a good show. The result was the minutely rehearsed and perfectly drilled royal ceremony that we have come to regard as anciently and archetypically British. In fact it was neither, but Esher's Edwardian invention.

In the next reign, the monarchy faced the still greater challenges of the First World War and the Russian Revolution. But George V – like William IV a sailor-king – was equal to the test. Indeed, the changes introduced by this unassuming man were greater than any the monarchy had undergone since the Glorious Revolution. But their nature was very different: for they were existential, not political. The name of the royal house was changed from Saxe-Coburg-Gotha to Windsor, and its marriage customs ceased to be German as well. Ever since the Hanoverian accession, the British royal family had stuck with the German rule that required wives to be of equal status to their husbands. But in 1917 George declared that his children could marry Englishmen and women. It was, as he noted in his diary, 'an historic day'. At a stroke, the monarchy had been anglicized and humanized: royal weddings could be presented as love affairs, rather than affairs of state, and the royal family became the archetypical British family, with an appeal that transcended boundaries of wealth and class.

The family monarchy was born.

And it served the House of Windsor well, carrying it through the General Strike, the Depression and the Second World War. It even took the Abdication – when King Edward VIII, who refused to play by the family rules, was disposed of in days – in its stride.

But it was shipwrecked by Diana, Princess of Wales. Like Edward VIII she was a star and a clothes horse and a natural in front of the camera. And she too thought that personal happiness should come before public duty. But whereas Edward was ahead of his time, she was perfectly in tune with hers. And she won the battle for public opinion hands down. For the first time in over a century and a half, the monarchy faced widespread and deep-seated unpopularity. Still worse, its most effective means of controlling public opinion, the idea of the family monarchy, was broken as well: never again could the House of Windsor present themselves as the guardians of hearth and home and marriage.

In the short term, as the celebrations of the queen's Golden Jubilee showed, the monarchy has weathered the storm. But it still lacks a new Big Idea. Nor is there any sign of one emerging. No doubt residual respect and mere inertia will keep the show on the road. But the British monarchy is too big, and has too large a place in the national consciousness, to survive only on habit. Its royal characters are in search of an author. Will one appear, as has always happened in the past, to tell us what they are for?

INDEX

INDEX

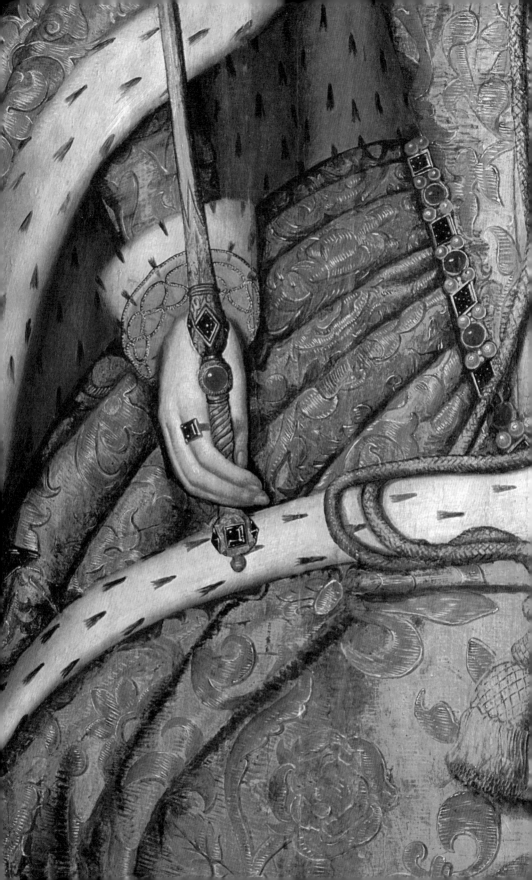